János Thuróczy
Chronicle of the Hungarians

Indiana University Uralic and Altaic Series

Editor: Denis Sinor
Volume 155

Medievalia Hungarica Series

Editor: Emanuel J. Mickel
Volume II

JÁNOS THURÓCZY
HRONICLE OF THE HUNGARIANS

Translation by Frank Mantello
Foreword and Commentary by Pál Engel

Indiana University
Research Institute for Inner Asian Studies
Bloomington, Indiana
1991

Book design by Elena Fraboschi

Library of Congress Catalog Card Number 91–061993
ISBN 0–933070–27–6

CONTENTS

ACKNOWLEDGMENTS

This annotated translation of the fourth part of János Thuróczy's chronicle was supported by a grant from the Division of Research Programs (Translations Category) of the National Endowment for the Humanities. It is the second in the series and the result of close collaboration between American and Hungarian scholars, under the guidance of the Medieval Studies Institute and in cooperation with the Hungarian Chair at Indiana University. Professor Denis Sinor deserves special mention for his willing intellectual and administrative contribution to the project as a whole and to each volume in the series. Lisa Mosele has been instrumental in overseeing the various phases of the project and in providing expertise in word-processing, and she has contributed significantly to the difficult tasks of revising and editing.

The translator is greatly indebted to the general editor of this series of translations, Professor Emanuel Mickel of Indiana University, for his patience, encouragement, and kind assistance, and he wishes to thank his colleagues at The Catholic University of America, Professors John Petruccione, Thomas Halton, William McCarthy, and William Klingshirn, all of whom responded cheerfully to many requests for help. He would also like to acknowledge a very special debt of gratitude to the Reverend Edmund Colledge, O.S.A., whose vigilance considerably reduced the number of inaccuracies and infelicities.

TRANSLATOR'S PREFACE

For this translation of the fourth part of János Thuróczy's *Chronica Hungarorum*, we have used the edition of the chronicle prepared by Elisabeth Galántai and Julius Kristó (Budapest, 1985), pp. 204-293. Except for a version in modern Hungarian, there is no other translation of this work or any part of it.

Our aim has been to provide an aid for the modern student who cannot understand Latin, or whose command of Latin is insecure. To permit easy comparison, when desired, with the Latin text, we have tried to produce a fairly literal translation, while seeking to convey some sense of the characteristic "style" of this chronicle. Thuróczy's narrative can be quite vivid, but there are several self-conscious attempts to write as a great stylist that are bombastic and intrusive. These we have often sought to render in a less turgid fashion, with a view to producing a reasonably smooth English version. Many of his very long sentences, for example, have been reduced to a series of shorter, more easily comprehensible English statements.

Readers who consult this translation alongside the Latin text of the chronicle prepared by Galántai and Kristó will observe that we have subdivided the English version into paragraphs and supplied, in parentheses beside the number for every chapter (except the preface) of the fourth part of the 1985 edition, a reference to the Roman numeral assigned this same chapter in the first volume of the earlier editions (1746, 1765, and 1766) of Joannes G. Schwandtner, *Scriptores rerum Hungaricarum veteres ac genuini*. Hungarian spelling has usually been preferred for most Hungarian personal names. It should also be noted that we have introduced several emendations into the text of the 1985 edition, among which the following may be noted:

P. 211,
lines 17-18: *reading* variasque per illecebras *for* variaque per illecebra

      19: *reading* cogunt. Rex *for* cogunt Rex

216   26: *reading* virentibus spoliatas foliis *for* virentibus foliis

222   4-5: *reading* diabolus que *for* diabolusque

224   33: *reading* dicti *for* ducti

225   9: *reading* intorta *for* inter orta

226   30: *reading* congregavit *for* c ngregavit

228   7: *reading* Istum *for* Is tum

239   15-16: *reading* reperissent ultramarittimum *for* reperissent, ultra marittimum

240   6: *reading* fore *for* fuisse

243   10: *reading* iuvamini *for* iuvamine

246   36: *reading* gerendis sui regni rebus *for* gerendarum sui regni rerum

249   34-35: *reading* tumescentem? Nonne *for* tumescentem, nonne

      36: *reading* potest? *for* potest.

251   18: *reading* invaderent *for* invadrent

260   27: *reading* regni de potioribus *for* regni potioribus

261   11: *reading* genere ⟨oppugnationis⟩ excogitato *for* genere excogitato (cf. p. 266, lines 20-21)

      23: *reading* nationes, que omnem *for* nationes, omnem

262   4: *reading* gravamine *for* gravaminibus

268   18: *reading* funebri *for* funebra

269   20: *reading* modice illos animositati *for* modica illos animositate

270   12: *reading* veniet *for* veniat (cf. Ps. 120 [121]: 1)
272   17: *reading* provisus est? *for* provisus est.
       21: *reading* extremum? *for* extremum.
       21: *reading* uberi *for* ubero
       30: *reading* crisporum *for* crispium
273   14: *reading* qua conditum *for* quo conditus
274   34: *reading* locentur, tuque *for* locentur. Tuque
276   24: *reading* rubea de purpura *for* rubeo de purpuro
278   1: *reading* comitetur *for* comitet
       20: *reading* quodam *for* quondam
       30: *reading* altoque *for* altaque
281   2: *reading* amictum *for* amictus
       27: *reading* recta *for* recto
282   13: *reading* uno et eodem *for* uno eodem
283   8: *reading* wayuode *for* wayuoda
       10: *reading* arbitrabantur se *for* arbitrabantur illos se
       11: *reading* vindictam *for* vindicte
       34: *reading* prorumpens *for* dissoluta
284   5: *reading* primeva *for* primevo
       14: *reading* tristi *for* tristo
       21: *reading* multaque *for* multeque
288   33: *reading* clament: *for* clamant,
289   1: *reading* summit. Celicis *for* summit, celicis
       14: *reading* pressos, reprimatque, *for* pressos repri-
            matque,
       18: *reading* Arcturus *for* arcturus
292   5: *reading* regis! *for* regis,
        6: *reading* Ledere *for* cedere
       28: *reading* neminem? *for* neminem.

Foreword

János Thuróczy *Chronicle* marks the end of a long period in Hungarian historical writing. It must be considered a medieval chronicle, for it shares the characteristic features of that genre, and it is in fact the last of a series of medieval works. The year of its publication might even be viewed symbolic, for it is not too distant from the date of the discovery of America, traditionally considered the end of the Middle Ages. By the time a new generation of Hungarian historians would appear some decades later, history was already being written all over Europe in the new style characteristic of humanist historiography, and such was the case in Hungary. But there is a great difference between the historical attitudes and aptitudes of that new generation and the medieval mentality which so thoroughly shaped Thuróczy's work.

We shall return to that difference later. Here one should note only that both Humanism and its parallel in the arts, the Renaissance, began in Italy in the early fifteenth century and entered Hungary very soon thereafter. These developments were especially predominant at the court of King Matthias Corvinus (1458-90), whose incomparable library in Buda and in the palace at Visegrád played an important role in the history of Hungarian civilization. It is very striking that the imprint of this lavish Renaissance court can hardly be perceived in Thuróczy's chronicle, even though he lived and wrote in its immediate vicinity.

This incongruity is surprising, however, only if one subscribes to the widely-held opinion that the Renaissance spirit of

King Matthias' court was typical of Renaissance culture common in Hungary at that time. It has often been written that, by the end of the Middle Ages, the Hungarians had attained a level of cultural sophistication almost equal to that of the leading countries of Europe, and that Hungary would have kept pace with other European states, had it not suffered a severe reverse at the hands of the Ottoman conquerors in the sixteenth century. Although this notion seems quite plausible, it is contradicted by the facts. On the one hand, an unprecedented cultural flowering can be observed in Hungary in the decades just following the catastrophe at Mohács and the collapse of the kingdom (1526). On the other hand, however, what little we know about the cultural level of the elite in King Matthias' time does not correspond exactly with our idea of a society imbued with Italian humanism. Instead, one has the impression that the emulation of Italian models was dictated by the king's personal ambition and interests and did not spread much beyond the court. One might even say that, except for a handful of intellectuals, it was generally considered a princely extravagance.

Fifteenth-century Hungarian society was dominated both in politics and cultural matters by a social stratum called the nobility. This group represented three to four percent of the population, i. e. about 20,000 families or 100,000 people. "Noble" status in Hungary did not imply wealth. The majority of the nobility were "peasant" nobles who possessed nothing but a simple house and a small piece of land without tenants. As a separate group they were distinguished from the class of unfree tenants in three important ways: their noble birth, their tenure as freeholders, and the privileged status such tenure conveyed. Unlike the commoners, the nobles were considered free men to whom even the king himself could not issue orders. They were in theory exempt from any kind of tax and were compelled to go to war only in those rare instances when the country itself was attacked. Yet they had the right to intervene in political affairs.

From the 1440s the affairs of the kingdom were the responsibility of the diet, a general assembly of nobility whose members were either represented by elected deputies or, in exceptional cases, appeared personally. This new role of the nobles in politics encouraged them to identify themselves as the "people" and to deny to commoners any claim to the same identification and any effective exercise of political rights. Because of this new point of view, which originated in the mid-fifteenth century, *Hungarian* came to mean the Hungarian noble and his peers, all of whom collectively were the "nation," sharing a common origin and certain carefully protected privileges. According to a contemporary definition, "every nobleman is a member of the nation by 'the power of his blood.'" This assertion reflects the prevailing myth that the nobles were descended from those free-born Hungarian warriors who had conquered the country in the ninth century and thus held their estates and enjoyed their privileged status by right of conquest. This was the status of the nobility in the fifteenth century, as reflected in legal theory, but the reality of their position differed in certain respects. As for their privileged social status, the exemption of peasant noblemen from payment of taxes was denied more than once after 1439, and King Matthias imposed taxes upon them almost in the same way as he did upon peasant tenants. Moreover, most of them were not their own masters. They often served wealthier lords as armed retainers, and although they did not lose their personal freedom because of this service, they had to become accustomed to obedience. As for politics, it is fair to say that the affairs of the kingdom really concerned only the wealthiest of the nobility. About forty percent of the land and population belonged to the estates of some forty high-ranking and powerful dynasties whose heads actually ruled the country by monopolizing the higher offices of state and by exerting supreme influence in the royal court. In practice, the authority of the diet was illusory, consisting for the most part of voting in support of new taxes that had already been imposed by the king and his lords. In their attitude toward Humanism, neither the magnates nor the landed gentry accepted its new cultural values. Since they had remained deaf to the lyric of the troubadours and the Minnes ngers a few centuries before, even though both were a product of nobles like themselves, it is hardly surprising that they were unsympathetic towards a cultural movement initiated by merchants and artisans. "Our Pannonians prefer wielding the sword or following the plough to reading Cicero, Livy, Sallust or Aulus Gellius," the lawyer István Werbőczy remarked indulgently in the epilogue of his *Tripartitum* some decades later (1514). Hungary was, indeed, a harsh, warlike society, scarcely susceptible to other values, a society in which a genius like the humanist poet Janus Pannonius (d. 1472) could not help feeling isolated. When in 1491 peace was made in Pozsony with the Habsburgs, none of the Hungarian delegates could sign his name, though they were among the chief men in the country. István Bátori, for example, was then Lord Chief Justice and Voivode of Transylvania, and his father had also been Chief Justice some fifty years before; Ladislas Ország of Gut, one of his companions, was the only son of the Count Palatine Michael Ország, the first lay dignitary of the realm, and himself held the high office of Royal Marshal. If men such as these did not acquire the basic elements of culture, one should have no illusions about the level of education and refinement of the mass of lesser noblemen. It is therefore no surprise that János Hunyadi, the father of the great Renaissance king, Matthias Corvinus, and the famous champion of Christendom, was not only illiterate, but was elected regent or governor of Hungary by the nobility. In fact, literacy must have been rather exceptional among the nobility until the end of the fifteenth century. Acquired usually by those few people who earned a living by it, it remained a professional requirement. Educated officials were especially needed to serve in offices of administration, e. g. in chancelleries and courts of justice and in the *loca credibilia*, i. e. ecclesiastical bodies entrusted with notarial and administrative functions. The magnates, too, needed more and more men able to read and write. Literacy, however, meant competence not in the vernacular but in Latin for this was the language of administration. For those who aspired to any administrative post, it was necessary to learn to compose Latin documents and even private letters with a fairly high level of accuracy. Such administrative careers, however, conveyed little prestige, and attracted not the wealthier members of the nobility, but only its poorer ones, individuals whose means allowed them to receive some formal education and for whom even a modest position at court or in the chancellery meant a higher social rank and increased prosperity.

In the fifteenth century members of the poor or lower middle-class gentry with not more than twenty tenants commonly found posts as professional administrators. Chronicler János Thuróczy came from this class. His ancestors had been small landowners since the thirteenth century in northern Hungary in the village of Szentmihály (Turóc county), and his uncle was granted another piece of land in Hont county by King Sigismund. Even the name by which the chronicler became known is evidence of his social position. At that time any nobleman of importance was named for his principle estate. Only a county gentleman of modest origin like Thuróczy would have been named not after an estate but after the region from which he came.

Thuróczy's name is recorded in the sources from 1459, and he may have been born about 1435. Nothing is known about his education, but it is almost certain that he learned Latin, as was customary, at a church school. It is highly improbable that he ever attended a university. Before 1467 he found a position as a court clerk in the office of the Lord Chief Justice in Buda and, from that time until his death, he practiced this profession. From 1470 to 1475 he was employed as a lay clerk (*notarius*) at the

Premonstratensian convent of Ipolyság. Later he managed to return to the staff of the Lord Chief Justice where he worked for more than ten years. At the end of his life he attained a position that was possibly the highest to which people of his rank might ascend: in 1486 he was appointed deputy judge (*protonotarius*) of the most important central law-court, the so-called "court of royal appeals." The last notices of him were recorded in 1488, the year in which his chronicle was published. He had probably died by the summer of 1489. The best representatives of Hungary's intellectual elite, of which Thuróczy was a distinguished member, were not the humanist courtiers of King Matthias, who were mostly foreigners, but the functionaries at the chancelleries and central law-courts in Buda. Thuróczy owed his historical preoccupations and literary interests to his position as clerk and judge, which no doubt provided him with regular access to documents and other materials of historical significance, such as copies of charters issued by former kings of Hungary. Of himself and other staff members he writes: "During conversations we sometimes had friendly disputes with each other. It occurred more than once that, during the discussion, we had minor quarrels because of differing views about the history of the Hungarian nation. . . ." It was clearly this environment that inspired him to become a chronicler, for about 1480, at the encouragement of his superior, the protonotary István Hásságyi, he began his chronicle, later continuing it at the instigation of Chief Justice Tamás Drági. As far as can be determined, he was considered by his colleagues to be the most likely person to bring such a work to a successful conclusion. It is also fair to assume that his chronicle reflects the demands and expectations of this group, as well as its intellectual aspirations. By the time Matthias had become king a "modern" history of Hungary was long overdue. The recording of past events had ceased with the death of King Louis the Great (1382), when the last historian before Thuróczy, John Küküllei, put down his pen. For nearly a century no one had undertaken the task of chronicling current events, which were preserved only in the fading memories of contemporaries and in chancellery documents. Though there had been an active interest in these events, it seems to have been confined to conversations. The need for a written account of the last century was great. In the Buda Chronicle, the first-known product of Hungarian printing, produced in 1473 by the printer Andrew Hess, one can see an enormous lacuna in the published knowledge of Hungarian history. This book contained a version of the ancient chronicles up to about 1382 but, apart from a few meagre details, offered nothing to the reader about recent times. Thuróczy's work, *The History of the Hungarian People up to the Rule of King Matthias*, printed in 1488, was originally intended to fill this gap. Apart from the unity of its theme, Thuróczy's chronicle was not a single literary work in the modern sense. It in fact consisted of four different works brought together only in Thuróczy's text. That they were originally individual works is shown by separate forewords at the beginning of each section. We know from these that in the early 1480s Thuróczy first wrote about the reigns of Queen Mary (1382-87) and King Charles II the Little (1385-86), her adversary, as a separate work. He next composed the first part of the chronicle (perhaps complete by 1486), which reached to 1342, and in 1487 he completed the book that treated of events from King Sigismund's accession (1387) until the author's own age. To these three works, all of which bear Thuróczy's own distinctive literary mark, another text was appended to complete the narrative. This was the *Gesta* of John Küküllei concerning the reign of King Louis the Great (1342-82), which Thuróczy adopted in its entirety.

Thuróczy's borrowing of Küküllei's work throws some light on his outlook and methods. He did not intend to create an original work. Nor did he have the slightest intention of being independent of previous authors, either in style or in attitude. He instead did what had been done for centuries by all historians:

he made free use of other texts and, when he found them correct, borrowed from them generously for his own work.

This is the feature which most distinguishes him from his humanist followers. A decade after his death, the Italian Antonio Bonfini (d. 1503) did essentially the same thing Thuróczy had done: he wrote a history of Hungary based on former writers (Thuróczy among them) who had been better acquainted with the subject. Yet there is a difference between the literary attitudes of Bonfini and Thuróczy. When writing about centuries that he did not know firsthand, Bonfini also assembled information from the available sources. But he thoroughly reworked his material using a uniform Latin style of his own to create a work which, though not more valuable than Thuróczy's work as a historical source, has stronger literary claims. This new approach on the part of the humanist writer was completely alien to Thuróczy's personality.

To consider the components of Thuróczy's text in chronological order, one must turn first to the compilation that ends in 1342. This in fact consists of two parts: the first treats of the history of the Huns; the second considers the history of the Arpadian rulers from the conquest of 895 to 1301, to which is appended an account of the reign of King Charles I (or Charles Robert, 1301-42). In its present form this section is a synthesis of a number of older chronicles written between the eleventh and fourteenth centuries.

In this first part Thuróczy's interests and critical acumen were aroused principally by the history of the Huns and especially by the question of their origin and that of the Magyars. The view that they were related and even essentially the same people, which was accepted until recent times, was propounded in the 1280s by Simon Kézai in his *Gesta*. The so-called "Anonymous," one of the oldest Hungarian historians, writing ca. 1200, had alluded to the kinship between the Árpáds and Attila, but he did not suggest any relationship between the two peoples. It was

Kézai who invented the twins, Hunor and Magor, and declared them to be the ancestors of the Huns and the Magyars respectively. Thus in Kézai's *Gesta* the foundation of the empire of the Huns in the Carpathian Basin in the middle of the fifth century A.D. was considered simply the "first conquest of the Magyars," and the great immigration of 895 was viewed as their return to a country that their ancestors had inhabited. Similarly, the deeds of Attila and his hordes formed an organic part of Hungarian history, and Attila was as entitled to be considered their ruler as was rpád. The heritage of the great empire of the Huns and all the dubious glory associated with it found favor with the Hungarian nobility, and the story as presented by Kézai did not raise the slightest doubts for centuries, until the birth of modern historical research.

Thuróczy of course accepted Kézai's theory and included it in his work. The only problem was that the story was poorly documented. Thuróczy had had an opportunity to read ancient authors in King Matthias' library and elsewhere and seems to have formed the opinion from his reading that the past glory of the Hungarians must have been greater than in the version presented by Kézai. He found much new data, especially about the Scythians, considered the common ancestors of the Huns and the Magyars. He therefore thoroughly reworked Kézai's text, revising it where necessary and completing it by interpolating new chapters. Elemér Mályusz has observed that "the procedure he followed when using his sources appears to be quite simple; he incorporated everything flattering or favorable to the Scythians and Huns and left out all abusive language."[1] He made a special point of exploring as many details as possible about Scythia, the country of origin, a preoccupation that suggests that this theme was probably popular among his contemporaries. Thuróczy was

1. Elemér Mályusz, A Thuróczy-krónika és forrásai [*Thuróczy*'s Chronicle and its sources] (Budapest, 1967), p. 119.

not in fact a man of great reading, but on this particular point he spared no pains to find all attainable information. He not only checked a Latin version of Herodotus (he did not know Greek), but also studied several classical texts–Pompeius Trogus, Pomponius Mela, Iulius Solinus, Diodorus Siculus, and Dionysius Periegeta. These he proudly cited, along with others of whom he had only second-hand knowledge, a commonly accepted practice in his day amongst historiographers.

He took less pain to present Hungarian history proper. Here he limited his efforts to providing the reader with the most comprehensive version possible of the extant chronicles. His work was needed because available manuscripts preserved only chronicles covering various periods. These were related to one another in different ways and overlapped to some degree. Thuróczy admittedly made use of two manuscripts copied during the reigns of King Charles I (1310-1342) and Louis the Great (1342-1382) respectively. These he combined, thereby providing a single more complete version than any of the earlier ones. Beyond blending the two into one, he reduced his compositional activities to a minimum and only in one or two places deemed slight correction necessary. For his first part therefore, Thuróczy produced a text containing earlier chronicles that had themselves been woven together by many generations of writers living between 1050 and 1350. Modern philological scholarship has managed to distinguish the following strata: a so-called 'proto-*gesta*,' composed about the middle of the eleventh century; two of its continuations from the age of King Ladlislas the Saint (1077-95) and from the middle of the twelfth century; the revision of Master Ákos, made about 1270; Kézai's *Gesta* of the Huns and Magyars, written between 1282 and 1285; its continuation compiled about 1333 and attributed to Friar John, provincial of the Franciscans in Hungary; and, finally, the illuminated Chronicle, written in 1358 and sometimes attributed, without good reason, to the court chaplain Mark Kátai. This last text was never finished and ended with the events of the year 1330.[2]

This compilation of historical texts to 1330 was completed by Thuróczy from a manuscript that narrated events up to the death of King Charles I (1342). To this he added, as a separate work and without a single change, preserving even its original foreword, John Kükülleí's biography of King Louis the Great. Kükülleí was a contemporary of Louis, and though he finished his book in the 1390s during the reign of King Sigismund, he was able to provide an eye-witness account of his subject, a fact valued more by modern historians than by Thuróczy. What Thuróczy admired about Kükülleí's work seems to have been the author's tone and his attention to worldly exploits. Although Kükülleí was a priest and even vicar-general in Esztergom for a time, he had come from close to the same class as Thuróczy, from a minor noble family in northern Hungary, and his social background was apparent in his work. He was influenced by the Pseudo-Aristotelian *Secret of Secrets*, and he thought that a proper king's purpose in life was to increase his own fame and glory by military exploits. For Kükülleí God was mankind's principal source of glory, the transcendent power that "orders the battles and breathes courage into the spirits." It is plain that the layman Thuróczy would have found nothing to reject in Kükülleí's presentation. Since the period following King Louis' death in 1382 was largely untouched by historians, Thuróczy's contribution as a chronicler actually began with his continuation of Kükülleí. For this purpose he decided to revise an extant work, which narrated events from 1382 to 1386. Its author was a contemporary Venetian, Lorenzo

---

2. One may note the omission from this list of the work of the "Anonymous," who is probably the best known medieval Hungarian writer today. Curiously enough, his work remained virtually unknown almost until the eighteenth century and thus did not have any influence on subsequent historical writing or on Thuróczy, who was unaware of it.

Monaci, who visited Hungary as an ambassador of the Republic several times. He later became governor of Crete and died in 1429. Monaci had all the qualities to guarantee acceptance in Hungary: he was well disposed toward the Hungarians, he wrote in Latin, and his work was accessible. His text, however, could not be borrowed word for word because it had been composed in hexameter verses. Since Thuróczy's superior, István Hásságyi, and his colleagues preferred prose to poetry, Thuróczy recast the poem as an ordinary, straightforward narrative. To make it even more attractive, he supplied a few anti-Italian remarks and interspersed some episodes he had invented, but otherwise he remained faithful to his source.

Thus, from a modern point of view, Thuróczy's talents as a historian can be assessed only upon examination of the last, "original" part of his work, that which begins in 1387. This represents Thuróczy's own account of his times and is not drawn from or dependent on other extant texts. The present volume contains an English translation of only this part of his chronicle. It is this part of the chronicle that can provide us with a picture of the level attained by Hungarian historiography in the 1480s after a hundred years of silence.

It must not have been an easy undertaking to write the history of four generations without literary antecedents. Thuróczy himself could have had memories at best only from the 1450s. Moreover, in his youth he could have had a view of politics only "from beneath," as he was not at that time moving about in the company of those who made national policy. He was compelled to look for sources, but his age was not rich in them. It is instructive to note here the contradiction between the historical interest of his contemporaries and their literary achievements. Their interest cannot be denied: once writing had become an established attainment in Hungary in the eleventh century, historiography was the only secular literary genre that received attention. The audience for the texts may have been small, but the volumes themselves are evidence of the unchanging desire and need to know the past. However this impulse was not pronounced enough to produce a wide variety of historical records in Hungary was often the case elsewhere. One finds no chronicles recording the deeds of the leading families; there are no *gesta* about the principal figures of the age; and there was no tradition of keeping annals at the royal court or in monasteries. King Sigismund, from the House of Luxemburg, the Hungarian monarch for fifty years (1387-1437), became the leading statesman of contemporary Europe and died with the Roman imperial crown in his possession, yet not a single line was written in Hungary to record his exploits. For this reason, Hungary almost conveys the impression of being an illiterate, prehistoric society. But although events were not methodically recorded, some memorable episodes became subjects of an oral tradition, commemorated in ballads sung by minstrels all over the country. Some of these survived in sixteenth-century elaborations, such as the story of Nicolas Toldi, the Herculean knight of King Louis' household who went on a pilgrimage to Spain and Ireland. The ballad of István Kont of Hédervár and his thirty-two valiant companions, who were beheaded by Sigismund for rebelling against him, was preserved by Thuróczy himself, who was compelled to borrow occasionally from popular tradition.

Having no historical works to serve as sources, Thuróczy had to rely primarily on the memories of contemporaries such as Mihály Ország, as he tells us in the preface to this part of his chronicle. But their memory was limited. Ország, who was Count Palatine from 1458 until his death in 1484, was one of the leading men of the age of the Hunyadis, but he was a young man in the 1420s when he joined Sigismund's court as a royal squire. Some of Thuróczy's sharp remarks about the general features of Sigismund's reign probably derive from Ország, but the Palatine obviously was not in a position to give a detailed account of the expedition to Nicopolis (1396) or of the rebellion of the barons (1403).

Fortunately Thuróczy also had opportunities to exploit other sources. There were documents kept in the royal chancellery for official use as well as register-books (*registra*) into which the contents of other records were copied. As a clerk of the Lord Chief Justice and later himself a judge, he had easy access to every kind of document, some of which he no doubt carefully examined.

In contrast with the scant literary production of the period, official records were used everywhere in medieval Hungary. While contemporaries were reluctant to take up the pen for their own pleasure or for private purposes, they did not question that administrative affairs and legal procedures required careful documentation. One has an idea of the extent to which formal written documents were used, when one considers that, from the five decades of King Sigismund's reign alone, almost fifty thousand such pieces have survived. And this must have been only a small portion, probably not more than one or two percent, of what was in fact produced. The modern historian, whether studying everyday life or the details of a military campaign, obtains his information almost exclusively from these archival sources. Thuróczy himself did the same, but he limited his research to only one kind of document, the royal charters, and of these he used only a few.

Royal charters in Hungary had a feature which was probably unique in Europe and met the chronicler's needs exactly. Besides their legal content, they contained long narratives reporting colorfully on military events, and in this way they could almost serve as substitutes for missing chronicles. Since the thirteenth century it had been customary in the Hungarian chancellery to include in a charter conveying some kind of royal favor, such as the grant of an estate or the right to hold a fair or administer justice, an account of all the services by which the grantee merited the privilege. It was the practice to provide a colorful description of the heroic deeds of the beneficiary to demonstrate his unsurpassed excellence and unquestionable right to the gift. This requirement gave birth to a unique kind of literary production, and chancellery clerks developed a surprising skill in composing texts for this purpose. Some of their products are in length the equivalent of minor chronicles. An example is a charter of King Sigismund, dated March 4, 1397, by which he granted the castle of Simontornya to his Lord Chancellor, John Kanizsai, archbishop of Esztergom, and the chancellor's brothers. The presentation of their merits covers here all the important events of an eight-year period, thus providing a comprehensive picture of the first decade of Sigismund's reign. Thuróczy was familiar with this document and relied on it fully for three chapters of his chronicle and partly for another three. Textual parallels also prove his use of other documents, and one may surmise that he knew some that are no longer extant.

It must be remembered that these texts were not written with a view to aiding future chroniclers. As far as concerns the precise dates of the events reported in them, Thuróczy could have found only vague indications. The surprising unreliability of his work in this respect may therefore be ascribed to the lack of chronological precision in his sources, but his innate indifference toward chronology was also partly to blame. He supplied his narrative sparsely with dates, for he knew he was likely to make a mistake. He was wrong in dating Sigismund's campaign to Moldavia in the fourth year of the king's reign, i. e. in 1390/91, instead of the beginning of 1395; he misdated Sigismund's coronation, which occurred not on Pentecost in 1386 but on Palm Sunday in 1387. He was also at times confused about the chronology of his own age, e. g. he recorded 1455 as the year of the famous victory at Belgrade. His presentation of the sequence of events is also often faulty. Although the thirty-two knights' execution happened in 1388, Thuróczy records it after the events of 1395; the punishment of the Lackfis (1397) is placed after the rebellion of 1403; and he reported the battle of Galambóc/Golubac

(1428) earlier than the death of Jan Hus or the unlucky campaign against Hrvoje/Hervoja (both in 1415). This last event is followed in the narrative by the defeat of István Losonci in Wallachia (1395) and by the two battles of Nicholas Péterfi of Macedónia, at least one of which occurred in 1396-97. All of these are followed by the coronation of Sigismund as King of Bohemia in 1420. Thuróczy's method of redaction is immediately apparent: he seems to have woven together the events found in his sources almost at random without considering chronological inaccuracies, even when his source could have helped him resolve the problem.

Thuróczy did not strive for chronological accuracy, for such a goal was far from his purpose and capacity. One must not expect from him a work like that of his older contemporary, the Polish writer Jan Dlugosz (d. 1480). Dlugosz had to tackle a similar task, that of writing the annals of Poland from the beginning to the fifteenth century. He, too, had to rely mainly on archival materials. But he had an almost modern scholarly attitude to research. For years he searched the documents of the chancellery, not satisfied until he had succeeded in reconstructing the history of Poland as accurately as possible, following it year by year and almost day by day. He was thus able to write an excellent source book replete with data indispensable for modern scholarship. When leafing through his work today, one cannot decide what is more admirable, his determined objectivity, his critical acumen, or his tireless diligence.

In the work of Jan Dlugosz one may observe that modern notions of historiography were not unknown in Eastern Europe in the fifteenth century. In Hungary, however, no one with such an approach to historical research and composition was yet writing. This is especially unfortunate, because the royal archives in Buda, where a scholar of Dlugosz's insight and stature could have found rich treasures, were to be annihilated during the Ottoman invasions of 1526 and 1541. Of this invaluable collection practically nothing has been preserved in Thuróczy's chronicle. One is left with his often vivid and dramatic narrative and his jumbled chronology. His text is also characterized by the medieval notions of universal historical time and the progressive unfolding of a providential scheme. The innate superiority of Hungarian Christianity is assumed and Thuróczy takes the side of the Hungarian nation against its pagan enemies and even against outside Christian influences when they are contrary to Hungarian interests. "The Huns or Hungarians came from some part of creation at the beginning of time, but their glorious fame, spread far and wide throughout the world because of the greatness of their exploits, proclaims that they are devoted to the Catholic faith, that because of their uprightness and moral integrity they shine brightly and flourish, and that they by far surpass other nations in military prowess and armed valour." Thuróczy's chronicle is marked by the medieval historiographical tradition which places temporal events within a providential perspective. When Hunyadi is successful against the Turks, it is because God has bolstered the Hungarian cause even against great odds. When he fails, it is because the papal legate has persuaded him to betray the peace he negotiated with the enemy in good faith.

Thuróczy appears to adopt the familiar medieval topos of humility when he proclaims his own poor abilities as a writer. In the preface he wrote that "such great events deserved a greater writer," and in the prologue of the last part he described himself as an insignificant man with feeble Latin, much in the same spirit as Gregory of Tours. After reading his work, however, one wonders whether these remarks are in fact an honest acknowledgement of his own real limitations.

Though modern scholars must be careful when using Thuróczy's work as a source book, in its own time it was a success. It went to press immediately after it was written, and it was issued by March 20, 1488. This was an amazingly short time, if

we consider the fact that the text referred to the occupation of
Wiener Neustadt by King Matthias' armies, an event which occurred on August 17, 1487. The first edition was published in
Brünn (today Brno) in Moravia. This town belonged at that time
to the empire of Matthias and its printing office had been patron-
ized by the king's Moravian chancellor, John Filipec, bishop of
Várad/Oradea. The work was probably recommended to Filipec
by Thuróczy's superior, Tamás Dragi, who undoubtedly found
the work worthy of high esteem. The volume seems also to have
been a profitable undertaking, for it was published again two
months later in Augsburg, Germany. Theobald Feger, a book-
seller in Buda, obtained the services of Erhard Ratdolt, a well-
known typographer of the time, for a new edition. As Mályusz
has observed: "It left the press on June 3, 1488, in two versions.
One of them was identical with the Brünn edition, but in the
second, *Austriae dux* was omitted from among the titles of King
Matthias, and there was no reference to the occupation of Vienna
and Wiener Neustadt. Moreover, in one of the illustrations, Austria is absent from among the arms of Matthias, which were to
declare his glory. This second version was obviously published
for the German reading public and designed so as not to offend
their sensibilities."[3] Both editions were enhanced by representations of Hungarian rulers or battles. But one must not assume
that these are true likenesses. The thirty-six portraits in the Augsburg edition evidently represent generic figures rather than individuals, for only twenty-four blocks were used for them. Thus
the same picture, with an appropriate change of background,
served to represent more than one person. The portraits of King
Peter (1038-1046), István II (1116-1131) and Wladislaw I (1440-
44) are identical except for some differences in background elements. The printer's approach was similar when illustrating
battle scenes. Mályusz has noted that "these represent only four

3. Mályusz, p. 93.

scenes: the combats of armoured knights, of Hungarian and Turkish cavalry, of mounted troops and infantrymen, and of infantrymen alone; but the first of these scenes is repeated eight times, the second six, the third five times, and the fourth twice."[4]

Copies of the chronicle intended for presentation to King Matthias and his court were lavishly produced to convey the impression of illuminated codices. They were not printed on paper but on parchment, with decorated initials, illustrations painted in color, and the dedication to the king printed in gold.

Thuróczy's original manuscript has not been preserved. Its text, known only from the printed versions, was later reedited by Johann George von Schwandtner, the librarian of the Imperial Library in Vienna for his three-volume collection of the sources of Hungarian history.[5] The annotated translation that follows is of the "contemporary" fourth part of the chronicle, the part written by Thuróczy himself, who has covered the period between 1387 and 1487.

Recent works concerning the last part of Thuróczy's Chronicle and the political history of XVth century Hungary (since 1386; scholarship in Hungarian not included):

Bak, Janos M., and Béla K. Király, eds. *From Hunyadi to Rákóczi: War and Society in Medieval and Early Modern Hungary.* Brooklyn, 1982.

Bartl, J. "Political and social situation in Slovakia at the turning point of the 14th and 15th centuries and the reign of Sigismund of Luxemburg." *Studia Historica Slovaca* 9 (1979): 41-84.

---

4. Mályusz, p. 93.

5. Ioannes Georgius Schwandtnerus (ed.) *Scriptores rerum Hungaricarum veteres ac genuini,* vol. I (Vindobonae, 1746), pp. 39-291. A new critical edition was published recently: Johannes de Thurocz, *Chronica Hungarorum,* vol. 1 (Budapest, 1985), ed. Elisabeth Galántai and Gyula Kristó. Volumes 2 and 3, containing the commentary in Latin of E. Mályusz and Gy. Kristó, are now being prepared for publication.

Cvetkova, Bistra. *Pametna bitka na narodite. (Evropejskijat jugoistok i os-manskoto zavoevanie - kraj na XIV i pĕrvata polovina na XV v.) [The memorable battle of peoples. South Eastern Europe and the Ottoman conquest - end of the XIVth and first half of the XVth centuries].* 2nd ed. Varna, 1979.

Deletant, Dennis. "Moldavia between Hungary and Poland, 1347-1412." *The Slavonic and East European Review* 64 (1986): 189-211.

Djurić, Ivan. *Sumrak Vizantije (Vreme Jovana VIII Paleologa 1392-1448) [The decline of Byzantium. The epoch of John VIII Palaeologus].* Beograd, 1984.

Fahlbusch, F. B. *Städte und Königtum im frühen 15. Jahrhundert. Ein Beitrag zur Geschichte Sigmunds von Luxemburg.* Köln, 1983.

Fügedi, E. *Castle and Society in Medieval Hungary 1000-1437.* Budapest, 1986.

Hohlweg, Armin. "Der Kreuzzug des Jahres 1444." *Die Türkei in Europa.* Ed. Klaus-Detlev Grothusen. Göttingen, 1979, 20-37.

Koller, Heinrich. "Sigismund 1410-1437." *Kaisergestalten des Mittelalters.* Ed. Helmut Beumann. München: Beck, 1984, 277-300.

Köpeczi, Béla, ed. *Kurze Geschichte Siebenbürgens.* Budapest, 1990.

Kubinyi, András. "Ethnische Minderheiten in den ungarischen Städten des Mittelalters." Ed. B. Kirchgässner, and F. Reiter. *Städtische Randgruppen und Minderheiten.* Sigmaringen: Thorbeke, 1986, 183-199.

Mályusz, Elemér. *Kaiser Sigismund in Ungarn 1387-1437.* Budapest, 1990.

Matthias Corvinus und die Renaissance in Ungarn 1458-1541. (Katalog der Austellung des Niederösterreichischen Landesmuseums, Schallaburg) Wien, 1982.

Rady, Martyn C. *Medieval Buda. A study of municipal government and jurisdiction in the kingdom of Hungary.* Boulder, 1985.

Szakály, Ferenc. "Phases of Turco-Hungarian warfare before the battle of Mohács (1365-1526)." *Acta Orientalia Academiae Scientiarum Hungaricae* 33 (1979): 65-111.

Živković, P. *Tvrtko II Tvrtković. Bosna u prvoj polovini XV stoljeća [Tvrtko II. Bosnia in the first half of the XVth century].* Sarajevo, 1981.

Chronology of Events

The chronological order of the events reported in Thuróczy's work is inaccurate and confused. Explanatory notes can rectify individual errors, but they cannot supply readers with the guide they need to find their way among them. A chronological table to the work has therefore been supplied here, so that the true sequence of events can be followed easily. References to individual chapters in the chronicle have been provided within parentheses.

1382   Death of Louis the Great, last Angevin King of Hungary (1342-1382) and of Poland (1370-1382). He is succeeded by his elder daughter, Mary (b. 1371), under the regency of her mother, Elizabeth.

1384   János of Horváti, former Ban of Macsó, rebels against the queens and invites King Charles III of Naples as the last male representative of the House of Anjou to the Hungarian throne.

1385   Civil war in Hungary. (August) Marriage of Queen Mary to Sigismund of Luxemburg, Márgrave of Brandenburg, brother of King Wenceslas of Bohemia and Germany. (October) Charles arrives in Hungary; flight of Sigismund into Bohemia. (December 31) Coronation of Charles as King of Hungary (Charles II). The queens appear to submit.

1386 (February 7) Their adherents make an attempt on the king at Buda Castle and send him, severely wounded, to Visegrád, where he dies in prison (February 24). The queens resume power but Horváti refuses to submit. (April) King Wenceslas invades Hungary and forces the queens to acknowledge the rights of Sigismund. (June 10) At Pentecost, Sigismund returns to the royal court and is solemnly presented as prince consort (ch. 197).

1387 (January) Queen Mother Elizabeth is strangled at Novigrad (see ch. 196). (March 31) On Palm Sunday, coronation of Sigismund as King of Hungary at Székesfehérvár (ch. 198). (June or July) Siege of Pozsegavár and escape of János of Horváti into Bosnia (ch. 199). (June 4) Release of Queen Mary from prison (see ch. 197). (August) King Tvrtko I of Bosnia invades Croatia and Dalmatia (see ch. 199).

1388 (February or March) Victory of Sigismund's commanders over an army of the Horvátis between the rivers Sava and Bosut. Execution of the "thirty-two knights" (ch. 202).

1389 (June) Battle of Kosovo Polje. Serbia becomes a vassal state of the Ottomans. (September to November) First campaign of Sigismund against the Turks.

1390 Turkish raids into south Hungary begin.

1394 (June-July) Siege of Dobor Castle and execution of János of Horváti at Pécs (ch. 199).

1395 (January-February) War against Voivode István of Moldavia (ch. 200). (March 7) Voivode Mircea of Wallachia vows allegiance to Sigismund in return for Hungarian support against the Turks. (April) Hungarian army sent into Wallachia defeated (ch. 212). (May 17) Death of Queen Mary (ch. 201). (July-August) Sigismund's war against the Turks in Wallachia; capture of Little Nicopolis. During his absence, an attack of the King of Poland is repelled by the regents (ch. 201).

1396 (July to September) Crusade against the Ottomans. (September 28) Battle of Nicopolis (ch. 203). (October to December)

Sigismund flees to Constantinople and returns by sea to Dalmatia. Rebellion of the Lackfis (ch. 204). Victory of Miklós of Macedónia over the Bosnian pretender Ikach (ch. 213).

1397 (February 22) Killing of Lackfis at Kőrös (ch. 207). (October) Diet at Temesvár. Laws for the defense of the kingdom.

1401 (April 28) Baronial coup d'état at Buda. Arrest of the king (ch. 204). (August 31) Agreement of the rebels with Miklós Garai; Sigismund released (ch. 205).

1402 (January) Sigismund leaves Hungary (ch. 205). (February 4) King Wenceslas appoints him Regent of Bohemia.

1403 (January) Last and greatest revolt of the barons against Sigismund. (February 4) King Ladislas of Naples invited to the throne. Sigismund returns to Hungary. (October 8) After suppressing the rebellion a general amnesty is proclaimed. (November) Ladislas of Naples embarks for Italy (ch. 206).

1405 (April 15) Promulgation of royal statutes for the benefit of cities and trade.

1408 (December 12) After a great victory over Bosnia, foundation of the Order of the Dragon rallying King Sigismund, Queen Barbara, and twenty-two of their chief supporters.

1410 (September 20) Election of Sigismund as King of the Romans (i.e. of Germany) by three electors at Frankfort (followed by a unanimous election on July 21, 1411, ch. 208).

1413 (July) Sultan Mehmed I sole ruler of the Ottoman Empire (ch. 213).

1414 (November 8) Coronation of Sigismund as King of the Romans at Aachen (ch. 218). (December 24) Arrival of Sigismund at the Council of Constance, opened on November 5.

1415 (July 6) Execution of Jan Hus at Constance (ch. 210). (July or August) Defeat of a great Hungarian army at Doboj Castle in Bosnia (ch. 211). (December 13) Treaty of Narbonne between Sigismund and the King of Aragon.

1416 (March) Visit of Sigismund to Paris. (May to August) Sigismund's stay in England. (August 15) Alliance with King Henry V at Canterbury.

1417   (January 27) Sigismund returns to Constance. (November 11) Election of Pope Martin V. End of the Great Schism.

1419   (August 16) Death of Sigismund's brother, King Wenceslas (ch. 214).

1420   (March 17) At the Diet of Wroclaw a crusade against the Czech Hussites is proclaimed. (June) After a ten-year war with Hungary, the Republic of Venice completes the conquest of Dalmatia by taking Trau and Spalato. (July 28) Sigismund is crowned as King of Bohemia at Prague (ch. 214).

1422   (January) Sigismund's defeat by the Hussites at Kutná Hora (ch. 210).

1426   (May) Treaty of Tata between Sigismund and Despot István Lazarevic of Serbia (ch. 215).

1427   (July 19) Death of Despot István. The treaty of Tata comes into force, but Golubac Castle falls into Ottoman hands.

1428   (February) First Hussite raid into north Hungary. (June) Defeat of Sigismund by the Turks at Golubac (ch. 208).

1431   (March 3) Beginning of the Council of Basle. (August 14) A huge imperial army defeated by the Hussites at Domazlice (Taus). (November 28) Coronation of Sigismund as King of Italy at Milan (ch. 218).

1432   (June) A Hussite band takes possession of the royal city of Trnava (ch. 216).

1435   (March) Diet at Pozsony. Administration of justice and defense of the realm reformed (ch. 218).

1436   (August 23) Sigismund enters Prague after being recognized King of Bohemia (ch. 219).

1437   (June to January 1438) Peasant revolt in east Hungary and Transylvania (ch. 217). (December 9) Death of Sigismund at Znojmo in Moravia (ch. 219). (December 18) His son-in-law, Duke Albert V of Austria, elected King of Hungary.

1438   (January 1) Coronation of Albert at Székesfehérvár (ch. 220).

1439   (May 23) Plebeian revolt against the German merchants in Buda (ch. 220). (May 29) The diet of Buda gains the upper hand over the king by abrogating much of Sigismund's reform statutes and measures. (August 18) Sultan Murad II takes Smederevo after a siege of two months. The Hungarian army encamps around Titel (ch. 222). (October 27) Death of King Albert (ch. 222).

1440 (February 22) Birth of Ladislas Postumus, son of King Albert and Queen Elizabeth, daughter of Sigismund (ch. 223). (March 8) King Wladislas of Poland elected King of Hungary in Kracow by a delegation of the Hungarian Estates without success (ch. 223). (April-May) Sultan Murad besieges Belgrade without success (ch. 230). (May 21) Wladislas of Poland enters Buda (ch. 223 and 224). (June 29) The Estates swear an oath of fealty to Wladislas (ch. 225). (July 17) He is crowned King of Hungary (Wladislas I, 1440-1444) with a substitute crown, the Holy Crown being in Queen Elizabeth's hands (ch. 226). A civil war between the two parties follows. (November 22) Queen Elizabeth forms an alliance with King Frederick IV of Germany at Wiener Neustadt (ch. 224).

1441 (January) Victory of Miklós Ujlaki and János Hunyadi over an army of the queen at Bátaszék (ch. 227). (February) King Wladislas appoints Ujlaki and Hunyadi as voivodes of Transylvania (ch. 225). (February) Unsuccessful siege of Esztergom by Wladislas (ch. 228). (March to May) His victorious campaign against the queen's partisans in southwest Hungary (ch. 228). (Summer) Hunyadi's victory over the Turkish troops of Ishak bey in Serbia (ch. 231).

1442 (March) Cardinal Giuliano Cesarini arrives as papal legate in Hungary with the task of organizing a crusade against the Ottomans (ch. 234). (March 22) Hunyadi defeats Mezid bey at Gyulafehérvár (ch. 232). (September 2 or 6) He wins a new victory over the Beylerbeyi Sehabeddin at the Ialomita River (ch. 233). (December 17) Death of Queen Elizabeth at Győr (ch. 234).

1443 (October) Beginning of the Long Campaign of Wladislas and Hunyadi into the Balkan Peninsula. (December 12 and 22) Hungarian victories over Sultan Murad at Zlatica and over the Beylerbeyi Kasïm at Melstica (ch. 235).

1444 (January 2) Victory over Turakhan bey at the Kunovica Pass. (January 25) The Hungarian army returns to Belgrade (ch. 235).

(April 24) At the diet in Buda Cesarini proclaims a crusade against the Turks. (June 12) Preliminary peace treaty between the Sultan and the Hungarians at Adrianople. (August 4) King Wladislas takes an oath at Szeged, declaring null and void any treaty which might be made with the Sultan's ambassadors. (August 15) Peace treaty between Hungary and the Ottoman Empire at Nagyvárad, ratified in bad faith by the oath of Hunyadi in the name of Wladislas, and invalidated immediately after that by Cardinal Cesarini. (August 22) In accordance with the terms of the treaty of Nagyvárad, Serbia together with Smederevo and other castles is handed over by the Turks to Despot George Brankovič. (September 22) Launching the crusade, Wladislas and Hunyadi invade Bulgaria (ch. 236). (November 10) Battle of Varna; death of Wladislas and Cesarini (ch. 240).

1446 (June 6) At the diet in Pest, Hunyadi is elected regent with the title of Governor during the minority of King Ladislas V (ch. 239). (November-December) Hunyadi's campaign against King Frederick in Austria (ch. 240).

1447 (December) Expedition of Hunyadi against the Voivode Vlad of Wallachia (ch. 239).

1448 (October 16-18) Second battle of Kosovo Polje (ch. 241). (December) Hunyadi, arrested in Serbia after the battle, is set free by Brankovič after being compelled to agree to a treaty with him (ch. 242).

1451 (February 8) Death of Sultan Murad. His son Mehmed II the Conqueror succeeds (see ch. 247). (August 7) Defeat of Hunyadi by the Czech mercenary leader Jan Jiskra at Losonc (ch. 243).

1452 (June to August) Hunyadi's campaign against Jiskra in north Hungary (ch. 243). (September 4) King Ladislas V (also Duke of Austria), ward and prisoner of his kinsman King Frederick since 1440, is liberated by a revolt of the Estates of Austria (ch. 246). (December) In Vienna Hunyadi pays homage to the king and resigns the office of governor (ch. 246).

1453 (February 1) In exchange for his resignation, Hunyadi receives from the king the hereditary title of Count, and retains his control over Hungary as Captain-General of the kingdom (ch. 246).

(May 29) Conquest of Constantinople by Sultan Mehmed II (ch. 249).

1454   Hunyadi's victory over the Turks at Kruševac in Serbia (ch. 245).

1455   (June) The Franciscan Giovanni da Capestrano begins proclaiming a crusade in Hungary (ch. 247).

1456   (February 6) King Ladislas V arrives in Hungary (ch. 248, and see ch. 253). (July 4-22) Siege of Belgrade by Sultan Mehmed. Hunyadi and the crusaders of Capestrano liberate the castle and win a great victory (ch. 250). (August 11) Death of János Hunyadi at Zimony near Belgrade (ch. 251). (October-November) Negotiations between the king and László Hunyadi, elder son and heir of the regent (ch. 253). (October 23) Capestrano dies at Ujlak (ch. 252). (November 9) Count Ulrich of Cilli, uncle and guardian of the king, is murdered at Belgrade by László Hunyadi and his followers (ch. 253). (December) King Ladislas V, then prisoner of the Hunyadi party, promises impunity to the murderers of his uncle (ch. 254) and invests László Hunyadi with the office of Captain-General.

1457   (March 14) Because of a coup d'état, László Hunyadi is arrested at Buda Castle along with his younger brother Matthias and his chief supporters. (March 16) Execution of László Hunyadi (ch. 255). (April to September) Civil war between the parties of the king and of the Hunyadi family, the latter being headed by Mihály Szilágyi, maternal uncle of the Hunyadi brothers (ch. 256). (November 23) Death of King Ladislas V at Prague (ch. 257).

1458   (January 24) Matthias Hunyadi, called Corvinus, is proclaimed King in Buda (ch. 258). (February 9) The Regent of Bohemia, George Podiebrad, sets free King Matthias, who had been brought to Prague on the order of the king (ch. 259). (February 14) King Matthias I (1458-1490) enthroned in the church of St. Mary in Buda instead of being crowned, the Holy Crown being in Emperor Frederick's hands (ch. 259).

1459   (April) Frederick, after being proclaimed King of Hungary by a handful of barons, is defeated by Matthias' armies at Körmend (ch. 260).

1463 (June) Ottoman conquest of Bosnia. (July 19) Treaty of Wiener Neustadt with Emperor Frederick. At the expense of accepting harsh terms, Matthias recovers the Holy Crown, taken by Queen Elizabeth in 1440. (October to December) Campaign of Matthias against the Turks into Bosnia. Siege of Jajce. (December 25) Surrender of Jajce to the Hungarian King (ch. 260).

1464 (March 29) Crowning of Matthias at Székesfehérvár. (November) Unsuccessful siege of Zvornik in Bosnia (ch. 261).

1467 (January) Punishment of Jan Svehla's mercenary band at Kosztolány (ch. 261). (September) Revolt in Transylvania suppressed (ch. 261). (November) Expedition against Voivode István the Great of Moldavia (ch. 261).

1468 (April) Ten-year war against Bohemia begins (ch. 261).

1469 (May 3) King Matthias elected King of Bohemia by Czech catholics at Olomouc (ch. 261).

1471 (Autumn) Baronial plot against King Matthias, led by Archbishop János Vitéz of Esztergom. Prince Kazimierz of Poland, candidate for the throne, invades north Hungary (ch. 262).

1474 (October-November) Matthias blockaded by the Kings of Poland and Bohemia in Breslau (ch. 262).

1476 (February 15) Capture of Sabač from the Turks (ch. 262).

1479 (July 21) Peace treaty between Hungary and Bohemia ratified by Matthias and King Wladislas at Olomouc (ch. 262).

1482 (September 30) Capture of Hainburg. Hungarian conquest of Austria begins.

1485 (June 1) The city of Vienna surrenders to Matthias (ch. 262).

1487 (August 17) By entering Wiener Neustadt Matthias completes the conquest of Lower Austria (ch. 262).

1488 (March 20) Thuróczy's Chronicle printed in Brno and (June 3) in Augsburg.

JÁNOS THURÓCZY

Chronicle of the Hungarians

✠ 195:   HERE BEGINS THE PREFACE TO THE CHRONI-
CLE OF SIGISMUND, WHO BECAME KING AND EMPEROR,
AND WHOSE OTHER ACCOMPLISHMENTS ARE ALSO HERE
RECOUNTED ✠

B ecause there is good reason to do so, or rather because
an old friendship which has not yet wavered compels
me, I have thought it fitting to comply more fully with
your wishes than you required when you asked that I tell afresh
the forgotten deeds of men, to prevent their being snatched away
by manifest neglect. And in order that the work, which I have
at your prompting rashly commenced, should not lack a conclusion, I have, in preference to every other course, presumed

like a typical madman to treat also of matters beyond my powers, namely the times of our late prince Sigismund, king and Roman emperor (whom above I called margrave of Brandenburg), which the mind perceives to be linked, so to speak, to the work I have already concluded, my purpose being to ensure that events which someone's pen has not written down may not disappear from the records of mankind. With an apology in advance for my pen and simple, unadorned poetry, I have undertaken to touch on those events that occurred within the living heart of Hungary following the sad end of King Charles, during the celebrated reign of our modern prince, particularly those that are worthy of the honor of immortality, in so far as I have been informed of these events, first by his magnificence, the lord Mihály Ország, palatine (whom the emperor raised up, not without obvious merit, from the humble dwellings of the lesser nobility to the lofty palaces of the baronage), and then by a certain register[1] of this emperor, which was daily compiled as a record of his times. And to you, who did not feel ashamed to write pressing me to begin this work, though I am such an insignificant man with feeble Latin,[2] I have undertaken to dedicate my narrative of these events. Farewell!

⎯⎯⎯⎯⎯⎯⎯⎯⎯⎯

1. For its own use, the royal chancellery had the text of the documents issued there copied into register books, to which Thuróczy, as a chancellery clerk, had easy access. The use of registers was a custom introduced first by Charles I of Anjou about 1320, after the Sicilian model and resumed later by Sigismund. All such register books were destroyed during the two Ottoman conquests of Buda in 1526 and 1541.

2. Like Gregory of Tours and other writers, Thuróczy employs the humility topos in exaggerating his own insignificance and the poverty of his Latin.

✠ 196 (I): CONCERNING THE VENGEANCE EXACTED BY THE BAN, JÁNOS OF HORVÁTI, FROM THE QUEENS AND THE PALATINE[3] ✠

3. Here begins, preceded by the short preface above, the third and last part of the Chronicle (see *Introduction*). The story begins in 1386, immediately after the assassination of King Charles II the Little, whose fortune was recounted in the previous chapters. A brief background necessary for an understanding of the chronicle is as follows. King Louis I of Hungary (1342-1382) and of Poland, known as Louis the Great, died in 1382. He had been the last male descendant of the Hungarian branch of the House of Anjou and he left only two minor daughters: Mary, born in 1371 and successor in Hungary under the regency of her mother Elizabeth, and Hedwig, born in 1373 and eventually (1384) Queen of Poland. Mary had been betrothed since 1379 to the young Margrave of Brandenburg, Sigismund (b. 1368), younger brother of the Bohemian, Roman, and German King Wenceslas of the House of Luxemburg. It had been arranged that Sigismund should ascend the Hungarian throne after his marriage, but, in the meantime, other plans were being made. The queen mother, Elizabeth, supported by the Count Palatine, Miklós Garai senior, and by her other favorites, made efforts to break up the engagement and to enter into a new alliance with the French royal court. Another faction of the barons, resenting female rule as well as the favoritism of the queen mother, rose in open revolt. In 1385 one group, led by János of Horváti and his brothers, invited King Charles III of Naples, the sole male offspring of the House of Anjou, to the Hungarian throne. From that point events followed rapidly. In June a Bohemian army invaded Northwest Hungary to assert Sigismund's rights, and, faced with a dual menace, the queen mother was forced to yield. She dismissed Garai, who was replaced as Count Palatine by one of the rebellious barons, and, in August, Sigismund celebrated his wedding with the young queen. In September, however, Charles landed in Dalmatia and, by the end of the year, was crowned king (Dec. 31). Sigismund fled into Bohemia, and the queens and their party submitted to the new king without resistance, although Charles had brought no army from home and his partisans in Hungary were not numerous. One finds an explanation for this peaceful attitude on the part of the queens in subsequent events. Only forty days after his coronation, on February 7, 1386, King Charles, who was separated on some pretext from his followers, was assaulted in the royal palace of Buda by Garai and other men loyal to the queens. Taken captive and severly wounded, he was sent to Visegrád Castle, where he died soon afterwards (Feb. 24), either from his wounds or by assassination. It is after these events that Thuróczy's narrative begins.

After King Charles[4] had been wickedly slain and the queens[5] had again seized control of the kingdom, those who were the king's aids shook with great fear and searched for regions where they might be safe, while remaining no less fervent to avenge the king who had been killed. The queens and the palatine,[6] however, reckoned that they had smoothed away and overcome all opposition to them after the king had been slain. And when that time of the year arrived when the hot sun was entering the sign of the lion and beating down with its burning heat[7] upon the reapers, the ill-fated queens and the palatine foolishly left Buda[8] led on by madness, with only their retinues of household attendants[9] to escort

4. Charles of Durazzo (1354-1386), King of Naples (Charles III) and of Hungary (Charles II), son of Duke Louis of Durazzo from a younger branch of the House of Anjou. Brought up in the court of his second cousin, King Louis of Hungary, he became, with his support, King of Naples in 1381 and was invited to the throne of Hungary in 1385. For his fate see note 3.

5. Mary (1371-1395), elder daughter of King Louis I, reigning Queen of Hungary from 1382, and her mother Elizabeth (1339-1387), of Bosnian origin, who led the regency for her. See note 3.

6. Miklós Garai (i.e. of Gara) senior (d. 1386), Hungarian magnate, principal supporter of the queen mother, called here Palatine because he held this office previously (1375-1385); see note 3. The possessions of his family lay in South Hungary, centered around Gara (today Gorjani, Yugoslavia), whence his family derived its name. *Count Palatine (regni Hungariae palatinus)*: the first in rank among the lay office-holders of Hungary (called *barones regni*, "barons of the realm"), of unparalleled prestige and power due partly to his judicial authority (he was chief justice of the realm) and partly to his great "honours," i.e. to royal castles and revenues which he was accustomed to hold and receive (until 1402) "during the King's pleasure" by virtue of his office. [For the institution of royal "honours," see Pál Engel, "Honor, vár, ispánság. Tanulmányok az Anjou-királyság kormányzati rendszeréről" ("Honours, Castles, and Counties. Studies on the System of Government in Angevin Hungary"), *Századok* 116 (1982), 880-920].

7. In the middle of July, 1386. Thuróczy had a penchant for dating events in zodiacal terms, a habit he learned from the thirteenth-century writer, Guido della Colonna, who was one of his models. He obviously thought it a proof of his erudition.

8. The walled royal city of Buda with a fortified royal palace next to it,

them, and they wandered through the southern counties[10] of the
kingdom. And when on the most solemn feast day of blessed
James the Apostle[11] they were proceeding, untroubled by any
suspicion of an ambush, through the middle of a field toward
the town of Diakó,[12] the ban, János of Horváti,[13] who had col-

---

both on Castle Hill (today part of Budapest). It was one of the king's main
residences in the Middle Ages, and eventually capital of the kingdom.

9. *Aulici* was a comprehensive term in Thuróczy's own age for the
knightly members of the royal household (the *aula*). Up to about 1450 they
were called respectively "knights" or "squires" of the household (*milites* or *iuvenes aulae regiae*) according to their rank. They were almost exclusively of noble
origin, belonging for the most part to well-to-do knightly, sometimes even to
baronial houses, and they were bound to the king by ties of personal fidelity,
probably by a fidelity oath. Their function was the same as that of parallel insti-
tutions in medieval Europe: besides providing an escort to the ruler, who was
permanently on the move, they executed his will at any time and in any matter,
public or private. (See the thesis, now in print, of Ágnes Kurcz, *A magyarországi
lovagi kultúra kérdései* [XIII-XIV. sz.] [*The Problems of Chivalry in Thirteenth and
Fourteenth-century Hungary*], 1975; for English parallels cf., e.g. J. O, Prestwich,
"The Military Household of the Norman Kings," *The English Historical Review*
96 (1981), 1-35).

10. In Latin the southern counties were called simply *partes inferiores*, "the
inferior parts," a general term never exactly specified. The northern ones were,
in the same uncertain way, called "the superior parts."

11. July 25, 1386.

12. Diakó (today Djakovo, Yugoslavia), market and castle in Valkó county,
residence of a bishop, called "bishop of Bosnia" (*episcopus Bosnensis*), who was,
at that time, a partisan of the Horváti brothers (see notes 3 and 13).

13. János of Horváti (d. 1394), Hungarian magnate who held the office of
Ban (see below) of Mačva (1376-1381 and 1385-1386). With his two brothers,
László and the bishop Pál of Zagreb, he led the baronial opposition against the
queens and the Count Palatine Garai, and he was the chief promoter of King
Charles (see note 1). They did not submit after the king's death, but considered
Charles's minor son, Ladislas, the legitimate heir. *Horváti*: an extinct village in
Valkó county (to the east of Djakovo, Yugoslavia) that gave the family its name.
Ban (banus): title of governors appointed to the southern frontier provinces
in medieval Hungary. In the fourteenth century there were four of them: the
Ban of Slavonia in the region of Zagreb, of Dalmatia and Croatia to the south
of the Kapela mountains of Severin (today Turnu-Severin, Romania), and of
Mačva. All four were counted among the principal officials (the *barones*) of the

lected a large hostile host and was burning for revenge, rushed in a rage against the escorting attendants. The two enemies confronted each other in a harsh struggle; and when the partisans of the queens and the palatine saw that the enemy had them outnumbered, those who had not yet fallen turned their backs and precipitately fled. It was in fact Balázs Forgách[14] who, because of his boldness, received the first-fruits of the conflict: thrown from his horse by a blow from an enemy lance into the midst of the combatants, he was taken captive and, as the queens looked on, beheaded. And when Garai the palatine had reflected that for so critical a situation death alone was the remedy, he got down from his horse, joined the queens in their carriage, and, wielding his sword against the enemy, defended himself and the queens with all his strength. But what good was the protection afforded by one hand alone?

When enemy arms pressed him on all sides, wounding him with deadly arrows, he snapped like reeds the ones that had become lodged in his body, so that they would not get in the way of his sword-hand. And all the while he held off a very large body of men until his feet were seized by a certain knight from beneath the royal carriage, who from that position feared no injury. Garai was thrown to the ground and was there decapitated, as fear of their imminent death and the shrill screams of the queens and their servants increased. Once the palatine had been slain, and some of the queen's household attendants had been killed and others put to flight, the fierce Croats,[15] knowing nothing of the

───────────────

kingdom. As a territory the Banate (banatus) of Mačva, in Hungarian Macsó, comprised the northwestern part of present-day Serbia, basically the region west of Belgrade, as well as five southern counties of Hungary that were also governed by the Ban, though they did not belong to the Banate proper.

14. Balázs Forgách, knight and, as Cup-bearer to the King (*magister pincernarum regalium*, 1382-1386), one of the principal officials of the household. He had played a leading part in the assault on King Charles (see note 3).

15. Horváti's followers are described as Croats because the majority of

respect accorded royalty, attacked the queens' carriages and simultaneously overturned them, dragging out of them the queens as well as their ladies-in-waiting without any allowance for their sex and deference to the royal dignity. And subjecting them to many insults, they brought them as prisoners into the presence of their ban.

When with many reproaches the ban charged them with the murder of King Charles, the elder queen at once fell to her knees, raised her hands in supplication, and said: "Be merciful, my lord Ban, be merciful! And remember the fief you once received from our King Louis[16] and do not be so angry with his blameless daughter! It was on my authority that the crime was committed; but the partisan who perpetrated it and who also brought me to this extremity has paid the penalty for it. Please, then, as a man of honor, have pity on one of the fragile sex, for it was not without cause that I did wrong." Although the queen wished to speak at greater length, the ban withdrew from her sight.

Now when that day's light had been made to flee, and night had fallen and spread its darkness everywhere, Queen Elizabeth was carried off, strangled, and drowned[17] in the deep waters of the River Bosut.[18] As for the maidens of the royal palace, who were remarkable both for their nobility of birth and for

them came from regions south of the river Sava, an area largely inhabited by a Croatian population. The fact that the rebels were, for the most part, Hungarian nobles was deliberately ignored by Thuróczy in order to stress the ferocity (*feritas*) of the Croats and thereby to show his aversion to an alien-speaking people, a feeling shared by most of his contemporaries.

16. Thuróczy alludes to the fact, mentioned by him previously, that the Horváti brothers owed their career and fortune to the favor of King Louis.

17. An error of Thuróczy concerning time and place. Elizabeth was killed six months later in the early days of January, 1387, in the Dalmatian castle of Novigrad near Zadar on the Adriatic Sea.

18. The little river Bosut, a parallel branch of the Sava. This river is near Djakovo where, according to Thuróczy, the capture of the queens took place. In contemporary sources the place of the skirmish is said to have been "in the environs of Gara (Gorjani)".

their beauty, they are said to have been shamefully violated that same night, a story which, in my view, is quite trustworthy. At length, as dawn was announcing the rising of the nearby sun which lightens the day, the Croats arose in haste from their beds and, reining their horses round, headed quickly across country towards Croatia,[19] taking the younger queen with them as a prisoner.

Alas for the human condition! How changeable is its fate! For who would have thought that chance, which long smiled upon the queens, could be changed so quickly into adversity, that vengeance, itself recently exacted, should be followed in so short a time by an unexpected retaliation for their crime? Such were the penalties paid by the queens and the palatine for the murder of Charles. For He who created all things and is mindful of them all also leaves nothing untouched by his judgment.

✠ 197 (II): CONCERNING THE RETURN TO BUDA OF THE MARGRAVE SIGISMUND AND HIS LIBERATION OF THE QUEEN ✠

At the same time when King Charles poured forth both his blood and his spirit, Queen Elizabeth's newfound joy had induced her to arrange for a detailed narrative of what had been accomplished to be written up for dispatch to Margrave Sigismund,[20] and she had had her messengers request that he come quickly. For that reason Margrave Sigismund,

---

19. Medieval Croatia was not identical with the territory of the present-day Republic of Croatia. As a frontier province of Hungary (see note 13), it comprised the region between the Kapela mountains and the Adriatic Sea.

20. Sigismund of Luxemburg (1368-1437), Margrave of Brandenburg, son of Emperor Charles IV, husband of Queen Mary from August, 1385 (see note 3). He had left Hungary before King Charles arrived.

who had not yet heard news of the queens' very great misfortune, marched speedily down to Buda with a great armed band of Bohemians, attended also by many nobles from the northern counties[21] of the kingdom of Hungary. And he was admitted without resistance to the citadel.[22]

Now during this same period the younger queen was being held in a fortress called Krupa,[23] situated in the territories of Croatia. After the ban, János of Horváti, heard that the margrave was in Buda and had the support of the nobles, he became discouraged, dispirited, and gravely anxious. So he went to the queen and addressed these words to her: "I repent of all the things done to you and your mother—even if you both deserved them well enough—though it was my intention for you both to die in the same way. For I have no doubt at all that if you are kept alive, at some time or other your mother's fate will be mine. But so that my hands are not stained by the blood of my benefactor, I have decided to set you free, on condition, however, that you swear to me a loyal oath that I shall never be sorry for having done so. Otherwise I shall be certain to finish what I have started; and if necessary I shall settle the whole affair by exacting of you the same penalty your mother paid." And with these words he withdrew to his residence.

The queen's heart was rent by the proud words of the tyrant, and for that reason copious tears welled up in her eyes and

---

21. See note 10.
22. Thuróczy is in error. It was by no means at the invitation of the queen mother that Sigismund returned to Hungary. He was escorted by a huge Bohemian army led in person by his brother, King Wenceslas, who, by the treaty of Győr (April, 1386), forced the queens to restore to Sigismund his rights. When they conceded, Sigismund was reinstated in June as prince consort at the court in Buda. All this happened, contrary to Thuróczy's statement, before the capture of the queens (see appended *Chronology of events*).
23. Krupa (today Bosanska Krupa, Yugoslavia), royal castle on the river Una, held by the Ban of Slavonia as part of his office (see note 13). Thuróczy's statement about the queens being held here for a time is not supported by other sources.

flowed down her pale cheeks. Finally, when she had wept enough, she dried her eyes and asked that he be called to her. When he came, the queen shook with fear and promised not only to swear an oath to him but also always to revere him like a father for saving her life. Holy relics were then brought in and all the terms demanded by the ban were confirmed by the queen in the oath that she swore. Because of her action the queen's carriage was prepared and she herself, as if snatched from the river, was escorted to Buda, the city she longed for.[24]

✠ 198 (III): CONCERNING THE CORONATION OF KING SIGISMUND ✠

1n the course of three years or a little more after the death[25] of King Louis, the course of events took a violent change, with considerable bloodshed and plundering. At length the nobles of the kingdom, preferring the joys and pleasures of peace to the torments of harsh warfare, assembled in the year of our Lord 1386, at Székesfehérvar,[26] on the great feast of Pentecost.[27] It was that time of the year when spring,

─────────────

24. Thuróczy had a tendency to invent not only speeches which were never delivered but, at times, scenes which never happened. Mary was not set free by Horváti, but released by an army of Sigismund and a Venetian fleet from the castle of Novigrad (see note 17) on June 4, 1387. At that time, Horváti himself was fighting far from there, in South Hungary, against Sigismund's commanders (see note 41). After her liberation Mary did not go to Buda but to Zagreb, where, on July 4, she met her husband, then already crowned king.

25. Louis the Great died on September 10, 1382. From then to the coronation of Sigismund more than four years passed.

26. Székesfehérvár, royal city (southwest of Budapest) where, according to ancient custom, the coronations of Hungarian kings took place.

27. Here and below Thuróczy seems to have merged two different events. Except for the fact that he speaks of a coronation at Székesfehérvár, the story he tells in this chapter may be accepted as a colored account of what happened af-

that most agreeable season because of the sweet singing of little birds, was drawing near its close, to make way for the approaching summer heat. Springtime had adorned dwelling-places with red peonies;[28] and Gemini, the twins, carrying the chariot of Phoebus,[29] were ascending higher in the heavens.

When Queen Mary, her cheeks previously wet from streams of tears, stood in the midst of the general assembly of nobles that had been convoked, she addressed these words to the people, interspersed with deep sighs: "My lords and brothers, you who on recalling the merits of my father have been well-disposed towards me and have not undermined the exercise of my authority, which was given me by you! To God and to you I express my profound gratitude. You know how violent were the wars that in recent days have troubled our reign, and how many stormy dangers I have myself endured. It is by no means necessary for me to relate them to you here in your presence, or for you to hear them, for you have either seen or heard them all. Nor do I think you have forgotten the kind of agreement that has bound me in a marriage compact to this prince"—Sigismund was standing there and she pointed to him—"an agreement made before

ter Sigismund's return from Bohemia in Spring 1386 (see note 22). It is known from other sources that from about mid-June he sojourned with the court at Buda and took some part in governmental affairs. It is therefore not at all improbable that, as we are told here, at Pentecost (June 10, 1386) his rights were in fact solemnly restored to him by the queens at Buda, an act which Thuróczy recorded but confused with Sigismund's subsequent coronation. This latter act did indeed take place at Székesfehérvár, as Thuróczy tells us, not in 1386 but in 1387, and not on Pentecost but on Palm Sunday (March 31). Queen Mary was not then present, as she was confined in prison (see note 24).

28. Peonies, once considered a kind of rose in Middle Europe. The Hungarian name for them is still "roses of Pentecost" (see also German "Pfingstrose").

29. In zodiacal terms (see note 7), the period when the Sun stands in the sign of the Gemini, i.e. between May 12 and June 12. Phoebus was an epithet of Apollo as the god of light; his chariot symbolized the sun.

the passing of my father of happy memory, which was in accord with your wishes. Indeed I believe that those arrangements
which you then found acceptable are acceptable now also. Behold, then, I make a king of my betrothed; and to him I yield
jurisdiction over the kingdom together with the diadem. I do
this chiefly because I am aware that you do not like the rule of
a woman and that such a rule is not strong enough to guide the
reins of so violent a people, as events demonstrate."[30] With this,
placing the margrave at her side before all the people, she said:
"This is my lord and husband; this is your king. Refrain, then,
from harming the kingdom; and do not destroy yourselves in
mutual slaughter. For peace everywhere on earth is the ultimate
blessing, and it is a people living in harmony that the neighboring kingdom fears." The queen's speech pleased everyone there
present. And so on the most solemn feast of Pentecost, Margrave Sigismund, in his twentieth year,[31] was with great jubi-

30. Thuróczy frequently pointed out to his readers the perils that female
rule would bring to the country. In writing his chronicle he was motivated by
the beliefs of his age and by court intrigues. King Matthias Corvinus (1458-
1490), whom he served, was laboring then to assure the succession for his il-
legitimate son at the expense of his own wife. Thuróczy's attitude reflects the
view of the nobility and is intended to bolster the king. Resistance to the political activities of women must have been especially strong among the Hungarian nobility, where patriarchal customs of ancient origin survived far into
modern times and where, accordingly, the social and legal status of women
was inferior when compared with the status they enjoyed in western Europe.
This was apparent, above all, in rules regulating inheritance. Heirs to landed
property were as a rule the male descendants or, when they were lacking, the
next closest relatives in the male line. Female succession and the transmission
of property rights through daughters were made possible, in certain cases, by
legal reforms of the fourteenth century (for these, see Ferenc Eckhart, "Vita a
leánynegyedről" ["On the dispute concerning the *quartalicium*"], *Századok* 66
[1932, 408-415]) but they always remained the exception. Under such circumstances, Hungary was not, as Thuróczy correctly stated, a country where a
queen could count on lasting loyalty.

31. Sigismund was born on February 15, 1368, and was indeed crowned
in his 20th year. In 1386, however, he was only eighteen.

lation solemnly anointed and crowned king, after the fashion of the other kings of Hungary.[32]

✠ 199 (IV): CONCERNING THE PENALTIES EXACTED FROM THE BAN, JÁNOS OF HORVÁTI ✠

nce King Sigismund had successfully acquired the sceptre of the kingdom of Hungary, Queen Mary, who some time ago conceived the hope of revenge for the misfortune she had suffered and was burning with desire for its fulfillment, very frequently appealed to him to seek revenge against those who had wronged her; she wearied him with repeated tearful suggestions and reproached him for the countless and various hardships she had endured.

At the same time the ban, János of Horváti, to safeguard his life, had by stealth entered the royal fortress called Pozsegavár.[33] Therefore King Sigismund, roused by the continual complaints of his wife, readied his troops and pretended to send them to the regions across the Danube, in the direction of Bulgaria, before having them change direction to besiege the aforementioned fortress. When the war machines were fiercely storming it during the siege, and the attackers were doubtful of its speedy capture, the ban, János of Horváti, found that he was free to flee one night, when darkness covered the earth everywhere, providing an appropriate opportunity for clandestine deeds. He leapt

32. The circumstances of the coronation ceremony in Hungary were prescribed, as elsewhere, by established custom. In order to be valid it had to be held at Székesfehérvár and performed by the first in rank among the prelates, i.e., normally the archbishop of Esztergom, who was Primate of Hungary. The holy crown of Saint Stephen was also essential to the ceremony. Sigismund was in fact crowned by the bishop of Veszprém, the archiepiscopal see being vacant.

33. Pozsegavár (today Slavonska Požega, Yugoslavia), royal castle and borough in Pozsega county.

from that part of the fortress where Voivode István Lackfi,[34] and another István, of Simontornya,[35] were keeping watch, having joined the king's expedition in bad faith. That same night he crossed the river Sava[36] —it is not known whether he did so by boat or by swimming—and entered a fortress named Dobor,[37] situated in the territories of Bosnia[38] that are called Usora.[39] There he found Pál,[40] bishop of Zagreb, and more of his partners in crime.[41] At the same time the Bosnians, Dalmatians, and

---

34. István Lackfi senior (d. 1397), head of the family of the Lackfis (i.e. "sons of Lack"), then the wealthiest noble house in Hungary. He was called "voivode" because he had held for a time (1372-1376) the high office of Voivode of Transylvania. He was Count Palatine in the beginning of Sigismund's reign (1387-1392). *Voivode*: title of the governor of Transylvania, a large eastern province of medieval Hungary that is today part of Rumania. At that time he was considered next in rank after the Count Palatine among the "barons of the realm."

35. István Lackfi junior (d. 1397), nephew of the Voivode Stephen (see note 34), and called "of Simontornya" after a castle of his family in Tolna county (south of Székesfehérvár). As Master of the Horse (1368-1387) he was a principal official of the royal household and counted among the "barons of the realm."

36. The river Sava (Száva in Hungarian) formed the southern frontier of Hungary in the Middle Ages.

37. Dobor was a castle in the northern part of Bosnia on the river Bosna (north of Sarajevo, Yugoslavia).

38. Bosnia was a principality (kingdom since 1377) and a neighbor south of Hungary. Though the Hungarian kings tried more than once to bring it under their control, it remained practically independent until its Ottoman conquest in 1463 (see note 555).

39. Usora (Ozora in Hungarian), a northern region of the Kingdom of Bosnia between the rivers Drina, Sava, and Vrbas.

40. Pál of Horváti, bishop of Csanád (1377-1378) and of Zagreb (1378-1387), brother and supporter of János of Horváti (see note 13). In 1387 he was deprived of his see and died in exile, probably at Naples, at an unknown time.

41. The events reported above took place about June/July 1387. Thuróczy's statement that István Lackfi junior was in some way responsible for Horváti's escape from Pozsegavár, when it was under siege by Sigismund's commanders, is supported also by the fact that, soon after (i.e., before August, 1387), he was relieved of his office as Master of the Horse, although, as yet, he was not accused explicitly of treachery. On the other side, the charge against

Croatians, corrupted by the persuasive powers of János the ban and of the great men of his band, had rebelled[42] against the fealty they owed to the sceptre of Hungary, and with fire and sword were causing considerable devastation to the very borders of the kingdom. King Sigismund therefore increased the number of his troops with the intention of subjecting those kingdoms to his own suzerainty and also of storming the fortress[43] that was sheltering his disloyal vassals. Escorted on all sides by a large force of armed men, he crossed the river Sava and forced his way into the kingdom of Bosnia. Terrified by the great size of the king's expedition, János the ban placed his trust in flight (an action he had previously found satisfactory) more than in the fortifications of the castle; and before it could be blockaded, he left the fortress with a number of his confederates, all infected with the same contagion as himself; and he made his way, a fugitive, through hills and steep mountains. But this flight did him no good at all, for he fell into an ambush arranged for him by the king and was captured. As for King Sigismund, he returned home, having captured the fortress of Dobor and bound the king of Bosnia as well as the kingdoms of Dalmatia and Croatia to himself by the yoke of fealty. And he gave orders to put János the ban to death in the city of Pécs,[44] using a terrible method of execution, as the queen in her rage demanded. For to begin with he was

---

Lackfi senior (then Count Palatine) is unsupported by other sources and appears to be an arbitrary addition to the facts by Thuróczy. For the trial of the Lackfis, see below, Chapter 207.

42. King Tvrtko I of Bosnia (1377-1391) remained loyal to the queens and to Sigismund until August, 1387, when he chose to attack Croatia and the Dalmatian cities on the pretext that they were supporting the Horváti party. His entry into the war was considered rebellion by the Hungarian court, the Kings of Hungary having claimed for themselves suzerainty over Bosnia (see note 38). By 1390 King Tvrtko had occupied the greater part of Croatia and the Dalmatian coast, and it was not until 1394 that King Sigismund succeeded in inducing these regions to recognize his rule.

43. I.e., the castle of Dobor (see note 37).

44. *Civitas Quinqueecclesiensis* (meaning "city of five churches") is the me-

tied to the hindquarters of a horse and carried round through the streets of the city. In the end, tortured with glowing pincers and then divided into four parts and hung piecemeal from the gates of the city as a terrifying lesson for future malefactors, he experienced that severity with which he treated others.[45] Moreover, although not put to death when many others were killed, the bishop of Zagreb[46] could never during his lifetime be reinstated in that episcopal see.

✠ 200 (V): CONCERNING THE ARMY SENT BY KING SIGISMUND AGAINST MOLDAVIA ✠

When previously the affairs of Hungary were subject, under a woman's leadership, to the vicissitudes of fierce warfare, the Moldavians together with the transalpine regions showed contempt for the queen's authority, and they

dieval Latin name of Pécs, a city in Baranya county (in South Hungary) with an episcopal see.

45. The above account refers to events of the year 1394. According to his itinerary, Sigismund stayed in that part of the kingdom from mid-June until the end of July. Leaving Buda after June 11, he was at Pécs on June 23, at Djakovo from July 5 to 12, and at Erdut on the Danube on July 29. The siege of Dobor must have taken place immediately before his stay at Djakovo, about the end of June. It was probably at Djakovo that King Stephen Dabisa of Bosnia (1391-1395), Tvrtko's successor, solemnly paid him homage and received the honour of Somogy county in return. [Cf. Sima Cirkovič, *Istorija srednjovekovne bosanske drzave* (History of the Medieval Bosnian State) (Beograd, 1964), pp. 173 ff.] The fact of Horváti's execution is not mentioned by contemporary royal charters and is therefore rejected by some authorities (Mályusz 1984, 279, note 50) as a pure invention. It is more probable, however, that Thuróczy's story is truthful: the unusually cruel form of execution may have been an act of retaliation on the part of Queen Mary for her mother's death, an act for which the king himself bore no responsibility, and that is why he did not boast of it in any of his charters.

46. Pál of Horváti, cf. note 40.

were not yet sensible enough to support King Sigismund.[47] It was for this reason that, in the fourth year after his coronation,[48] the king renewed hostilities and attacked them, in order to reduce them to subservience. During this same period Voivode Stephen[49] was governor of Moldavia. To bar the king's approach, Stephen roused to action all the fighting force of his people, and both with defensive works[50] and with a body of archers he fortified the Alps[51] and the rough winding pathways through which the king had to march. And when the king had travelled down the Alps not apprehending any ambush, he was soon attacked by a large band of archers. Their missiles struck men as well as horses, and almost all the king's expedition was overpowered

47. From the fourteenth century to modern times two principalities existed in the territory of today's Rumania (apart from Transylvania, which belonged to Hungary). *Moldavia*, between the East Carpathians and the river Dniester, came into being about 1360, and *Wallachia*, between the South Carpathians and the Danube,had been formed a few decades earlier. In Hungarian the latter had been called "Havaselve", i.e. the province "beyond the Alps", the *partes Transalpinae*, of the Latin sources. Both countries were inhabited by Rumanians, and ruled by native princes who bore the title *voivode*. Before their rise the region was ruled by the nomadic Kumans and, in thirteenth-century sources, it was accordingly named Kumania. From the 1220s the kings of Hungary had claimed suzerainty over that territory and assumed the title of "King of Kumania." King Louis I (1342-1382) led numerous campaigns against the Rumanian *voivodes* in order to assert these claims, and succeeded in reducing them to a sort of loose subordination, which they renounced after his death.

48. Like most medieval rulers, Sigismund counted his regnal years from his coronation day, March 31, 1387. Accordingly, his "fourth year" means the time between April 1390 and March 1391, and it was indeed in that period in November 1390, that a minor expedition was led, or at least planned, against Moldavia. Sigismund, however, did not take part in it, and the events related here took place four years later, in January/February 1395, with a major campaign conducted by the king in person.

49. Stephen I, Voivode of Moldavia (c. 1394-1400).

50. Primitive frontier defenses built mainly of tree-trunks, and called 'gyepü' in medieval Hungarian.

51. The woody and snow-capped ranges of the East Carpathians, impassable except in a few places.

by showers of closely packed arrows. In an effort to save themselves by summoning all their strength, the king's knights dismounted and very courageously charged and attacked the Wallachians, whom after many had been killed they compelled to retreat, putting them to death as they fled down the steep Alpine slopes. Once the king had by the sword recovered for himself the route of access, he made his way right up to the residence[52] of Stephen the voivode. The latter realized that he had no choice but to seek pardon, and coming to the king he fell prostrate before him together with the magnates of his domain. And in these words he begged the king not to exact the punishments due for his grave transgression: "Most glorious prince! May your royal clemency forgive us who now seek your pardon, and punish with welcome benevolence what we in our impudence rashly presumed to do, in contravention of the fealty we owe. For an act of mercy towards those who are here prostrate, rather than the crushing of brazen disobedience, brings just as much glory to the royal office you hold. To be sure, we are the dust under your feet. You are our king and lord. May you with royal compassion therefore generously bestow upon us the forgiveness that is not merited by our crimes." When he had finished speaking, they together all humbly bowed their heads and awaited some expression of the king's goodwill. And to these words King Sigismund made this reply: "Although these offenses against our royal power must be deemed worthy of retribution, we nevertheless do spare and forgive you, lest our good name be smirched by an accusation of excessive harshness; and since you have not in the past been guilty of any offense, we restore you to our favor." And so Voivode Stephen and his followers fell down at the king's feet, kissed the hem of the royal robe, and then promised

---

52. On February 3, 1395, Sigismund issued a charter "before the castle of *Nempch* in our province of Moldavia." The castle of Neamţ, today in ruins not far from the Tirgu Neamţ (in Rumania), was one of the residences of Moldavian rulers. Thuróczy is probably here referring to it.

true fidelity and the payment of an annual tribute; and all these promises were strengthened by oaths of loyalty. King Sigismund therefore returned home and gave his knights and weapons one year's respite.[53]

✠ 201 (VI): What follows concerns the expedition of King Sigismund's Army against the Transalpine regions, and the death of Queen Mary ✠

After these events, King Sigismund in the sixth year[54] of his reign made war on the transalpine peoples, who had hired a powerful band of Turks[55] to defend them because they did not think they could rely on their own strength alone. When the royal troops had crossed the Alps[56] and descended to the level ground of that region, and when the two enemies had arranged themselves in formation and engaged in a pitched battle, each eager to put their own strength to the test, both the Turks and the Wallachians at once sought protection in flight, terrified by the flashing of the brightly shining armor that shielded the troops of the royal expedition. The king's army pursued them as long as it could. The Turks and the Wallachians were falling left and right, and many more would have been added to the fallen had the horses of the king's knights, weighed down by the enormous load of armor on their backs, been able

---

53. This is not true. Sigismund was far too bellicose at that time to rest a whole year. See the next chapter.

54. I.e. in 1392 or early 1393, according to Thuróczy. In reality, the following events took place in 1395, in the eighth regnal year. (See Mályusz 1969, 232 ff.)

55. On the rise of the Ottoman Turks, see chapter 203 below.

56. The South Carpathians, passable only at two points, at Braşov (Brassó, Kronstadt) and Sibiu (Nagyszeben, Hermannstadt). As a rule, Hungarian armies made use of the former pass during the Middle Ages.

to catch up with those in flight, and had the arrival of nightfall not provided the enemy with a safe crossing of the Danube.

After the dispersal of the opposing forces, King Sigismund encircled the fortress of Little Nicopolis[57] in a ferocious siege. Both Turks and Wallachians were at that time guarding this fortress, and during their frequent sorties from the walls they caused much disorder in the royal army. After, however, the king had recourse to siege-machines, he reduced a great part of the fortress to ruin, captured it, and, having executed some of its defenders and taken others captive, he handed it over for safe-keeping to a Hungarian garrison. At length the successful king returned to Hungary in triumph, having imposed the yoke of obedience upon the people of these regions.

Yet before Sigismund had arrived home, Queen Mary succumbed to a grave illness, which ended both her reign and her life.[58] The queen's death was the cause of no little concern to him, for Wladislas,[59] king of the Poles, was happily married to her twin sister, whose name was Hedwig. Believing that the sceptre of her dead sister belonged to his own wife, Wladislas sent a large army against King Sigismund. And had the most reverend

───────────────

57. The Fortress of Little Nicopolis was situated on the northern (Wallachian) side of the Danube facing the fortress of Great Nicopolis (today Nikopol) in Bulgaria. According to the king's itinerary, the campaign described here took place in July/August 1395.

58. The sequence of events is given here erroneously. Queen Mary died on May 17, 1395, shortly before the beginning of the Wallachian campaign. She was buried at Nagyvárad (Oradea–Mare, Rumania) and the king, on his way to Wallachia, attended her funeral. Thuróczy's reference to her "grave illness" is purely rhetorical: she died as the result of an accident, falling from her horse while hunting.

59. Wladislas II (1386-1434), founder of the Jagiellonian dynasty, former Grand Prince of Lithuania under his pagan name Jagiello. In 1385 he married the heiress of Poland, Hedwig (Jadwiga), daughter of Louis I of Hungary and the younger sister of Queen Mary (see note 3). After Mary's death in 1395, he claimed Hungary as an Angevin inheritance for his wife.

father, lord János Kanizsai, archbishop of Esztergom,[60] not fortified the borders of the kingdom with a great armed force, the ambitious prince would have been able to throw into confusion the government of King Sigismund, for he was then absent.

✠ 202 (VII): WHAT FOLLOWS CONCERNS THE BEHEADING OF THE THIRTY-TWO KNIGHTS ✠

Kings as well as humble men of meagre possessions, who are required to keep silence because of their standing, are by success in their affairs impelled to behave in unaccustomed ways. It alters their characters and exposes them to various enticements. For when it is a man's destiny to be directed along the path to success and prosperity, this fate will encourage him; yet it will likewise bring him troubles. As long as good luck was on his side, King Sigismund was puffed up with unaccustomed self-confidence, and he turned his attention to certain distinguished noblemen from among his subjects who previously had seriously offended him, as also the queens, while they were so disastrously reigning. These men he was concerned either to put to death or to associate willingly with himself by means of the bond of fealty, although they were under the influence of an insane and obstinate impudence, and preferred death to life under an unwelcome prince. These men were those nobles whom we today call the thirty-two knights.[61] Among them was that

---

60. János Kanizsai, bishop of Eger (1384-1387), then archbishop of Esztergom (1387-1418) and Lord Chancellor (*summus cancellarius*, 1387-1403), a favorite of Sigismund and a leading politician during the early part of his reign. In summer 1395, during the king's Wallachian campaign, he acted as regent and was able to stop the invading Polish army near Eperjes (Presov, Slovakia).

61. Thuróczy is here presumably hinting at a folk ballad, still known in his time, and below in this chapter he supplies some passages which seem to be quotations from or paraphrases of it.

very illustrious knight, famous and often greatly praised among all Hungarians, István Kont by name, a descendant of the exalted family of the lords of Hédervár.[62] Of him our generation, which is no less outstanding for its vigor and excellence of character, is not content merely to speak; no, it also sings his praises to the accompaniment of the lyre.

These knights were wandering about like vagabonds through the regions of the kingdom, thereby causing King Sigismund no little humiliation. Suspecting that they were plotting a revolution, he decreed that they should be surrounded, and he appointed György Lackfi,[63] a faithful vassal whose power was based on deceit as much as on strength of arms, to bring the knights to him by force or guile.

Now these knights suspected no hostility and, having been provided with lodging on the open land alongside the river Sava,[64] were sleeping soundly as dawn approached. Not with them was János Korpádi,[65] who, people say, was never found asleep in dawn's first rosy light. It was while they slept that György Lackfi rushed upon them, but they rose at once and snatched up their arms. He countered with promises to influence the king in their favor, all the while inspiring fear in them, for he was stronger than they in arms and men. Indeed, when they perceived that their physical powers were not a match for their enemy, they accepted his assurances and submitted. But

62. Hédervár in Győr (today Győr-Sopron) county, a village with a castle and the seat of a ranking family in the fourteenth and fifteenth centuries. István, with the surname Kont, was one of the leaders of the Horváti party.

63. György Lackfi (d. 1393), son of Voivode András of Transylvania, cousin of the Count Palatine István Lackfi (see note 34), later Ban of Mačva (1392-1393). The events recorded here happened in early 1388 and formed part of the military operations against the Horváti party.

64. The river Sava (Száva); see note 36.

65. Korpád (today Nagykorpád), a village in Somogy county. János Korpádi, a minor nobleman, was beheaded in spring 1388 and his estates were given to the Kanizsai family, i.e. to Archbishop János and his brothers.

when they reached a town called Karom,[66] they were consigned to harsh imprisonment and conveyed in carriages to the city of Buda.

During their journey these nobles had conferred amongst themselves, concluding that although they would be coming into the king's presence, they would nevertheless not consider themselves obliged to give him any respectful greetings. And this is in fact what happened. For when King Sigismund took his seat in their midst, surrounded by his subjects, and these nobles were brought into his presence, none of them opened his mouth to greet him, nor did they show him any honor by bowing their heads or bending the knee. This disgraceful behavior roused King Sigismund to greater anger. And so, in a fit of fury he had them beheaded in the city of Buda itself, in the square of St. George the Martyr.[67] Some say that when István Kont had to suffer decapitation, he chose to lie on his back and face the executioner's blow: he said that he had fearlessly witnessed many deaths close at hand and that he was certainly not afraid of what was about to happen—indeed, he wanted to watch. Not a few people also say that these nobles were thirty-one in number. But when at their execution a swordsman of István Kont called Csóka dissolved irrevocably into tears and wept without ceasing, the king caught sight of him and said: "Control your tears, my son, and stop your weeping. Behold me, your lord, who have the power to bestow more upon you than does he who has been beheaded." To this they say the boy replied: "I shall never serve you, you Bohemian swine!"[68] Finally, at the king's command,

66. Karom (today Sremski Karlovci, Yugoslavia), a market in Szerém county.

67. St. George's Square, named after a chapel founded by King Louis I, was located in the south end of the medieval city of Buda (see note 8) next to the royal palace. In medieval times it was the scene of festivities and various important events.

68. The passage certainly comes from the folk ballad (see note 61). The

the boy endured the same sentence as his master and completed the number of thirty-two mentioned above.

Now after these knights had shed their blood and offered up their spirits, they were buried in the consecrated earth of the cemetery of the Blessed Sacrament Chapel,[69] situated in a suburb of the city of Buda, which will serve as their permanent dwelling until the angel sounds the trumpet. The deaths of these knights provided those sparks which, though hidden under such distinguished ashes, afterwards flared up and blazed between King Sigismund and the Hungarian people. As a consequence his government was never again secure as long as he lived.

✠ 203 (VIII): CONCERNING THE WAR KING SIGISMUND UNSUCCESSFULLY WAGED AT THE FOOT OF THE FORTRESS OF GREAT NICOPOLIS ✠

D uring the prosperous reign of the late King Louis, a great disagreement arose among the Greeks[70] that led to violent turmoil and civil dissension. The Greeks had two rulers. Although not born of the same parents, each one nevertheless kept claiming that he was the one of imperial descent and that the prerogative of rule therefore belonged by right to him. Likewise other Greeks took sides at will, supporting and following one or the other of these claimants, and aggressively contending in a civil war for the disputed name of emperor. And

person named Csóka (meaning "jackdaw" in Hungarian, a species of bird in the *corvidae* [raven, crow] family), is otherwise unknown. The explanatory address, "Bohemian swine," alludes, in a crude way, to Sigismund's origin.

69. The Chapel of the Blessed Sacrament in the medieval St. Peter suburb of Buda, between Castle Hill and the Danube. Its exact site is not known.

70. The term "Greek" denotes here the subjects of the Byzantine Empire. The following passage refers, in a somewhat confused way, to the civil war between the rival emperors, John V Palaeologus (1341-1391) and John VI Cantacuzenus (1347-1355), in the 1340s and 1350s.

when one of the claimants saw that his own side was faltering, he was seized by a desire for revenge, and with the offer of a reward along with other promises he invited into Greece from Asia Murad I,[71] the third of the Turkish sultans after they had begun their rule, to bring assistance to his cause. Persuading this sultan to help was not particularly difficult, for he had previously been eager to intervene and was ready to bring all his military strength to bear. And so the Greek claimant brought the sultan and his troops in ships across the Dardanelles[72] into Thrace,[73] on condition that once the war was over, he would be shipped back home again. It was by this agreement that the Turkish race migrated[74] from Asia into Europe.

This misguided action of the Greeks set alight the inextinguishable pyre now constantly blazing throughout regions of Europe; it germinated the seeds of our miseries, which are sending forth abundant new sprouts in our fields. For Murad was intending to do not what he had promised, but what he hoped could be to his advantage. When occasion offered, he always from one day to the next dragged out the war he was supposed to be fighting, so that, without any losses to himself, he could attack the Greeks, who were weakened by mutual slaughter, and the more easily overpower and crush them. Nor was he deceived by his expectations. For when he discerned that the Greeks were

71. Murad I, ruler of the Ottoman Turks (1362-1389). Contrary to Thuróczy's statement, it was his father and predecessor, Sultan Orhan (1326-1362), who was engaged in 1344/1345 by Emperor John Cantacuzenus to fight against his rival.

72. The Dardanelles or the Hellespont (*mare Helesponti*), the strait connecting the Sea of Marmara with the Aegean.

73. Thrace was a province of the Byzantine Empire between the Balkan Mountains, the Black Sea and the Aegean.

74. The Ottoman Empire, which by Thuróczy's time stretched to the southern border of Hungary, was, until the reign of Murad I, a minor principality in the northwest corner of Asia Minor, founded by Murad's grandfather Osman (d. 1326) in the early fourteenth century.

faltering in the long war and could little help themselves because they had exhausted their domestic resources, he at once contrived an opportunity to turn his arms against them. And after he had at a very favorable moment seized the town of Gallipoli,[75] located on the Hellespont, he did not hesitate to besiege the other cities of Greece, to ravage the fields, and to seize possession of everything indiscriminately, persisting until he had subjected a great part of Thrace to his authority.

As Turkish fortunes hereafter continued daily to prosper, sovereignty in Hungary passed to King Sigismund upon the death of King Louis. Thereupon Murad's son, Bayezid,[76] sultan of the Turks, who was as acutely talented and qualified as his father and more audacious than he in taking on difficult enterprises, in a short time captured the whole of Thrace,[77] and Thessaly,[78] Macedonia,[79] Phocis, Boeotia and Attica,[80] forcing

75. Gallipoli (today Gelibolu, Turkey), Byzantine city on the Dardanelles. It was captured by Orhan's son Süleyman in 1354 after an earthquake that ruined the city walls. Gallipoli was the first important acquistion of the Ottomans on European soil.

76. Bayezid I, sultan of the Ottomans (1389-1402).

77. Thrace was conquered by Murad I between 1362 and 1375, but a small part of it had remained in Byzantine hands.

78. Thessaly, an ancient province of Greece, formed a separate principality until 1392 or 1393 when it fell under Ottoman control.

79. Macedonia, a former Byzantine province, was only a geographical term by the end of the Middle Ages. Its territory was considerably larger than the modern Republic of Macedonia (part of Yugoslavia), and was divided among several Serbian princes when the armies of Murad I (and not of Bayezid I, as Thuróczy suggests) conquered it between 1375 and 1389.

them to capitulate and incorporating them in his domain. He also savagely attacked the Mysians, whom we call Bulgarians[81] and who were subject to the authority of King Sigismund. To this Bayezid the king is said to have sent his heralds and to have communicated his wish that the sultan cease his hostilities against the kingdom, which by right belonged to the king. It is also said that for a while Bayezid, as it happened, kept Sigismund waiting for a response until the sultan had made himself master of all Bulgaria. In the end Bayezid is said to have had various arms, namely spears, shields, and quivers used by the Turks against their enemies, hung on each of the walls of a house. And when Sigismund's heralds were ushered into his presence, it is reported that he said to them, while at the same time showing them the arms hanging on the walls: "Return to your king and tell him that I, too, as you see, have a sufficient right to this land." This did not cause King Sigismund to feel at all fearful of exacting retribution. And so, in the 1396th year of the Lord's Incarnation and the tenth of his own reign, Sigismund mustered all the military resources of his realm and assembled an enormous army. Indeed, to this great royal expedition the duke of

---

80. Phocis, Boeotia, and Attica were ancient names, rarely used, if at all, in the Middle Ages for provinces of central Greece. Humanist literature revived them in the fifteenth century, and Thuróczy borrowed them from his main source, the *Cosmography of Aeneas Silvius Piccolomini* (Pope Pius II, 1405-1464). These parts of Greece were occupied by the Ottomans later in the fifteenth century.

81. Moesia, province of the ancient Roman Empire between the Balkan Mountains and the Danube, was inhabited by Bulgarians in the Middle Ages. It is confused here with Mysia, another Roman province in Asia Minor. Three Bulgarian principalities existed in the second half of the fourteenth century: Dobrudja in the east, Tirnovo in the middle, and Vidin to the west of Bulgaria. From 1271 the numerous titles of the kings of Hungary also included that of Bulgaria (*rex Bulgariae*), but from 1369 they held only suzerainty over the "Emperor" (*tsar*) of Vidin. Bayezid I subdued Tirnovo in 1393 and Vidin in 1396 or 1397.

Burgundy,[82] among other nations, and the Frankish or Gallic people brought a considerable supply of arms and companies of mighty warriors. Representations of their armorial bearings, painted on panels and attached to the walls in the Dominican cloister of St. Nicholas the Confessor[83] in Buda, have endured as a memorial down to my own time. Having then set in motion his great armed host, King Sigismund crossed the Danube. Not only did he show no fear of the sultan of the Turks, but some report that he said: "Why should we fear this man? Were the immense weight of the heavens above us to tumble down, we could hold it up with the spears we are carrying and thus not be harmed."

At length he reached the borders of Bulgaria, having passed through the kingdom of Rascia[84] with savage cruelty, considerable depredation, and an excessive din of shocking proportions. Next, not without his supporters shedding much blood, the king stormed the towns of Oriszum[85] and Vidin[86] and other fortifications in the same areas where a hostile band of Turks was on guard. Finally, in the summer of that year, when vines were for their cultivators producing very sweet fruits, about the time of the feast of St. Michael the Archangel,[87] he pitched his camp on

---

82. Duke Philip the Bold of Burgundy (1363-1404). It was not he but his son and eventual successor, John the Fearless, Count of Nevers (d. 1419), who took part in the expedition.

83. The cloister of St. Nicholas, the principal house of the Dominican province of Hungary, stood in the center of the city of Buda (see note 8). Its remains are still visible today.

84. As is plain from his itinerary, King Sigismund did not visit *Rascia*, i.e. Serbia, at this time. He crossed the Danube at Orsova on August 15, 1396, and immediately invaded Bulgaria.

85. Rightly Oriakhovo on the Danube in Bulgaria.

86. Vidin, on the Danube, then capital of a Bulgarian principality (see note 81)

87. The feast day of St. Michael the Archangel is September 29; the battle was fought on the 28th.

the plain below the fortress of Great Nicopolis.[88] But the Turks kept bursting out of the fortress and challenging the king's army to fight them. And after wounding a number of men, they would retire to the fortress, very often wounded themselves.

Now when the sultan of the Turks—called Bayezid by our elders, as I mentioned above, although Niccolò Sagundino,[89] when writing to Aeneas, bishop of Siena,[90] concerning the family and the origin of the Turks, specified that he was called Chalapinus[91] —heard that the king had entered his realms with great engines of war, he, too, roused to arms all the military might of his people, and in an effort to block the king's expedition, he approached with main force. In fact, moved to action by the reputation of the approaching enemy, the Gauls or Franks came to the king and requested that he allow them to take for themselves the first-fruits of the war, which are commonly associated with greater ferocity. So when the sultan, whose hordes of troops were raging everywhere and who was bringing along with him a large body of heathens, was seen taking his position opposite the royal encampment, at once the Franks, insolently eager to begin fighting first, came rushing out of the camp before all the king's forces could be drawn up in battle-formation and the sign to commence battle had been given. They leaped off their horses, as is their custom, intending to fight as foot-soldiers, and charged the cavalry troops who were ranged opposite. A dreadful battle continued to be vigorously fought by both sides, when the Hungarians, not yet acquainted with Frankish war strategy, observed the saddled horses of the Franks change course and head for the royal encampment. Believing they would be completely annihilated at

88. Great Nicopolis, today Nikopol, on the Danube in Bulgaria (see note 57). The castle was in Turkish hands from 1393.

89. Niccolò Sagundino, Italian humanist scholar of the mid-fifteenth century.

90. The humanist, Aeneas Silvius Piccolomini (see note 80), was bishop of Siena in Italy (1450-1458) before being elected pope as Pius II.

91. Latinized form of the Turkish word, čelebi, meaning "prince".

the hands of the enemy, the Hungarian forces became gravely confused and simultaneously abandoned the fortress and their engines of war. Routed everywhere on the plain, they were forced to flee, with the enemy in hot pursuit. The greatest slaughter followed, with many Hungarians killed and many taken prisoner. And had the king himself not contrived to escape safely by ship, he would have been crushed there and then, not beneath the weight of the heavens, to quote what the exalted prince himself is reported to have said, but beneath the arms of the enemy.

✠ 204 (IX): CONCERNING THE ENMITY STIRRED UP AGAINST KING SIGISMUND, AND HIS CAPTIVITY ✠

Alas! When under the guidance of step-mother Fortune human affairs are directed along undesired paths, how are the enmities they provoke and how great is the hatred to which they give rise! They sometimes even make enemies of welcome friends, especially among men of Hungarian stock.

After the grievous disaster suffered by his people, King Sigismund was hated by them, although hitherto they had loved him. And in fact he was afraid he would be punished for his improvidence by those he had ineptly led, just as once Xerxes,[92] king of the Persians, was, after the ill-fated end of the war he waged in Greece. Like a fugitive, therefore, Sigismund had recourse to oars and over the deep waters of the Danube and the sea sailed[93] to the city of Constantinople,[94] and from there to

92. Xerxes I, Achaemenid King of Persia, the Ahasuerus of the Bible (486-465 B.C.), defeated by the Greeks at Salamis. He did indeed die a victim of murder, but it was fifteen years later.

93. Sigismund landed at Ragusa (today Dubrovnik, on the Dalmatian coast in Yugoslavia) on December 21, 1396, and issued charters dated from Spalato (today Split) on January 4, 1397.

94. Constantinople (today Istanbul, Turkey) was until 1453 capital of the Byzantine Empire.

Rhodes,[95] and thereafter to the coasts of the kingdoms of Dalmatia and Croatia. Accompanying him were men of power in the kingdom, the Lord János, archbishop of Esztergom, and the archbishop's brother, István Kanizsai,[96] who were also, by means of intermediaries, devoted to promoting the king's best interests with the leading men of the kingdom.

In the meanwhile, however, Voivode István Lackfi, and another István, of Simontornya,[97] both of whom I mentioned above, had become arrogantly ambitious because of the success of their previous villainy, and together with many accomplices in crime whose heartfelt desire it was that King Sigismund reign no longer, dispatched messengers to the illustrious young man Ladislas,[98] son of the King Charles who not many years before had been killed, as I mentioned earlier. To this Ladislas, then reigning in the kingdom of Apulia in his father's place, they promised to hand over, with as little violence as possible, the sceptres of the kingdom of Hungary. But he never lost sight or recollection of the wretched lot that had been in store for his father as king of Hungary, and was rather more dilatory than he in taking charge of Hungarian affairs, in spite of the fact that the messengers promised him to remove King Sigismund and to hand over to him a realm at peace. When they observed that he was responding with some reluctance, they did not for that reason cease their efforts; to achieve what they wanted more easily, the two Istváns themselves through intermediaries had received from King Ladislas an oath and a letter in which he swore that whatever they might do in his place in the kingdom would, until

95. Rhodes, an island in the Aegean Sea, at this time the center of the Order of the Knights of the Hospital of St. John of Jerusalem.

96. Kanizsa (today Nagykanizsa), market and castle in Zala county, seat of the ranking Kanizsai family. As Steward of the Household (1395-1401), István Kanizsai (d. 1427/1428) was one of the "barons of the realm." For his brothers, see notes 60 and 101.

97. For the two Lackfis, see notes 34 and 35.

98. King Ladislas of Naples (1386-1414), son of King Charles (see note 4).

such time as he received the sceptre, be acceptable to him. This treacherous arrangement led a large number of nobles astray; many because of this ignominious crime were vilified, and their descendants, even in our own times, lament that because of this they are still condemned to live obscure, rustic lives.[99]

This arrangement was made secretly, but it did not escape the notice of King Sigismund. Several days passed in their usual way, and after having himself delayed for a year and a half in the coastal regions,[100] King Sigismund was restored to the royal throne with the aid of certain magnates, especially the archbishop of Esztergom, the lords of Kanizsa,[101] and the ban, János Maróti.[102] And although he was aware that the two Istváns were planning and plotting against him, he did not however have the power to avenge himself against them because of the throng that had joined them. Another three and a half years[103] passed after the king's return, and meanwhile the number of those conspiring against him always kept increasing. It was as if the whole

---

99. After the failure of the baronial revolts in 1397 and 1403, many participants were declared guilty of felony and were deprived of their estates. None of them was executed, but as a consequence of the confiscation they lost their noble status and their families sank into obscurity. Only a few were later pardoned and able to regain some of their fortune.

100. Coastal regions, here a reference to Dalmatia and Croatia (see note 19). On this occasion Sigismund spent only two months here (January/February 1397).

101. See note 96. A third brother, Miklós Kanizsai (d. 1404), held the office of Chief Treasurer (1388-1398) and ranked also among the *barones regni*.

102. Marót (today Morovic, Yugoslavia), a market in Valkó county, seat of the knightly family Maróti. János Maróti (d. 1434/1435) was a favorite of King Sigismund, held the office of Ban of Mačva several times between 1397 and 1428, played a significant role in the consolidation of Sigismund's rule, and was rewarded with an enormous fortune.

103. Thuróczy's chronology is false. In chapters 204 to 207, he confuses three different plots against the king between 1397 and 1403. The first one, in early 1397, was led by the two Lackfis assisted by only a handful of magnates. Its suppression in February 1397 will be related in Chapter 207, falsely connected with events of the year 1403. Chapters 204 and 205 deal with the plot of 1401, led by the Kanizsai brothers. By then the Lackfis were no longer alive.

Hungarian people, corrupted by the power of suggestion, were regarding him with suspicion. Not only had the deaths of the thirty-two knights especially inflamed the Hungarians to hatred of him, but so had the disastrous outcome of his expedition against Nicopolis. And the king himself, too, indulging his lust, dissolute and wanton, and given to the violent seduction of maidens, was a source of scandal to the Hungarians. What is more, the frequent and persuasive arguments of the two Istváns also carried great weight with the people. And so everyone who considered the problem argued that they should hand the king himself over to captivity, when a suitable opportunity presented itself to them for this purpose.

Therefore, in the 1401st year after the Lord's Incarnation, during that part of the year when that most fruitful season of spring was providing mild middays under Taurus's leadership,[104] and had covered with flowering boughs the trees that had by winter's icy rigor been stripped of their verdant leaves, and on that day when Mother Church recites the glorious triumph of the struggle of St. Vitalis,[105] the barons of the realm approached the royal palace,[106] pretending to seek a parley, and expressed their wish that the king himself come into their midst. When he came, they first threw in his teeth all the reasons they had contrived against him for their misdeeds, and then with a great clamor they seized him. And had they not been dissuaded by those who used to love him, he would there and then, like Julius Caesar,[107] have been fatally wounded many times and have poured forth at once his blood and his spirit.

104. An allusion to the second sign of the zodiac (see notes 7 and 29), that of Taurus, indicating the period between late April and late May.

105. The feast day of St. Vitalis, i.e. April 28, 1401, who was said to have been martyred at Ravenna during the second century.

106. Sigismund was arrested in the royal castle of Buda (see note 8).

107. Allusion to the murder of Julius Caesar in the Roman senate on March 15, 44 B.C.

At the same time there were in the Garai family two young men of pleasing character, whose father was the late Miklós Garai, the palatine, who was killed at the side of the queens.[108] One of these young men received his father's name, the other was called János.[109] Believing that these youths felt deep animosity towards the king because of their father's murder—for Sigismund had been especially responsible for his punishment—the king's captors handed him over to these young men for confinement in their fortress called Siklós.[110]

✠ 205 (X): CONCERNING THE RELEASE OF KING SIGISMUND ✠

nce King Sigismund had been made to suffer the hardship of imprisonment, those who were bitterly opposed to him made no secret of the plot they had previously devised against him. And now, with nothing to stop them, they

---

108. See note 6.
109. Miklós Garai junior (d. 1433), Ban of Mačva (1387-1390; 1393-1393), Ban of Croatia and Dalmatia (1394-1402) and of Slavonia (1397-1402), then Count Palatine until his death (1402-1433), and his brother János (d. 1428), governor of Usora in Bosnia in the 1410s. Both well over thirty in 1401, they were not exactly *iuvenes* any more, as Thuróczy suggests.
110. The castle of Siklós in Baranya county, one of the strongholds of the Garai family, which still exists in a restored form. In the fifteenth-century texts one finds a widely accepted misunderstanding, shared also by Thuróczy, about the role of the Garai brothers. In reality, both of them ranked from the very beginning among the strongest supporters of King Sigismund, as charters and other contemporary documents disclose. After his capture in 1401, Miklós left no stone unturned in an effort to have him released. In August, 1401, he managed to secure the king in his own castle of Siklós after handing over his own son and his brother János as hostages to the rebellious magnates. Thus the story about the king's liberation, told in the next chapter, must be considered a fiction.

were making plans to obtain what they wanted. Gathering together publicly in large throngs, they walked about full of self-esteem, and raising high the banner of King Ladislas himself, they made their way through the regions of the kingdom. And when with this banner they came to a city, no matter which city it was, the sacred order of clergy was compelled to meet them respectfully in procession. Meanwhile they made known to King Ladislas that they had smoothed away all difficulties in accordance with his wishes and that he should act quickly. Now when King Ladislas heard that Sigismund had been taken prisoner and that his own party was gaining in strength, he was moved by the prayers of those who were calling upon him, as if ready to take possession of the inheritance which was now at his disposal. And speedily taking provisions, he pursued his journey towards Hungary.[111]

King Sigismund, however, was living out his wearisome captivity in this fortress with sorrow, tears often welling up and flowing down his wan cheeks. When the mother of the young men responsible for the king's confinement had very often observed his unremitting bitterness of heart and the recurring flow of tears, she was profoundly moved with compassion for him. His sufferings moved her whole heart, as a woman's nature demands, and approaching her sons, she addressed them in the following way: "My dear sons! Can it really be that in this man you find reason for greater animosity than do other subjects of the realm? I say this because others are exempt from responsibility for his confinement, and you alone are obliged to watch over and keep him safe. I particularly recollect what your late father said in my presence. For he used to remark that one should not forsake a legitimately crowned king, even if he is like an ass.

---

111. Thuróczy here confuses two different events: the king's arrest in 1401 and the baronial revolt of 1403. Though King Ladislas of Naples was one of the possible candidates for the Hungarian throne during Sigismund's captivity in 1401, no revolt had yet broken out in his favor (see note 116).

How I wish you were not involved in these things, no matter what others have done! For if you kill him, as his opponents hope you will, the stigma of having shed royal blood will be imputed forever to your descendants. And although others always hope, by bringing in a new king, to take pleasure in his new acts of generosity, you will be detestable in his eyes. What accursed act are you thinking of, to shed the blood of kings? What office will you or your successors ever be worthy of in the kingdom, if you stain your hands by this impious crime? Sigismund has been crowned and regarded as king for so many years. But the one who is to benefit from your action, and not because he was our king, is in fact not yet acquainted with the kingdom. Desist, then, my sons, if you are conspiring to murder this man, and beware of defiling with this enormous crime the eminence of your family. You know how your father suffered death on account of that king; nor do I doubt that you have no knowledge of the one who is said to be the son of the murdered king. If he assumes the sceptres of the kingdom of Hungary, do you really think he will not remember his father's murder, especially since it was brought about by your father. But if that prisoner should be restored to power, and if you should be the ones to bring it about—which is the very thing I am seeking to persuade you to do—it is to be hoped that your affairs will always prosper, and you will always be considered especially deserving in the eyes of him on whose account your father poured forth his soul."

The young men listened to this and for a while were shocked. At length, having lost their resolve, they became greatly concerned about what their mother had said. While they next gave free rein to various considerations, that clever woman went to King Sigismund and said: "King Sigismund, know that your adversaries are anxious about the new king and about your execution. The tears falling incessantly down your cheeks have moved me, and I have taken to heart your endless weeping and feel pity for so young a man in such bitter distress. I am the woman who alone is taking pains to secure your release, but something frightens me when I think about it and frequently holds me back. For I am afraid of losing my two sons, whom you know, if I set you free. But if you promise faithfully to remember my kindness and not to forsake them and me when you regain the sceptre, I shall devote my every care to securing your release." At this King Sigismund immediately threw himself on the ground at her feet, and with outstretched arms rushed to embrace them. With a trembling and piteous voice he said: "Come, my lady and mother. If indeed the kingdom is restored to me, if I am to go on living, and if because of a greater misfortune than this present one I am handed over to you or your sons whenever I forget what you have done, may God not ever grant me liberty again. See, I this day adopt you as my mother and them as my brothers, and with an oath of loyalty I promise you and them to observe this pact." Afterwards this woman prevailed over her sons with frequent arguments, and she kept them, when they were arranging the king's release, from the ever-watchful eyes of their opponents, and had him taken surreptitiously to the borders of the margraviate of Moravia.[112]

---

112. Sigismund regained his liberty in October 1401, after promising full amnesty to all those who had taken part in the conspiracy of April. His confinement passed without consequences, and his brother, King Wenceslas of Bohemia, even judged him to be, after his liberation, "mightier than ever." Indeed he felt himself so secure in his royal position that, in January, 1402, he left Hungary for more than a year to fight his cousins, the margraves of Moravia.

✠ 206 (XI): CONCERNING KING SIGISMUND'S RETURN TO HUNGARY ✠

he rumor of the king's release created no little terror for his adversaries, and its influence in successfully promoting his affairs was not small. For the ones who found his arrest repugnant were awakened as if from a deep sleep when their prince obtained his freedom, and with all their strength they tried to exact retribution from his offenders and to restore the king himself to the exalted throne of the kingdom of Hungary. They therefore ravaged on a massive scale both the villages and the fields of those who did not share their feelings. Among the plunderers was that harsh man, the ban, János Maróti,[113] who was pompous, stiff, and unyielding. Though we are old, we have not yet forgotten his acts of devastation. The opposition on the other hand was putting their strength to the test, sometimes in their own protection and at other times on the offensive. Consequently, with wars raging all round and the pillaging of possessions becoming more and more savage, King Sigismund, escorted and powerfully assisted by strong companies both of armed native people and of the leading men of the northern counties of the kingdom of Hungary—for the northern counties had not yet strayed from their loyalty to him—came once again into Hungary.[114] It was not particularly difficult for the king to regain the royal sceptre, since the fortress of Buda and practically all the fortifications of the kingdom were in the possession of his own loyal supporters.

---

113. See note 102.

114. The open rebellion against Sigismund broke out in early 1403. It was headed by János Kanizsai, Lord Chancellor and Archbishop of Esztergom, who conspired with most of the magnates. Only the Garai brothers and some of their relatives remained with the king. By the time the king had returned from Bohemia in July, 1403, his partisans had succeeded in mastering the situation, though sparse fighting went on intermittently until the following spring.

At the same time the king of Apulia,[115] attracted by the repeated promises of those who were calling upon him, was on his
way to take control of what he had been promised, and he had already reached the frontier of the kingdom of Dalmatia, when he
heard that King Sigismund was waiting safe and sound in Buda
and enjoying unchallenged exercise of authority in Hungarian
affairs. He therefore at once put an end to his undertaking,
changed direction, and headed towards his father's kingdom.[116]
People say he was prompted by the unjust treatment first of this
father and then of himself to write a letter to King Sigismund
and therein to petition him to repay with some appropriate com-
pensatory gift the ones who, since he had survived, have always
customarily rejoiced at the succession of a new king.

✠ 207 (XII): CONCERNING THE PUNISHMENTS EXACTED
BY SIGISMUND FROM VOIVODE ISTVÁN AND THE OTHER
TRAITORS ✠

he king was so often overwhelmed by such sufferings
that he did not immediately after his return exact harsh
satisfaction by physically punishing the ones who were

---

115. King Ladislas of Naples, see note 98. Apulia was the most important
province of the Kingdom of Naples, and the name often, as here, could refer to
the kingdom itself. Its rulers also assumed the title of "King of Sicily," notwithstanding the fact that this island had been conquered by the king of Aragon in
1282.

116. King Ladislas was invited to Hungary by the rebels in late 1402, arriving at Zadar on the Dalmatian coast on July 19, 1403. There, with a substitute
crown, he was named King of Hungary by the legate of his supporter, Pope
Boniface IX. He embarked for Italy in November, 1403, after having realized
that the position of his partisans in Hungary had become hopeless. He afterwards (in 1409) sold his conquests in Dalmatia, consisting of several cities and
islands, to the Republic of Venice.

at fault. For he merely took their estates and conferred them on his own faithful followers. He did not vent his rage on those who frequently met with him, nor did he withdraw royal clemency and benevolence from those seeking his favor. And in fact to his humble subjects he held out a hook baited with the sweetness of feigned goodwill, so that with it he could more easily catch the great men who were tainted by what they had made him suffer. The clever king concealed his feelings of deep resentment, and in the meanwhile the number of those loyal to him was greatly increasing every day.

The king therefore became more confident after this and proclaimed to his faithful subjects his intention to hold a universal assembly in a town called Kőrösudvarhely,[117] located in a province of Slavonia.[118] A great throng of turbulent nobles gathered there on the appointed days, and there came Voivode István, son of Lackfi,[119] led by sinful intention, or with trust in the king's clemency or in the armed troops which he had, like the king, brought with him. One day, when the king and the chief men of the kingdom, as well as the voivode himself, had assembled in a residence, Voivode István was there and then dragged into the midst of the council, taken prisoner, and beheaded.[120] And when the report of his death reached his followers, at once they rushed to arms, inflamed with a desire for revenge. And there would doubtless have been much bloodshed, had not the voivode's corpse, hurled down from high up in the residence, presented them with a terrible sight, and had not someone also shouted at

117. Kőrösudvarhely or simply Kőrös (today Križevci in Yugoslavia), royal borough in Kőrös county in Slavonia.

118. Slavonia, province of medieval Hungary between the river Dráva and the Kapela mountains (today part of Croatia in Yugoslavia), was governed by a Ban (see note 13) in the king's name.

119. István Lackfi senior (see note 34).

120. Thuróczy gives here a false chronology (see note 103). István Lackfi senior and his nephew, István junior, were killed at Kőrös on February 22, 1397, immediately after Sigismund's return from the crusade at Nicopolis.

them, while they were exposed to so dangerous a situation: "Desist, you wretches; desist, you who are about to die. Behold, you see dead before you the man for whose sake you were obliged to take up arms." After this, their stern anger cooled, and each of them fled in search of places where he might be safe.

People were charging that when King Sigismund was staying in the coastal areas, after he had suffered the disaster at Nicopolis, this man István, the voivode, committed the crime that will be described, in addition to the other unspeakable villainies he had treacherously performed so as to injure the king's majesty. For he had dispatched messengers to Bayezid, sultan of the Turks, and had given his word to marry Bayezid's daughter to King Ladislas, whom he was seeking to promote, on condition that Bayezid provide him with help against King Sigismund. And in proof of this they said that he had led large hordes of Turks into the regions of Hungary located between the Sava and Drava[121] rivers and that he had there been responsible for heavy pillaging. Before these devastations the Turks had not yet traversed Hungarian lands.[122] That was their first hostile advance into Hungary, and it was then that they caused the considerable devastation we see in the cities of Szerém.[123] Even now these cities, with places deprived of their buildings, testify that the damage was great.

121. The river Dráva, western tributary of the Danube.
122. This is not true. Turkish marauders had been ravaging the southern borderlands of Hungary incessantly since their first invasion in 1390.
123. The region of ancient Sirmium, called 'Szerémség' in Hungarian, was Szerém county in medieval times, between the rivers Danube and Sava. Today part of Yugoslavia, it was a particularly rich and densely populated province of Hungary before the Ottoman conquest, reputed especially for its wine. From 1390 on and by the middle of the fifteenth century, it was almost ruined by the Turkish invasions.

✠ 208 (XIII): Concerning the election of King Sigismund as King of the Romans, and the siege of the Fortress at Golubac, which ended unsuccessfully ✠

A fter István the voivode suffered the ultimate punishment for the charge against him, some of his companions were condemned to death, others to exile, and all the plotting against the king everywhere ceased. And upon obtaining control of a kingdom that was thenceforth at peace, never as long as he lived was the king disturbed by civil violence in his realm.[124] And since, as a young prince, he had become a better person in his character and in his way of life for the very great misfortunes by which he had so frequently been troubled, and since he was considered even by foreign nations to exercise an imperturbable rule over his domain, he was elected king of the Romans when he had already reigned in Hungary for twenty-three years.[125] Moved by the high-minded heroism implicit in so pre-eminent a royal title, the king therefore assembled many armed men and again undertook to try out the fighting power of the Turks. With many a knight he encircled the stronghold called Golubac,[126] then subject to the Turks, which was located on a steep cliff above the banks of the Danube, in a Rascian field. Both enemies contended in battle, and the troops of Sigismund always

124. This proper remark about Sigismund's newly acquired authority in Hungary correctly describes the second part of his reign (after 1403), when the last revolt of the magnates was suppressed.

125. Sigismund was first elected "King of the Romans" (*Romanorum rex*), i.e. German king, on September 20, 1410, but by only three of the seven electors. His unanimous election took place on July 21, 1411, after the death of his cousin and rival, the Margrave Jost of Moravia.

126. The fortress Golubac (Galambóc in Hungarian, Tauenburg in medieval German) was on the right bank of the Danube in Serbia (today also Golubac, in Yugoslavia). The Turks obtained it in 1427 and Sigismund's offensive was aimed at its recapture.

had the upper hand, until Chalapinus,[127] sultan of the Turks, driven back when his men were overpowered, came at them with engines of war of great size and seemed a more powerful enemy than the king. The latter, therefore, after a great slaughter of his troops who were fighting to a finish all round, abandoned the plain, crossed the Danube, and got clear of the enemy. Although in this battle many lost their lives, it is the death there of that most famous man, called Zawisza "the Black,"[128] who was distinguished for his courage and his skill at arms, which is remembered with great anguish down to our own time.[129]

✠ 209 (XIV): CONCERNING THE ORIGIN OF THE HUSSITES ✠

Not only do the affairs of mortals end in reverses, but even the ordering of divine worship sometimes with God's acquiescence suffers eclipse. For towards the end of King Sigismund's reign, a great disagreement arose in the Christian religion, and the noxious corruption of heretical wickedness, infecting the minds of men and women, spread gradually and developed, its originators being John Wycliffe[130] in England and Jan Hus[131] in Bohemia. The adherents of this

127. A recurring Latin term for Ottoman rulers (see note 91). The Sultan in question was Murad II (1421-1451), a grandson of Bayezid I.

128. Zawisza Czarny ("the Black") of Garbów, a Polish knight who took part in the battle as the leader of an auxiliary force from Poland.

129. Sigismund's memorable defeat took place in early June, 1428, when he was retreating across the Danube from Golubac after its unsuccessful siege.

130. John Wycliffe (or Wyclif, d. 1384), professor of theology at Oxford University and a leading scholastic of the late Middle Ages, who, in his voluminous writings attacked the abuses, wealth, and immorality of the Church, papal claims to authority, vows and religious orders, indulgences, the liturgy,

sect, especially those who are our neighbors in Bohemia and its regions, we call Hussites. In addition to this monstrous wickedness challenging the Catholic faith, there had emerged at the same time, I know not at whose instigation, a certain unspeakable order, if it could call itself such, known as "Adamites."[132]
And it is said to have been particularly successful at luring to crimes of depravity people of both sexes, young and old, especially because, in my view, it was considered morally right for them to indulge the lusts of the flesh. For its adherents said that a supreme creator had established this order about the time of the creation of the world, and that all things were made as common property, and that he had given instructions for them to increase and multiply. They walked about naked and lived in the recesses of caves. And after the religious rites, if one may call them that, which they performed, they extinguished the lamps and consigned themselves to the shadows. And in Bohemian they called their chief "othecz", that is "father". The command "Increase and multiply!"[133] was given, and without distinction in age they rushed to embrace each other and simultaneously to satisfy the lustful desires of the flesh. And in spreading and increasing their nets the devil is considered to have been such a great

---

trans-substantiation, and the sacramental system. In 1377 Pope Gregory XI issued five bulls condemning his heretical teachings.

131. Jan Hus (d. 1415), professor of philosophy and theology at the University of Prague and a preacher of great skill who came strongly under the influence of Wycliffe (see note 130), attacked the primacy of the Bishop of Rome, and advocated a number of ecclesiastical reforms concerned with avarice, simony, and the general state of corruption in the Church. Following his death (see note 140), his name became the slogan of a revolutionary movement of social and religious impact, which by 1419 embraced all Bohemia. Its adherents were commonly called Hussites; the "official" term used by the royal chancellery seems to have been Wycliffites.

132. Throughout the Middle Ages and even later, "Adamite" was a name attached to different Christian sects whose members were accused of holding their services in paradisiacal nudity. Thuróczy tries to discredit the Hussites by associating the Adamites with them.

133. A quotation from the Vulgate, Gen. 1: 28.

help to this superstitious invention, which thereafter had spread to the human race, that when, among the other marvels he was performing, birds flying high in the air or wild animals lurking in dark forests were ordered by this company's chief to come, they were there at once and with bowed heads paid homage to him. If nothing else, this magician wanted with prodigies to catch in his nets the ones who had no desire to join his cult; and in this he was successful. For this pernicious subversion of holy religion had in a short time so grown, that afterwards these Hussites had to employ great force and many arms so as to overcome and destroy it.

✠ 210 (XV): CONCERNING THE WARS WAGED BY KING SIGISMUND AGAINST THE HUSSITES, AND THE BURNING OF JAN HUS ✠

Because of the office he had undertaken to discharge as king of the Romans, King Sigismund was bound to protect the Catholic faith. He felt a special obligation because the Hussites, battling fiercely with fire and sword against those who did not belong to their sect, had come together to form a large fighting force and were ravaging his native land. Against them the king more than once sent into action an armed force of both the Hungarian and the German peoples; and not sparing his hereditary land and people, he caused great devastation in the kingdom of Bohemia.[134] The Hussites could not be turned from their course, and as if ready to fight in the name of

---

134. The main reason for Sigismund's interest in pacifying Bohemia is ignored by the chronicler. In August, 1419, his elder brother King Wenceslas of Bohemia died, with Sigismund as his sole heir. The Czech diet was inclined to accept Sigismund as king only on condition that he acquiesce in Hussite hegemony. Sigismund responded by declaring war in March, 1420, and invading

the blood of Christ, their troops kept advancing under the leadership of Žižka,[135] a powerful one-eyed man, having had the picture of a chalice[136] painted as a military emblem on their banners, scutcheons, and shields, and on other battle paraphernalia. And as they continued to rage very fiercely against those who attacked them, both in religion and in human affairs the kingdom was subject to great confusion. For that reason the fighting between the two sides frequently entailed considerable danger for the people, especially, however, when one day both foes had assembled in a field not far from a mining town called Katumbánya,[137] and one side yielded to the other only after a great slaughter. For a long time the war raged on to the advantage of neither people, with many casualties on both sides, until finally Žižka got the upper hand. The king left the field, turned tail, and fleeing with his men who had survived, abandoned to the enemy what he possessed as well as his hostile inten-break tions.[138] When King Sigismund judged that he could with force by no means check the frenzy of this treachery, he concerned himself

Bohemia. On July 28 he succeeded in having himself crowned in Prague, but this was his last victory over the Hussites, as his armies were routed one after the other for the next fourteen years (see note 138).

135. Jan Žižka (d. 1424), the invincible leader of the Hussite armies. Due to his military prowess, he established for himself a kind of dictatorship over Bohemia.

136. The chalice served as a symbol for the Hussite movement because it represented one of its most distinctive tenets, namely, that priests and lay believers should receive communion under both kinds, *sub utraque specie*, i.e. both the body of Christ in the form of a host, and His blood in the form of the sacred wine. Catholic practice permitted the priest alone to drink from the chalice, which, came to be regarded as a panacea for all the evils of the time.

137. Katumbánya, a medieval Hungarian name for the Czech-German mining town of Kuttenberg (today Kutná Hora) in Bohemia. The Latin term *urbura* was used for the duty paid by the miners to the Treasury from the extracted gold or silver ore. *Civitas urburarum*: 'mining town'.

138. Sigismund suffered several defeats from Žižka and his Hussite followers in the years 1420 to 1422. The last of them was at Kuttenberg in January 1422.

with using the decree of a universal council to stifle the life out of so pestilential a movement, arranging for the whole of Christendom to hold the very famous Council of Constance.[139] It was there, at that council, that the aforementioned Jan Hus,[140] and Jerome,[141] the disciple of that heresiarch, were condemned along with their dogmas, sentenced, and punished by being burned to death. But the heat generated by the plague they had disseminated in the kingdom of Bohemia did not, because of their deaths, cease to be felt right down to our own time.[142]

---

139. Constance (Konstanz in German), imperial city on the Bodensee. Thuróczy confuses the two general councils of Constance (1414-1418) and Basle (1431-1449). The first was convened to end the Great Schism of 1378, and to carry out a wide-ranging reform of the Church. It was the second council whose main program was, after the failure of a military solution, to seek a compromise with the Hussites. In 1433 the moderate wing of the Hussite movement accepted the disciplinary articles proposed by the council (called the *Compactata* of Basle) which guaranteed certain freedoms (including the lay 'chalice,' see note 134). Now the moderates, called henceforth 'Ultraquists,' allied themselves with the Catholics against the intransigent wing of the Hussites (the Taborites) and routed them in the battle of Lipany (east of Prague) on May 30, 1434. This victory put an end to the Hussite wars, which had lasted almost fifteen years.

140. Jan Hus (see note 131) was summoned to appear before the council at Constance and, after much debate, was sentenced to death and executed as a heretic on July 6, 1415.

141. Jerome of Prague, an ardent propagator of Wycliffe's doctrines (see note 130) and a comrade of Hus. He was put to death in Constance on May 30, 1416.

142. Hussite doctrines remained popular in Bohemia until as late as the counter-reformation in the seventeenth century.

✠ 211 (XVI): WHAT FOLLOWS CONCERNS THE DEFEAT OF THE HUNGARIAN ARMY IN REGIONS OF BOSNIA ✠

many wars of various kinds raged during Sigismund's reign, not always ending the way the king wished. But what writer is able to pass cursorily over the age of so great a prince, who ruled for so many years?

Among other wars, there was in the 1415th year after the Lord's Incarnation a great military campaign by the Hungarian people against the duke of Spalato,[143] whose name was Hrvoje.[144] For that duke, previously loyal to the king, at this time insolently and treacherously attempted to attack the kingdom of Hungary and then, to strengthen his own region, he assembled large hordes of Turks and plundered extensively in the parts of the kingdom of Bosnia subject to the king. The king's long absence had inspired this man, for during these years Sigismund was at the Council of Constance, taking action against the heresy already mentioned and promoting his bid for the sacred crowns of the Roman hegemony.[145] When, therefore, the news of seditious activity came to the attention of the powerful men in the kingdom, whom the king had entrusted with its care, they appointed as leaders of their army the bans János Garai,[146] János

---

143. Spalato (today Split, in Yugoslavia), city on the coast of the Adriatic Sea in Dalmatia.

144. Hrvoje Vukčič (d. 1416), Bosnian magnate with the title of "Great Voivode," adherent of King Ladislas of Naples, who in 1403 appointed him to be his viceroy in Dalmatia with the title of Duke of Spalato (see note 116). Hrvoje won a leading position in North Bosnia and, in 1409, submitted to Sigismund, but he rebelled again in 1413 and made an alliance with the Ottomans.

145. Sigismund left Hungary in December, 1412, and returned there in January, 1419. He was crowned King of the Romans (i.e. of Germany; see note 125) in Aachen on November 8, 1414. In the previous summer, the first Ottoman raid into Slavonia had occurred.

146. See note 109.

Maróti,[147] and Pál Csupor of Monoszló,[148] and also a great many other important men, and sent an adequate Hungarian force into the kingdom of Bosnia against the duke. But he stationed himself against them in a field, defended both by his own people and by those he had hired. A pitched battle began, and with trumpets blaring loudly on both sides, each of the foes, thirsting for the other's destruction, attacked and fought with great valor and full fighting power. Loud battle-cries could be heard everywhere, lances were shattered, and as they broke in pieces, many riders were thrown from their horses, and the corpses of dead men from either army fell. But who could prevail over the cunning of the Bosnians? When they observed that the Hungarian troops were much stronger than they in this battle, those who had been specifically chosen for the task took up a position on some hill-tops and cried out, as they had been instructed, that the Hungarians were retreating. These words caused great confusion for the Hungarians. For although they were vigorously pressing on with the battle, as soon as the rumor of retreat was heard, they thought that a number of their fellows had fled, and they themselves abandoned the plain and turned tail, thereby occasioning in that place both a great slaughter and booty for the enemy. Nor did the generals themselves escape so great a danger; some indeed were taken prisoner there, others were killed.[149] For János Garai was captured and heavily fettered, obtaining his freedom only after many days of imprisonment. The huge iron weight

147. See note 102.
148. Monoszló (today Moslavina, in Croatia), market in Kőrös county in Slavonia, seat of the Csupor family. Pál Csupor of Monoszló was Ban of Slavonia (1412-1415).
149. The battle took place in Bosnia, in the valley of the river Bosna near the castle of Doboj, probably at the end of July, 1415, although its exact day is unknown. In September of the next year, a parliament was held at Pécs presided over by János Garai, who had been set free in order to raise a ransom for the captives (among them four barons) that amounted to 65,000 gulden. An extraordinary tax was imposed, but it seems not to have been exacted in the end.

with which he had been chained he left as a memorial for future generations in the monastery of Báta,[150] to the glory of the most precious blood of the Lord our Redeemer, to fulfill the vow he had made there. János Maróti, on the other hand, paid his enemy a large sum of gold in exchange for his freedom. And what should I say of the ban, Pál Csupor? He was sewn up in the raw skin of an ox, and did not deserve to have his life spared by the duke. For before this act of treachery, when Duke Hrvoje was an obedient ally of King Sigismund and frequented his court, he was observed to be brutish both in his way of life and in his behavior. When Pál the ban used to encounter him, he treated him as a laughing-stock, and instead of greeting him respectfully, he mocked him by bellowing like an ox, thus disparaging his rank. Duke Hrvoje could therefore say, when this same ban Pál had been decorated by him with the covering of ox skin I mentioned above: "When you looked like a man you made noises like an ox. Now you are both to look and sound like an ox!"

✠ 212 (XVII): CONCERNING THE WAR INITIATED BY THE BAN, ISTVÁN LOSONCI, IN THE REGIONS BEYOND THE ALPS ✠

D uring this king's reign there were also many wars in the regions beyond the Alps,[151] every time because the people there had rebelled. Especially worthy of enduring memory, however, is the battle that was joined in those regions under the leadership of the distinguished ban, István Losonci,[152] even though its outcome was unhappy. For at that time there were in this land two princes, Dan[153] and Mircea,[154] both born

---

150. Báta in Tolna county, a Benedictine abbey named after St. Michael.
151. In Wallachia (see note 47).
152. Losonc (today Lučenec, Slovakia), a market in Nógrád county, seat

of the same family. Since their powers as equals had become confused, each was striving to be sole ruler. And when Dan realized that his own forces were weakened, he at once sought the help of the Turks, with which he forced the other side to flee. But when Mircea recognized that his own resources were insufficient to repulse a foreign foe, he requested the aid of King Sigismund. So the ban, István Losonci, was sent by the king with many armed troops to provide Mircea with assistance. At length the ban became engaged in a bloody encounter, but since he was not a match for the enemy, he was beheaded, there and then both losing his life and ending the war, after considerable slaughter on both sides. For after the fall of their leader, his troops fled, providing the enemy with much booty and many prisoners.

A great miracle closely followed the conclusion of this war. When, after this disaster, two years or less had passed, and some people had gone on to the battlefield to view the bones of the dead, as they were in astonishment marvelling at the countless ribs of both men and beasts killed there, they at that moment heard from behind something like a human voice, thin and barely audible. Astounded, they looked round this way and that, but saw no one. They therefore thought their imaginations were playing tricks on them; but overcome as much by fright, they stood there for a long time. And when they noticed that that

---

of a ranking family. István Losonci (d. 1395), Ban of Croatia (1387), of Severin (1387-1388), and of Mačva (1390-1392), was an able commander who played prominent part in the wars against the Horváti party and the Ottomans.

153. A minor slip of the chronicler. Dan I, a brother and rival of Mircea (see next note), had been Voivode of Wallachia in the 1380s. The person referred to here was Vlad I (1394-1395), also a rival of Mircea, but of unknown origin.

154. Mircea I, Voivode of Wallachia (1386-1418), was expelled in 1394 by his rival Vlad I and his Ottoman allies, and, having acknowledged Sigismund's suzerainty, begged for his support (March 7, 1395). The king immediately sent Losonci with Hungarian troops to Wallachia, but in April 1395 Losonci was defeated and killed by the Turks. The campaign, like the stories in the next chapter, is recounted by Thuróczy, within a false chronological context, because it happened just before the events related in chapter 201.

voice kept on speaking, and that among the sounds they were hearing were the divine names, repeated over and over again, of our Lord Jesus Christ and his most glorious mother Mary, they returned to their senses and went so far as to ask what kind of miracle this was. At length they found some human bones from which the flesh had rotted and around which grass had sprouted, grown up, and become entwined, as well as one unblemished human head. Oh most glorious queen of heaven! With what public praises should we magnify your holy name? What thanks should we give to you? With what glory should we venerate you? For all human powers are wholly inadequate to praise you. Let him cease his praises of you who has not experienced your kindness when your holy name is invoked, for the fact is that no one seeking your aid and fleeing to your holy protection has been abandoned by you. This momentous miracle, sacred Virgin, which you have revealed to us in this man is a great example to us. For when people noticed that the entire body was lifeless and decayed, and that the head alone was alive and that its tongue was speaking, they were stunned and seized with great astonishment that for so many days the fierce heat of the summer and the harsh cold of the winter, as well as starvation and thirst, had kept the head alone alive, when the flesh of the entire body had been consumed. And to those who were staring in amazement it said: "Why are you astonished? I am God's creature and a Christian. If you are Christians, in the name of Him who died on the cross for your sakes, search for a priest for me that I may confess." Asked at length how he had lived up to that time, he replied: "The most glorious Virgin Mary watched over me and kept me from danger right until your arrival, so that I would not die without receiving the Church's sacraments. And if I do not confess, I am unable to die." In addition he was asked: "Why does the glorious Virgin herself honor you with so great a kindness?" He replied: "I always fasted on bread and water on the vigils of her seven feasts, and her feasts I observed with the greatest devotion. In her I placed my every hope in life and death." At length a priest was sent for, and when confession and the other rites that must follow it were completed, he was set free and rested in peace.

✠ 213 (XVIII): CONCERNING THE TWO WARS WAGED BY MIKLÓS, SON OF PETER ✠

ften in the same period the Turks, who were impatient of inaction and thirsty for continued plundering, with savage incursions caused grief in the regions on this side of the Danube and in the land we call Temesköz[155] in our language. The son of Peter Macedóniai, Miklós,[156] a vigorous man and one bold at undertaking great exploits, with the assistance of friends and a collection of knights twice decisively defeated the Turks, took spoils, and caused the enemy both to flee and to be plundered. At this time Mehmed I,[157] the fifth sultan of the Turks, had succeeded to the kingdom upon the deaths of the brothers who were, like him, the sons of the late Bayerzid mentioned above, who likewise had previously been sultan of the Turks. When

155. Temesköz, literally "between the Temes (rivers)" in Hungarian, medieval name of a fertile region in Temes county south of Temesvár (today Timişoara in Rumania), between the rivers Temes (today Timiş) and Béga. At that time the latter was also called Temes and considered a branch of the same river.

156. Macedónia (today Macedonia, in Rumania), a village in Temes county, seat of a knightly family. Miklós Macedóniai, Peter's son (d. after 1433), was probably a knight of the household who took part in several battles that are recorded below as his own victories. Thuróczy must have derived his information from a lost royal charter in which Macedóniai's military "merits" were enumerated in the style of the Hungarian chancellery.

157. Mehmed I, son of Bayezid I, Ottoman ruler (1413-1421). After a decade of civil wars among his brothers, he reunited the empire in 1413.

Mehmed had added to his realm on land and at sea, and had subjected to his authority a certain part of Mysia that we call upper Bosnia or, in the vernacular, Vrhbosna,[158] it pleased him to establish a new king in this land. So he named as king of Bosnia a certain man called Ikach,[159] of little wealth and humble reputation. Enticed by the newfound glory of his name, he roused all the strength he could of the people entrusted to him, and invaded and pillaged the aforementioned regions. With estates burning on every side and all the men of that land fearfully fleeing who had a chance to escape, Miklós, the aforementioned son of Peter, though not a match in troops to the enemy but inspired by the boldness typical of knights, opposed him. Battle was joined, and when the fight was raging on to neither side's advantage, and King Ikach had come up against Miklós in the midst of the combatants, the latter recognized him, immediately reined his horse against him, and so courageously attacked him with his lance that its blow seriously wounded King Ikach, who fell headlong from his horse, despite his own loyal troops. The angry knight did not spare the man lying prostrate on the ground; dismounting, he thrust an armored foot on his chest and, with no regard for the prayers of the man he had defeated, he unsheathed his sword and cut his throat. When they saw this, the entire company Ikach had himself assembled was put to flight. Miklós, son of Peter, returned with his men well supplied with booty; and to King Sigismund as a token of victory he sent the enemy's banners or military standards together with many prisoners.

---

158. Vrhbosna, meaning 'Upper Bosnia' in Serbian, town and castle in South Bosnia (today Sarajevo) and name of the district around it.

159. Ikach of Orljava, a Hungarian nobleman of obscure origin from Pozsega county, former partisan of the Horváti brothers (see note 13). After the death of King Dabisa in 1395, he seems to have laid claim to the Bosnian throne, but in the next year he was defeated by Hungarian troops. In this chapter Thuróczy confuses events of the 1390s with those of the 1410s.

This knight also fought a second time with the Turks when they were making incursions into the aforementioned border regions. And although he did not have sufficient manpower and arms to wipe out the enemy, he judged that night would help him and assembled what troops he could. This militarily astute man added as well some wandering herds of mares and other animals grazing in a field, placing before each herd drummers, pipers, and also men to shout. With this kind of assistance he made a rush against the enemy who had settled down on the open plain for a night's rest. He threw them into confusion, attacked, and caused them to flee headlong; and having obtained both a victory and the customary spoils, he is remembered by nobles of his rank right down to our own day and has for ever achieved for himself the best of reputations. Some have said that in this battle the previously noted knight, to recognize his own people, had instructed that the words "Isten! Szent Mihály!"[160] were to be shouted in the heat of the savage fighting, to prevent his own knights from striking one another in the darkness of the night. And as the combat raged on in the darkness that same night, with one side not fully recognizing the other, the Turks thought that these expressions were as much a help to them either with God or against their enemies; and when they were being keenly pursued by the foe, they omitted the word "Isten" while loudly shouting only "Mihály."

160. Isten, "God," and Szent Mihály, "St. Michael," Hungarian war-cries. The time of the fighting described here is not known.

✠ 214 (XIX): CONCERNING THE CORONATION OF KING SIGISMUND AS KING OF BOHEMIA ✠

Reassured by the glory he had earned as ruler of the kingdom of Hungary for 34 years, King Sigismund was crowned king of the kingdom of Bohemia in the 1420th year after the Lord's Incarnation.[161] For before these years, after the passing of his brother Wenceslas,[162] King Sigismund did not have in Bohemia the name of king but of governor. He raised to exalted positions not only nobles of humble family but also a great many men of plebeian rank, and made them powerful in his kingdom. For the houses of the lords of Pálóc[163] and of Rozgony[164] and of the late lord Mihály Ország,[165] palatine,

161. On July 28 (see note 134).

162. Wenceslas IV, King of Bohemia (1378-1419) and of Germany (1378-1400), elder half-brother of Sigismund. He died on August 16, 1419. He had appointed Sigismund regent of Bohemia in 1402, but he soon withdrew the commission.

163. Pálóc (today Pavlovce nad Uhom Slovakia), a village in Ung county, seat of a knightly family. Máté (or Mátyus) Pálóci (d. 1437), esquire of the household and a favorite of Sigismund, became Keeper of the Privy Seal (1419-1423), Lord Chief Justice (1425-1435) and Count Palatine (1435-1437). One of his brothers, György (d. 1439), was Bishop of Transylvania (1419-1423) and Archbishop of Esztergom (1423-1439), and, after Sigismund's death, also Lord Chancellor (1438-1439).

164. Rozgony (today Rozhanovce, in Slovakia), a village in Abaúj county near Košice, seat of the knightly Rozgonyi family. Simon Rozgonyi senior (d. 1414), originally a knight of the household, became Lord Chief Justice (1409-1414) and paved the way for his sons and relatives. His cousin János (d. 1438) held the offices of Royal Treasurer (1412-1436) and of Lord Chief Treasurer (*magister tavarnicorum regalium*, 1433-1437); his nephew Péter (d. 1438) was Bishop of Veszprém (1417-1425) and Eger (1425-1438), and was followed in both dignities by Simon's younger son, Simon junior (d. 1444, Bishop of Veszprém 1429-1440, and of Eger 1440-1444, and Lord Chancellor from 1440). Other members of the family were wardens or captains of many royal castles and counties during the reign of Sigismund, thus enjoying considerable political influence.

165. Mihály Ország of Gút (d. 1484), a man of modest background and an esquire of the household, was promoted to the rank of Royal Treasurer in 1433.

whom I remember mentioning above, came at the king's instigation into possession of large landed estates, and their survivors
now rejoice in the high title of "magnificus"[166] in the kingdom.
Indeed, Count Pipo of Ozora,[167] who died with no blood relative to succeed him, and the ban Matkó and his brothers Franko,
Petko, and Jovan, whose descendants now have a small share of
their paternal estate, were Ragusans.[168] Although they were of

He acquired a great fortune and, under King Matthias Corvinus, ended his
brilliant career as Count Palatine (1458-1484). By his own account, it was from
Mihály Ország, an important observer of contemporary events, that Thuróczy
obtained much of the information incorporated in his chronicle (see *Introduction*).

166. In Hungary there were no hereditary titles until the middle of the fifteenth century, János Hunyadi being the first to be rewarded in 1453 with the
title of Count (*comes perpetuus*). Thereafter, titles in the proper sense were still
exceptional until the seventeenth century. Formal addresses served as substitutes for titles, among which the highest, *magnificus*, was originally due to the
'barons of the realm'. After about 1430 members of the richest ranking noble
families also came to be called 'barons' and were addressed as *magnifici*. By
the end of the fifteenth century, this usage became accepted, and, thereafter,
the number of the new hereditary 'barons' or *magnifici domini* was officially
recorded. By his use here of the Latin term *magnificentia*, Thuróczy alludes to
that group.

167. Ozora, village in Tolna county with a castle built by Pipo Ozorai (d.
1426). Pipo, whose original name was Filippo Scolari, was the son of a Flo-
rentine merchant who came to Hungary about 1390 and gained Sigismund's
favors because of his abilities. From 1404 to 1426 he governed as ispán (*comes*)
the castle of Temesvár (today Timişoara, in Rumania) with the surrounding
seven counties, as well as the salt mines of Transylvania. He won numerous
battles against the Ottomans and was famous for his patronage of the new Flo-
rentine arts. Among others, the painter Masolino is said to have worked for
him, though none of his works in Hungary has survived.

168. Ragusa (today Dubrovnik, Yugoslavia), a tiny merchant republic on
the Adriatic coast, under Hungarian suzerainty since 1358. The four brothers
named by Thuróczy were sons of a Ragusan merchant and were engaged by
Sigismund in 1429. Their family name in Hungary was Tallóci, from an extinct
village, Tallóc (in Croatian Talovac, near Virovitica in Verőce county), which
they received as a hereditary grant. Matkó (d. 1445) became Ban of Slavonia
(1435-1445) and of Croatia (1436-1445), Franko (d. 1448) was Ban of Severin
(1436-1439) and of Croatia (1446-1448), Petko or Péter (d. 1453) assisted and

urban status, they nevertheless enjoyed the considerable good-will of this king, and as men well supplied with gold and landed estates they were powerful in the kingdom as long as they lived. It is, however, not an easy matter for me to count the nobles of middle rank whom the king raised up either from the country or from some obscure noble family. I also consider it wearisome to my readers to provide these names, for they are of no importance to my history.

✠ 215 (XX): CONCERNING THOSE WHO ATTENDED THE COURT OF KING SIGISMUND, AND HOW THE DESPOT SUR-RENDERED TO HIM THE CASTLE OF NÁNDORFEHÉRVÁR ✠

T he court of this king shone brightly with the great brilliance of the nobles who frequented it, and illustrious it always was, because of the remarkable flood of visitors from abroad. Many of the leading men of Germany and Italy, for example, attended the court. Likewise, with a numerous escort of nobles from his kingdom came a son of the king of Portugal[169] from the western extremities of the earth to pay his respects to so great a prince. His visit was an honor for Sigismund's court. People say that he was astonished because he had seen the Danube

_____

later succeeded his elder brothers as Ban of Croatia (1437-1453), and Jovan (or Zovan, d. 1445) was Prior of the Hospitallers in Hungary. During the mid-century wars the family lost most of its fortune and the sons and grandsons were to become simple members of the gentry in the southern counties (see Elemér Mályusz, "A négy Tallóci fivér" ["The four Tallóci brothers"], *Történelmi Szemle* 23 [1980], 531-576).

169. Dom Pedro, a younger son of King John I of Portugal (1385-1433) who came to Hungary to fight the "infidels" and escorted Sigismund on his expedition against the Turks to Wallachia in 1427. From 1404 to 1426 he governed as *ispán* (or *comes*, see note 317) the castle of Temesvár.

freeze during the winter's harsh cold and that he reported this to his father as a miracle greater than any he had ever seen in his travels in foreign parts.

The illustrious prince George, despot of Rascia,[170] had taken an oath of complete obedience to King Sigismund, and to him as a pledge of his absolute loyalty he surrendered[171] the fortress of Nándorfehérvár,[172] situated at the junction of the mighty rivers Danube and Sava, and said to have been called Taurinum[173] in a bygone age, but Alba Bulgarica[174] by our elders. It was occupied by his predecessors and himself all the time up to about A.D. 1425. Afterwards this fortress was of no small usefulness during the period of increasing Turkish power in Hungarian territory, as will be touched on briefly below. Because of this gift, King Sigismund was no less munificent to him, for in his kingdom of Hungary he rewarded him for his generosity and hospi-

---

170. George (Djuradj) Branković (d. 1456), ruler of Serbia (1427-1456) with the Byzantine title of *despot*, granted by Emperor Manuel II to his maternal uncle and predecessor, Prince Stephen Lazarevič, in 1402. *Rascia* was the current Latin term for Serbia in medieval Hungary.

171. A minor inaccuracy. It was George's predecessor, the Despot István, who, in May, 1426, made a treaty with Sigismund at Tata (in Komárom county) concerning the Serbian succession. By its terms the king accepted George as the future heir of István, on condition that both Belgrade and Golubac, the two strongest fortresses on the Danube, were ceded to Hungary after his death. István died on July 19, 1427, and the obligations of the treaty began, but Sigismund could take possession only of Belgrade. Golubac treacherously passed into the hands of the Ottomans (see note 126).

172. Nándorfehérvár in Hungarian, *castrum Nandoralbense* in Latin, i.e. the "White Castle of the Nandors," the name of Belgrade (today the capital of Yugoslavia) common in medieval Hungary, to distinguish it from the city of Székesfehérvár, called *Alba Regalis*, "Royal White Castle", where coronations occurred (see note 27).

173. Taurinum (more exactly Taurunum), a *castrum* of Roman Pannonia, lay opposite Belgrade on the other side of the river Sava, on the site of the present Zemun. In Roman times Belgrade itself was called Singidunum.

174. *Alba Bulgarica*, "White Castle of the Bulgars," the name of Belgrade in early Hungarian sources. Its meaning is similar to that of Nándorfehérvár (see note 172), Nándor being an ancient Hungarian name for the Bulgarians.

tality with the fortresses of Szalánkemén,[175] Kölpény,[176] Becse,[177] Világosvár,[178] Tokaj,[179] Munkács,[180] Tállya,[181] Regéc,[182] and the towns of Szatmár,[183] Böszörmény,[184] Debrecen,[185] Túr,[186] Varsány,[187] and a number of others, and a splendid house, appropriate to his rank, in the city of Buda.[188] He also frequented the royal court and was warmly welcomed by the king and the Hungarians.[189]

---

175. Szalánkemén or Zalánkemén (today Slankamen, Yugoslavia), town and castle on the Danube in Szerém county.

176. Kölpény (today Kupinovo, Yugoslavia), a fortress on the Sava in Szerém county.

177. Becse (today Novi Bečej, Yugoslavia), castle and market on the Tisza in Torontál county.

178. Világosvár (today Şira, Rumania), a castle and a market in Zaránd county. It was given to George not by Sigismund but by his successor Albert in 1439.

179. Tokaj, a market reputed for its wine in Zemplén (today Borsod-Abaúj-Zemplén) county, with a castle built by Despot István about 1425.

180. Munkács (today Mukačevo, in the Soviet Union), castle and market in Bereg county.

181. Tállya, castle and market in Zemplén (today Borsod-Abaúj-Zemplén) county.

182. Regéc, a castle in Abaúj county above a village of the same name (today in Borsod-Abaúj-Zemplén county), northwest of Sárospatak.

183. Szatmár (today Satu–Mare, Rumania), borough in Szatmár county on the Szamos.

184. Böszörmény (today Hajdúböszörmény), a market in Szabolcs (today Hajdú-Bihar) county.

185. Debrecen, then a market in Bihar county, today an important city in East Hungary.

186. Túr, today Mezőtúr, a market in Szolnok county.

187. Varsány or Tiszavarsány, formerly a market in Szolnok county on the Tisza. It lay between the modern villages of Rákóczifalva and Rákócziújfalu.

188. Though Buda (see note 8) was primarily a merchant city, magnates also maintained houses there where they could reside when visiting the royal court or attending a diet.

189. The domains listed above had been granted to Despot István between 1411 and 1423 and were inherited by his nephew George in 1427 (see note 171). István had first been a vassal of Sultan Bayezid I, but after 1402 he

✠ 216 (XXI): CONCERNING THE DEVASTATIONS CAUSED BY BLAZKO ✠

King Sigismund was frequently a source of consolation to Holy Mother Church, which was sometimes saddened by warfare and at other times disturbed by the great storms and whirlwinds of schism and heresy, and he raised her up when she was coming to grief.[190] And for her sake he very often expended his treasures and poured forth both the blood and the souls of his people.

At length, when old age was threatening that he had not long to live, he devoted all his efforts, before death could intervene to deprive him of the honor of the imperial title, to receiving those diadems of the Roman Empire, celebrated throughout the entire world, together with the insignia of the imperial dignity.[191] He therefore appointed for the protection of the kingdom guardians chosen from amongst its leading men, and directed his cavalry towards the city of Rome. But these guardians did not satisfactorily protect the kingdom of Hungary in the absence of its king. For in the 1431st year of our salvation, when the king himself was pursuing his own affairs in foreign kingdoms, a certain

allied himself with the Hungarian side, vowed fealty to King Sigismund, and became his loyal supporter.

190. The ending of the Great Schism at the council of Constance in 1417 was due, indeed, to the energy and diplomatic skills of Sigismund (see note 139).

191. After being elected in 1410 and crowned in 1414 (see notes 125 and 145), Sigismund became head of the Holy Roman Empire, but his title was only "king of the Romans." To become emperor (*imperator*), he had to be, according to a usage established since the tenth century, crowned in Italy by the pope himself or by his representative. Not every Roman king was able to achieve such a coronation because an expedition to Italy was, at that time, as expensive as it was dangerous. Sigismund's father, Charles IV, was, in fact, the last German ruler before him who bore the imperial title. Both Wenceslas (1378-1400) and Rupert (1400-1410) died without having ever seen Rome. Sigismund left Hungary in July 1430 with the intention of acquiring at last the imperial crown.

Blazko,[192] of meagre wealth and reputation, assembled a large band from a group comprised of Hungarians and Bohemians eager to plunder, and having encircled first the town of Trnava,[193] which had high towers connected by a wall of baked bricks, he entered it by stealth at night while its citizens were sleeping. Once he had seized the fortification, he collected more arms, and like a most violent tornado flung himself upon the northern counties of the kingdom, which we call the Mátyusfölde.[194] Not sparing even holy things or sex or age, he ravaged everything with fire and sword as far as the Danube, exposing it to rapacious pillaging. And he would have done much more, had not the aforementioned guardians, after an assembly of all the nobles of the kingdom of Hungary, checked his voracious appetite and compelled him to be silent about his attacks and to pretend to keep the peace.[195]

---

192. Blazko of Borotín, a Hussite army leader.

193. Trnava, Nagyszombat in Hungarian, walled royal city in Pozsony county (today Slovakia). Its capture took place in June 1432, not 1431.

194. Mátyusfölde, "Matthew's land," was a medieval Hungarian name, not used in official documents, for the region around Nyitra (today Nitra) and Trencsén (today Trenčin) in West Slovakia. Matthew Csák (d. 1321) was a powerful Hungarian lord who had carved out a principality for himself in these parts that he was able to hold against King Charles I of Hungary.

195. From 1428 to 1434 the Czech Hussites led numerous devastating raids against the northern counties of Hungary. Blazko's enterprise was only one of them. He held Trnava until 1434, when it was redeemed for money by the Hungarians.

✠ 217 (XXII): CONCERNING THE PEASANT KINGS WHO AROSE IN THE KINGDOM ✠

Before these years two peasant wars raised an uproar in the kingdom of Hungary on two different occasions, instigated by certain peasants called Antal[196] and Martin.[197] Antal collected a large force of peasants in those parts of the kingdom in Transylvania; Martin did the same in the land of Nyír[198] and Szamosköz.[199] They usurped for themselves the name of king, and with standards raised burst out like a flood with considerable armed might, devoting all their efforts to subjecting the kingdom to their authority. They proceeded this way and that, killing all the nobles in their path. They sent messengers with blood-stained swords to the villages and towns to ensure that they would support them. Indeed, any unwilling to be disposed in their favor they robbed and killed. And the power of these peasants had become so strong that even armed men were afraid to attack them. They were finally crushed and subdued by a large expedition of the leading men of the kingdom and suffered appropriate punishments. The kings themselves were punished with death; of the others unable to escape, some lost their eyes, some their noses and lips, and some their hands.[200]

---

196. Antal, with the surname Nagy ("the Tall"), probably a minor nobleman from Buda, a hamlet in Transylvania northwest of Kolozsvár (today Cluj-Napoca, Rumania). He was one of the leaders of the peasant revolt in 1437.

197. Martin is not known from other sources.

198. Nyír, today Nyirség, part of the Hungarian plain between the Tisza and the Berettyó. In medieval times it was an archdeaconry and formed part of Szabolcs and Bihar counties.

199. Szamosköz, like Nyir (see note 198) a region of the Hungarian plain between the Tisza and the Szamos in Szatmár county. Today it belongs partly to Rumania.

200. This was the first major peasant revolt in Hungary. Details of the revolt in Transylvania are known from official records. It broke out in June, 1437, and sought to facilitate the transfer of peasants from one lord to another and to prevent transgressions in the exaction of the tithe. The revolt was finally sup-

✠ 218 (XXIII): How King Sigismund was auspiciously crowned first King and then Emperor of the Romans ✠

*M*eanwhile, having journeyed through the regions of Tuscany[201] and Lombardy,[202] King Sigismund was crowned in the city of Milan[203] with the second diadem of Roman rule by the princes and electors to this dignity, for he had previously received the first one in Aachen.[204] He then continued his journey and reached the city of Rome,[205] where the venerable grey-haired head of so great a prince as this was with great solemnity laudably adorned by the most holy father in Christ, the lord Pope Eugene IV,[206] who invested him with the sacred insignia of the imperial dignity. As a result, King Sigismund was now considered worthy to be called by his people not only king or emperor, but king and emperor. He next returned home through Italy and Germany, arriving in Hungary after prudently

---

pressed in January, 1438, with no major consequences, apart from subsequent reprisals against the rebellious peasants.

201. On his way to Rome Sigismund spent nine months in Siena from July, 1432, to April, 1433.

202. Most of Lombardy belonged then to the Viscontian duchy of Milan. Sigismund stayed in the Lombard cities of Milan, Piacenza, and Parma for half a year between November, 1431, and May, 1432.

203. Sigismund was crowned King of Italy in Milan on November 28, 1431. This coronation should be regarded as mere formality, because Italy was at that time made up of virutally independent principalities and city republics over which the king had no effective power.

204. Aachen, in West Germany, the city where German (Roman) kings were crowned (see note 145).

205. The journey to Rome was not so uncomplicated for Sigismund as Thuróczy suggests. He was then at war with the Republic of Venice, and both Florence and the pope were allied with his enemy. When his way was blocked, he was compelled to halt at Siena (see note 201) and to remain blockaded there until he could make peace with all his adversaries and continue his journey.

206. Pope Eugene IV (1431-1447) crowned Sigismund Emperor on May 31, 1433, ten days after he entered the Eternal City.

settling, in accordance with his desires, his own affairs as well as those of the Roman Church that came to his attention.[207] Because of his absence Hungary had been everywhere disturbed by many injuries, and had been made to suffer, as long as he failed to act, from the serious disagreements of the kingdom's leading men. So he established a residence for himself in the city of Pozsony[208] and all the princes and leading men of his kingdom of Hungary, as if representing the whole kingdom, flocked to him there to see their lord's new dignity. Sigismund thus with insight smoothed away every impulse towards discord and violent outburst with which his kingdom was troubled during the period it had been deprived of his royal presence; and what is more, to tear out by the roots any further disagreements among his subjects, and to ensure that peaceful relations among them would endure, he promulgated and strengthened new constitutions in the kingdom and new laws to be observed in perpetuity, issuing a charter by way of confirmation.[209]

---

207. Sigismund arrived at Pozsony (today Bratislava, Slovakia) on October 8, 1434. Previously he had spent seven months (from October, 1433 to May, 1434) in Basle where the general council was then in session (see note 139). Its purpose was to initiate an all-embracing reform of the Church, which was the desire of the Emperor himself, who worked in vain to achieve progress in that direction.

208. The royal city of Pozsony (Pressburg in German, see note 207) was the western gate to medieval Hungary. Its royal castle was rebuilt by Sigismund in the 1430s as a magnificent palace where he resided from October 1434 to May 1435. Because of its proximity to his other kingdom, he intended to make Pozsony his capital, a plan which his death prevented him from fulfilling.

209. Sigismund held a diet in Pozsony in March, 1435, and issued two important statutes concerned with questions of jurisdiction (March 8) and military affairs (March 12). (A critical edition by Ferenc Dőry et al., ed., Decreta regni Hungariae. Gesetze und Verordnungen Ungarns, 1301-1457 [Budapest, 1976], 258-82.)

✠ 219 (XXIV): CONCERNING THE DEATH OF THE EMPEROR SIGISMUND ✠

During the prince's absence, equally serious wars flared up and raged in the kingdom of Bohemia, particularly because the Hussites were rebelling against their Christian king and devoting all their efforts to subverting the Catholic faith, thirsty for both the possessions and the blood of those who disgareed with them. And since the Hussities had both strength and competence on their side, the Christians did not inflict as much violence on the pagans as the Hussites did on the Christians. The prince, a Christian, was moved by the discord in his native kingdom and not hindered by the burden of his great age, for having eagerly undertaken a journey to Bohemia to restore peace to those at war and to unite a people at variance among themselves, he entered the city of Prague.[210] When the aged prince began to suffer from the strain of his advanced age and the weight of his responsibilities, as well as from weakness induced by paralysis, he was overcome by his grave lack of strength. And recognizing that his physical weakness was because he was old and close to the end of his life, he secretly summoned the more powerful of the Hungarians who were his escort and addressed them thus:[211] "My dear sons! I think I have satisfied the supreme creator of the world concerning the days of my life, as I myself am aware from the infirmity of my body. And if death does

210. Sigismund entered Prague on August 23, 1436. Though both Catholics and Utraquists were inclined to accept him as king after the extreme Hussites had been crushed in 1434 (see note 139), his journey to Bohemia was delayed by lengthy negotiations. Once established on the throne, his policy in Bohemia did not altogether aim at restoring peace and order. He tried instead to curtail the rights of the diet and to restore the Catholics to their former position, with the result that growing discontent forced him to leave the country after a year (in autumn 1437).

211. Among so many imaginary speeches in the chronicle, the following one may be authenic, as Thuróczy's informer, the Treasurer Mihály Ország, was probably present. (See Introduction, and note 165).

here intervene, I am afraid that the Bohemians, who have always hated me and you, will make an attack on you and expose you and your possessions to rapacious pillaging. But I, who have loved you all along, have on your account taken the greatest care to ensure that you know I also love you very deeply now. So concerned am I that, ignoring both the illnesses with which I am oppressed and other concerns, I devote myself day and night to your liberty alone. I have therefore found a way to save you, by means of which I think I can restore you safely to your homes. For tomorrow, once you have arranged my beard and hair, adorn the grey locks on my head with a garland, seat me on the imperial throne, and then place me in a litter. Proceed with me through the middle of the city, and lead us all from the midst of those who are thirsting after your blood." No sooner had the emperor finished speaking than tears came to his eyes and flowed right down his face. The Hungarians were persuaded by the emperor's kind words. When, therefore, the shadows of the following night, which causes the stars to shine more brightly, had been dispelled by the rising of the sun, and the lofty turrets of the palaces had been suffused with the radiating light of the sun,[212] the Hungarians prepared everything needed for the journey and carried out all instructions in accordance with the emperor's plan. And when the aged prince, with a head-band of flowers then adorning his venerable grey hair, was borne through the middle of the city, everywhere men and women, young and old, gathered together, gazing at him with tears in their eyes, as if they would not see him any longer, and paying homage to him on bended knee and with pleasing words of prayerful greeting. The emperor responded to the eyes which devoured him on every side only with a nod of his head. Having

---

212. Thuróczy here uses the Latin adjective "*titaneus*" with reference to the sun-god, as son of Titan Hyperion. The chronicler's "*titaneum lumen*" is therefore a poetic allusion to the light of the sun (cf. notes 443 and 518).

left the city of Prague, he was unable to reach the fatherland he longed for. Carried into Znojmo,[213] a city in Moravia, he ended his days in the 1437th year of the Lord, on the feast of the conception of the most glorious Virgin Mary, in his seventieth year, his fifty-first as king of Hungary, his twenty-seventh as king of the Romans, his seventeenth as king of Bohemia, but his fifth as emperor.[214] Conveyed later into Hungary, not without the most copious weeping of his people, he was honorably buried, like his predecessors, in the church of Várad.[215]

The emperor Sigismund was a quite suitable man, as far as concerned the features of his countenance and the size of his person, having been endowed by the supreme creator of the world with a handsome face, curly grey hair, and a look of calm assurance. He wore a luxuriant beard, out of admiration for those Hungarians in the past with long beards.[216]

---

213. Znojmo, Znaim in German, city in Moravia on the Austrian frontier.

214. The date given here is slightly inexact. Sigismund died on December 9, 1437, the day after the feast of the Immaculate Conception. As for the regnal years, each of them was counted from the day of election or coronation (see notes 48, 125, 134 and 206).

215. Várad, or Nagyvárad (today Oradea–Mare,, Rumania), an episcopal see. Its cathedral was dedicated to the Árpádian King, Saint Ladislas I (d. 1095), who chose it as the place for his burial. A few other kings and queens followed his example, among them Queen Mary, Sigismund's first wife (see note 58). Most Hungarian kings, however, were buried at Székesfehérvár.

216. It was a western European fashion to have a clean-shaven face; wearing a beard was at this time then a Hungarian, or at least an Eastern European, peculiarity. The Florentine-born Pipo Ozorai (see note 167), who became a Hungarian baron, was described by his fifteenth-century Italian biographer as having "a long beard after the habit of the people living there" (See F. Polidori, ed., "Vita di messer Filippo Scolari,..composta...da Iacopo di messer Poggio," *Archivio Storico Italiano* 4 [1853], 176).

✠ 220 (XXV): CONCERNING THE CORONATION OF KING ALBERT AND THE PILLAGING IN THE CITY OF BUDA ✠

At his death the Emperor Sigismund had only one daughter, named Elizabeth,[217] as heir to the kingdom, whom he had begotten by the illustrious Queen Barbara,[218] his second consort and the daughter of the late Hermann,[219] count of Cillei, one of the "spectabiles." When still alive, the emperor had in a Christian ceremony given her to Albert,[220] duke of Austria, as his legitimate consort, on condition that his son-in-law and his daughter would together succeed him in the kingdom.[221] And since this arrangement by no means displeased the Hungarian people, as soon as the emperor had been buried, Duke Albert was immediately acclaimed. And on the first day of the new

217. Elizabeth, Sigismund's only child, was born in October, 1409.

218. Barbara (1392-1451), elder daughter of Count Hermann II of Cillei, second wife of Sigismund and Queen of Hungary from November 1405.

219. Hermann II, Count of Cillei (d. 1435), an ally of Sigismund from the 1390s, received from him the county of Zagoria and many other estates in Slavonia, thus becoming one of the greatest landowners in Hungary. He twice held the office of Ban of Slavonia (1406-1408; 1423-1435), married his younger daughter Anna to the powerful Count Palatine Miklós Garai junior (see note 109). "The Old Count," as he was called informally, or "Our most beloved father-in-law," as he used to be titled in royal charters, remained the most influential counsellor of Sigismund until his death. *Cillei* (today Celje, Yugoslavia), principal region of a county of the Holy Roman Empire, situated between Styria, Krain and Hungary. The Latin word *"Spectabilis"* (more exactly used in combination with *magnificus*) officially designated counts of the Holy Roman Empire. The barons of Hungary were addressed only as *magnifici* (see note 166).

220. Albert V, Duke of Austria (1404-1439), from the house of Habsburg.

221. From the beginning of his reign, Sigismund was on friendly terms with the dukes of Austria, his neighbors. In 1402 he made Duke Albert IV his regent and heir to Hungary, and after the duke's early death in 1404 he proceeded to raise his seven-year old son, Albert V. As soon as he had betrothed his daughter Elizabeth to Albert in 1411 on September 28, 1421, he celebrated their wedding and the following year he enfeoffed his son-in-law with the Margraviate of Moravia. From that point on the duke was considered his heir.

year next following, that is, on the celebrated feast of the Lord's Circumcision, in the 1438th year of the Lord, on the same day as the coronation of the earliest kings of Hungary, Albert was auspiciously crowned with much splendor.[222]

In the first year of this king a great disturbance arose in the city of Buda.[223] For because the city was inhabited by two peoples, Hungarian and German, the Germans, puffed up with pride to have a prince who spoke their language, devoted all their efforts to subjecting the Hungarians absolutely to their control, and to abolishing that custom observed from ancient times in the city whereby a Hungarian and a German were in alternate years appointed mayor. Sometimes, when an appropriate moment presented itself to them, they would offend the Hungarians, sometimes insulting them and sometimes actually using physical violence. But Hungarians, who from of old have usually been slow to rouse to vengeance, occasionally exact against their offenders a retribution which, though postponed, is as harsh in its execution as a powerful whirlwind. As if gripped by some oppressive somnolence, they pretended to ignore everything, while awaiting the outcome of some foolish presumption on the part of the Germans.

There was at that time in the city a certain Hungarian named John Ötvös,[224] a man of great eminence and importance there. He alone, more than everyone else, was indignantly enduring the shame of the whole Hungarian people, and he would vocally and physically protect the honor of Hungarian citizens as

---

222. Albert was elected King of Hungary by a handful of barons on December 18, 1437, at Pozsony, and he was crowned at Székesfehérvár on January 1, 1438. His wife Elizabeth was crowned on the same day, but, contrary to her father's intention, she did not receive a share in the affairs of the government, and her coronation was performed not by the archbishop of Esztergom but by the bishop of Veszprém.

223. The riot took place in May, 1439, i.e. in Albert's second regnal year.

224. Ötvös, "goldsmith" in Hungarian, was probably not only a surname but also an indication of the occupation of its bearer.

best he could. Since he was on that account considered quite troublesome in the eyes of the Germans, they took advantage of an opportunity secretly to take him captive, and subjected him as their prisoner to various kinds of instruments of torture in a secret place in their house. At length he died because of excessive torture, and tying a large, heavy stone to his neck they had him sunk in the Danube. For eight days this enormous crime was not mentioned, until the river exposed his corpse on its banks, freed of the stone that had weighed it down. When his lifeless body was found, plainly exposing to view the many scars of his misfortune, it provided convincing evidence of the identity of his murderers. At the same time the king's court was being frequented by many a nobleman. When, therefore, the Hungarians had set their eyes on the results of this enormous crime, they indignantly and unanimously shouted out their complaints. And with a great furious attack they charged into the city to avenge themselves, and when they were unable to find his murderers, they rushed into their palaces. And breaking through the armored barriers formed by screens of shields, they exposed the treasure-chambers of the Germans to rapacious pillaging.[225]

There was during these days in the city of Buda a certain friar named Giacomo,[226] a holy man and of faultless religious life, an Italian by nationality, and a member of the Order of St. Francis. When he preached, the Hungarians eagerly followed

---

225. Like most cities of medieval Hungary, Buda had a mixed population of Magyars and Germans, of which the latter tended to have the upper hand. The rich German patriciate controlled trade and city magistracies, and in the early fifteenth century they even formally excluded Hungarians from seeking the mayoralty, by prescribing that one had to have four German grandparents to be elected mayor. The city's plebians were mostly Hungarians, and the revolt of 1439 described in the Chronicle thus reflected both ethnic and social conditions.

226. Giacomo della Marca, 1391-1476 (Iacobus de Marchia), vicar of the Franciscan province of Bosnia. As inquisitor in Hungary between 1434 and 1439, he zealously and mercilessly carried out the extermination of the Hussite heresy.

his teaching. When roused by their loud shouts—for the details of the deed became known to him—he picked up the divine image of the crucified one and ran about bare-footed in the midst of the Hungarians. And showing them the image of Christ, with a voice that was both querulous and doleful, he asked them, in the name of him who had thus been crucified for them, to leave off what they had undertaken. Their shouts grew louder still and they kept saying: "Even God is with us!" And abandoning themselves to the plundering, they heeded his prayers not at all. And when the friar realized that he was achieving nothing and was in fact causing a greater uproar, he entered again the cloister of St. John the Evangelist[227] whence he had come. When the Hungarians had exacted this kind of compensation from the Germans for their wicked crime and could not find any more of their possessions to plunder, they ceased their pillaging of them.[228]

✠ 221 (XXVI): CONCERNING THE EXPEDITION OF THE ARMY OF KING ALBERT AGAINST THE HUSSITES ✠

After the emperor's death King Albert not only succeeded him as king of Hungary, but was also, following his coronation in Hungary, at once elected king of the Romans and of Bohemia.[229] When, after the emperor's passing, he heard that the Hussites were all the more bitterly venting their rage against the Catholics in the kingdom of Bohemia,

---

227. This Franciscan house in Buda, founded before 1268, was located near the royal palace on the site of the present Várszinház (Castle Theatre).

228. Following the riot, the city government was modified so that the Hungarians would elect a mayor of their own every second year. Six of the twelve aldermen were also to be Magyars.

229. Albert was elected King of the Romans (i.e. of Germany) on March 18, 1438, and King of Bohemia on May 6 of the same year.

he launched against them a large expedition of Hungarians and Germans. But although the Hussites also had bands of Poles to help them, they nevertheless withdrew within the walls of the city named Tabor,[230] when they noticed that the king's expedition, disposed on the plain, surpassed their own resources in size and fighting power. For this city in Bohemia was the fountainhead and nurse of the Hussites, established by them a little while ago, when their young superstition was still developing, on the open land where once their camp had been. New city walls were erected in a spot that was naturally strong, and nearby on the plain the king pitched his encampment. The Hussites would very often make sorties out of the city, as would the royal army from its camp, and either side in turn experienced cruel deaths. This fighting went on for three months, during which time a very great number from each side were killed, both in the conflict and from the missiles discharged by siege-machines. And when King Albert ascertained that starvation alone would be injurious to his enemy, and decided that he could not deprive so many people of food and bar from them the ways which brought them their supplies of victuals, he broke camp and yielded to the enemy. And that noble expedition of dukes ranking among the "illustres,"[231] of counts and other powerful nobles, assembled to overthrow the might and wickedness of the Hussites, and very strong in men and arms, was disbanded and surrendered the place to the Hussites, building morale and greater hope than before.

---

230. Tabor, in Bohemia, was founded by the Hussites in 1420 as a fortified camp and was named after the Mount Tabor of the Bible. Albert besieged it in August/September, 1438.

231. In contemporary documents the address *"illustris"* officially designated dukes, princes, and other persons of princely rank.

✠ 222 (XXVII): CONCERNING THE CAMPAIGN COMPLETED BY KING ALBERT IN TÜDŐRÉV, AND THE KING'S DEATH ✠

A fter these events, in King Albert's second year, the news spread everywhere that Murad,[232] sultan of the Turks, had launched a large force of his people and was endeavoring to invade the kingdom of Hungary. Consequently King Albert at an assembly[233] of the leading men of his kingdom resolved with them that this enemy ought not to be setting his sights beyond the borders of the kingdom, but should be forcefully resisted. The military might of the whole kingdom of Hungary was therefore roused to action, the king assembled a large army, and in a place commonly called Tüdőrév[234] he pitched his tents. But when the sultan of the Turks heard that the king was taking pleasure in the fact that he had enough men and arms adequately to protect and defend his kingdom, he stormed the fortress of Szendrő,[235] subjected to his authority almost all the land of Rascia, and caused the despot, master of that kingdom, to flee into Hungary. He then turned his sword and all his strength against the Greeks, and he took by force and completely looted that most splendid city, Thessalonica,[236] outstanding in Greece,

232. Murad II, Ottoman ruler (1421-1451), called *Chalapinus* above in chapter 208 (see note 127).

233. The diet was held at Buda in May, 1439.

234. Tüdőrév, a shallow part of the Danube in the Middle Ages, near Titel (today in Yugoslavia) at the mouth of the Tisza (rév means "ford" in Old Hungarian, "ferry" in the modern idiom). Albert and his army camped there from mid-August to the end of September, 1439.

235. Szendrő, Smederevo in Serbian, fortress on the right side of the Danube east of Belgrade. After the cession of Belgrade to Hungary in 1427 (see note 171), it was the residence of the Despot George of Serbia. Sultan Murad II took it on August 18, 1439 after a siege of two months.

236. Thessalonica or Salonica (today Saloniki, Greece), seaport on the Aegean and largest city of the Greek Empire after Constantinople, ceded to the Republic of Venice in 1423 (cf. Ivan Djurič, *Sumrak Vizantije [The Decline of Byzantium]* [Beograd, 1984], 245 ff.).

distinguished and most celebrated for its antiquity, wealth, the renown of its people, and the excellence and importance of its citizens. Next he attacked the important provinces of Epirus[237] and Aetolia,[238] annexing them upon their surrender to the rest of his realm.

The Hungarians on the other hand had grown weary of the long delay and the confinement in their camp on the plain, especially since many of them had lost blood and were thereby enfeebled. They therefore, in conformity with an old custom of theirs, announced that they were visited by plague, and in a scattered and disorderly manner withdrew and departed, against the wishes of the king, abandoning the royal encampment.[239] What is more, King Albert became ill when on his way to Buda, but since it was his intention to enter Vienna,[240] he absolutely refused to give into his physical weakness and continued his journey towards Austria. At length, when he had gone down into the village of Neszmély[241] on the feast of the blessed Apostles

237. Epirus, a region in northwestern Greece on the Albanian border, with its center in Yanina. It formed a separate principality ruled by despots of Greek and Italian origin. Thuróczy is wrong in dating the Ottoman conquest of these parts after the fall of Szendrő. Both Thessalonica and Yanina were taken by the Turks in 1430, i.e. nine years before.

238. Aetolia was a province of Greece south of Epirus and conquered by the Ottomans about the same time (see note 237).

239. Hungarian armies at this time consisted of two elements: the paid troops of the king and his lay and ecclesiastical barons, and the mass levy of the county nobility. The latter, which is probably referred to here, was mustered in case of external invasion only and had a very limited military value. What Thuróczy means by conformity with an "old custom" is a mystery. It seems that the troops dispersed after an epidemic of dysentery had broken out. The Hungarian equivalent of the Latin word *luppus* (translated here as "plague") is *"fene,"* meaning originally all sorts of nauseating diseases, especially cancerous ones, although today it is used only as a component of curses.

240. Vienna was Albert's residence in his capacity both as Duke of Austria and as King of Germany.

241. Neszmély, a village in Komárom county on the Danube, on the road from Buda to Pozsony.

Simon and Jude,[242] his illness grew worse, and after a reign in
Hungary of one year, nine months, and twenty-eight days, he
died there, in that village, in the 1439th year of the Lord, and
like his predecessors was with royal splendor accorded the final
honor of interment in the church of Székesfehérvár.[243]

King Albert was a man of adequate height, with a countenance more dark than fair. He was mild of manner and amenable
to the supplications of his people.

✠ 223 (XXVIII):   CONCERNING THE INTRODUCTION OF
KING WLADISLAS AND THE ACTIONS OF THE KING AND
OF QUEEN ELIZABETH ✠

A fter King Albert's death, Queen Elizabeth, who had
been left pregnant by him, was taking thought for herself and the kingdom, as is typical of the behavior of
women who have lost their husbands, and passing the days in
mourning. At that time in the kingdom there was a large number of magnates outstanding for their humane feelings and conspicuous for their excellence both in exercising judgment and in
performing military service. It was to these men, who were apprehensive about the next king, that the queen spoke as follows:
"My lords and brothers! It is your duty no less than mine to
take thought for the affairs of the kingdom. I am, as you know,
the kingdom's heiress, but I do not think I am strong enough to
guide the reins of the kingdom. If you are looking forward to
the birth of my child, I believe I shall deliver a daughter rather
than a son, to the extent that my woman's nature can know this

---

242. October 28, 1439. In fact, Albert died the day before.

243. The traditional city of coronations and royal burial place (see notes
27 and 215).

from experience. Try, therefore, to find for yourselves a prince who is more qualified than a woman to bear the responsibilities of so great a realm, keeping in your hearts and before your eyes the kindnesses of my father, lest you arrange for me to have no share in the kingdom of him whose daughter I am."[244] She finished her speech, sighed, and wiped the tears from her eyes.

This speech of the queen kindled a great torch that blazed in Hungary for many years. For as a consequence of these words of the queen, the magnates themselves came to a unanimous agreement concerning the introduction of a new king, having been led on by a piece of shallow advice.

There was then in the kingdom of Poland a certain young prince named Wladislas,[245] grand duke of Lithuania and brother of King Kazimierz.[246] When the virtues of this man's character were praised above all others in Hungary, he won the approval of a plenary assembly of the magnates. It was therefore agreed[247] that he should be acclaimed and that he should reign as king. Wherefore, the men who were powerful in the kingdom and enjoyed honorable reputations, the bishop of Knin;[248] Matkó,[249] ban of Dalmatia, Croatia, and all Slavonia; Imre Marcali,[250] son

244. The speech seems to have been invented by the chronicler to justify the subsequent election of a new king (see below). From the report of one of the queen's ladies-in-waiting (see note 272), it is known that Elizabeth never once considered renouncing the throne. Though she did give her assent to inviting Wladislas (see note 245) to assume the throne (in January, 1440), at the same time she reserved the rights of her future child to the crown, provided that child were a son.

245. Wladislas III (b. 1424), King of Poland (1434-1444) and of Hungary (Wladislas I, 1440-1444), son of Wladislas II of the Jagiellonian house (see note 59).

246. Thuróczy is in error. Kazimierz IV (1447-1492) was indeed king of Poland when he wrote his Chronicle, but in 1440 he was still Grand Duke of Lithuania. It was his elder brother, Wladislas III, who reigned in Poland.

247. On January 18, 1440, in Buda. The delegation elected there consisted of five members. The Lord Chief Treasurer, János Perényi senior (d. 1458), is omitted by Thuróczy, deliberately perhaps, as Perényi later became a partisan of Queen Elizabeth.

248. Knin, city and episcopal see in Croatia. In reality it was Bishop János

of the voivode; and László Pálóci[251] were elected and designated to convey to him the desire of the people and formally to present him for acclamation.

They had not yet discharged their responsibilities as legates to the aforementioned duke when they were forestalled by the queen's messengers, who announced that the queen had given birth to a son, and they were prevented from proceeding with the legation they had undertaken to the duke. But because they were within the walls of the city of Cracow[252] and their journey had come to the attention of King Kazimierz and his brother, Duke Wladislas,[253] who was its cause, they did not dare return home without carrying out the task entrusted to them. Furthermore, after they had fulfilled their duties as legates to the duke, the young prince at once was seized by an ambition to be king. Without any delay he immediately saw to the preparation of what was needed for the journey, assembled for himself a suitable escort of Polish knights, and came into Hungary.[254] The leading men of the kingdom of Hungary, who were delighted to rejoice in their new king, came with great throngs of people to meet him. Then the palatine, Lőrinc Hédervári,[255] who was custodian of the fortress

de Dominis of Senj, another Croatian prelate (d. 1444), thereafter Bishop of Várad (1440-1444), who took part in the embassy.

249. Matkó Tallóci (see note 168).

250. Marcali, village in Somogy county, from which the family took its name. Imre Marcali (d. 1448), son of Miklós Marcali, Voivode of Transylvania, had been Steward of the Household (1434-1437), ispán of Temes (1438-1439), and now (1440) was Gentleman Carver of the King (magister dapiferorum regalium). Later he served again as Steward (1447-1448).

251. László Pálóci (d. 1470), then Steward of the Household (1439-1446), later Lord Chief Justice (1446-1470), a nephew of Count Palatine Máté Pálóci (see note 163).

252. Cracow was the residence of the Kings of Poland in the Middle Ages.

253. Thuróczy is at least consistent in his errors (cf. note 246).

254. Wladislas accepted the offer on March 8, 1440; on April 23 he arrived in Hungarian territory.

255. See note 62. Lőrinc Hédervári (d. 1447), former Master of the Horse (1429-1437), was appointed Count Palatine (1437-1447) by King Sigismund.

in Buda, in accordance with an ancient custom of the realm,[256] also went out to meet the new prince when he came, and freely opening the gates of the fortress, admitted him as if he were king of Hungary to the lofty royal palace.

✠ 224 (XXIX): CONCERNING THE BIRTH AND CORONA-
TION OF THE BOY LADISLAS, AND THE REMOVAL OF THE
CROWN ✠

T he 1440th year of the Lord's Incarnation came round, and on the great feast of Pentecost King Wladislas was escorted to the citadel of Buda.[257] Now Queen Eliza-beth, who had given birth to a son while these events were tak-ing place, did not fail to organize such matters as were of con-cern to her partisans. For siding with her were many of the magnates whose heartfelt recollections of the kindnesses of the emperor Sigismund had not yet faded. And the actions of the new king altogether displeased them. Queen Elizabeth there-fore went to Székesfehérvár[258] with her company of barons, and she caused her little son Ladislas[259] to be anointed and crowned king. He was not yet four months old, and he howled long and loudly. The clergy chanted the customary praises,[260] and the

256. This was indeed an "ancient custom of the realm" in Thuróczy's time, but only after about 1438. For the castle of Buda, see note 8.

257. More exactly on the Saturday after Whitsun, i.e. May 21, 1440.

258. See notes 26 and 32.

259. Ladislas V, called "the Posthumous," King of Hungary (1440-1457) and of Bohemia (1453-1457), son of King Albert. He was born on February 22, 1440, and crowned on May 15.

260. The rite of the coronation ceremony was rigourously prescribed in most European countries. For that of medieval Hungary see Erik Fügedi, *Uram, királyom (My Lord the King)*. (Budapest, 1974), 52-71.

queen wept continually, as did the barons assembled there in attendance, profoundly moved by the tears of the queen. Present at the unseasonable coronation of this tiny infant was the distinguished man, the lord Dénes Szécsi,[261] cardinal archbishop of Esztergom, who, as required by his office and rank, anointed the little boy and placed upon him the holy diadem. Also there were the bishops, Mátyás of Veszprém[262] and Benedek of Győr,[263] and Ulrich, count of Cillei[264] and the queen's next of kin. This last, on behalf of the boy who had been crowned, took the actual oath sworn by other kings of Hungary at the time of their coronation, to guard the liberty of their people. Likewise Miklós Ujlaki[265] and László Garai,[266] bans of Mačva;[267] András Botos, also of

261. Szécs or Rimaszécs (today Rimavská Seč, Slovakia) was the original home of a ranking family called Szécsi. Their castles and domains lay, however, on the Austrian frontier, around Felsőlendva (today Gornja Lendava, Yugoslavia). Dénes Szécsi (d. 1465), former Bishop of Eger (1439-1440), became Cardinal Archbishop of Esztergom (1440-1465), and later Lord Chancellor (1453-1465). He was a devoted partisan of Queen Elizabeth and her son.

262. Mátyás Gatalóci (d. 1457), son of a minor nobleman in Slavonia, Lord Chancellor and Keeper of the Privy Seal (1433-1439), Bishop of Vác (1437-1440) and of Veszprém (1440-1457).

263. Benedek (d. 1442), former Provost of St. Mary in Székesfehérvár, was privy councillor under Sigismund and Bishop of Győr (1439-1442).

264. Count Ulrich of Cillei (d. 1456), grandson of Count Hermann II (see note 219) and first cousin of Queen Elizabeth, later Ban of Slavonia (1445-1456), which province he governed almost like a sovereign. Owing to the extensive holdings of his family both there and in Austria, he became one of the leading political figures in Hungary during the following two decades.

265. Ujlak (today Ilok, Yugoslavia), castle and market on the Danube in Valkó county, home of a ranking noble family. Miklós Ujlaki (d. 1477) was Ban of Mačva (1438-1472) and of Slavonia (1457-1466), and Voivode of Transylvania (1441-1465, with interruptions). He ultimately fulfilled his ambitions by obtaining for himself the royal crown of Bosnia in 1472.

266. László Garai (d. 1459), son and heir of the Count Palatine Miklós junior (see note 109) and cousin of Queen Elizabeth through his mother, Anna of Cillei, Ban of Mačva (1431-1442, 1445-1447), and Count Palatine (1447-1458); one of the wealthiest magnates of the kingdom.

267. For Mačva, see note 13. From the beginning of Sigismund's reign,

the Garai family;[268] László and Henrik, sons of the late voivode János Tamási;[269] Tamás Szécsi;[270] and a great many other nobles of the kingdom, were present to witness the glory of so impressive a spectacle and to signify their fidelity to the queen and the infant king.

After the solemn formalities of the coronation had been completed, the queen made her way to the citadel at Visegrád,[271] the keys and guardianship of which had been entrusted at that time to the aforementioned ban, László Garai, in order to put back in its place the royal crown. This fortress was in a place that was naturally secure, having been erected high up on a mountain alongside the Danube, with a delightful view and skilfully constructed walls. With its upper walls it touched the limpid sky and the clouds that floated beneath the heavens, and at the base of its embankment flowed the aforementioned river. Because of this location, in ancient times former Hungarian kings chose this citadel to safeguard their crown. After the queen entered this citadel, she deceived the barons who gathered round her when she was replacing the crown. For she pretended to put it back in its place, while in fact stealing it with womanly cunning and keeping it hidden on her person. And she had these barons safeguard and seal up the ancient repositories of this great treasure,

baronial offices were sometimes held jointly by two or even three dignitaries.

268. András Botos (d. 1441), of Harapk (formerly a village in Valkó county), a favorite of Elizabeth and *ispán* of Temes (1439-1441), called also "of Gara" because he was descended from a younger collateral branch of the Garai family.

269. Tamási, castle and market in Tolna county, seat of a ranking noble family. László (d. 1442/1443) and Henrik (d. 1444), sons of the Voivode János of Transylvania, were former Stewards of the Household (1417-1434; 1438-1439).

270. Tamás Szécsi (d. 1448), younger brother of Cardinal Dénes (see note 261), Treasurer of the Queen (1438-1442), and Warden of Komárom.

271. Visegrád, formerly a city (today a village) in Pilis county on the Danube north of Buda, had been a royal residence under the Angevin kings. Its citadel, now in ruins, was the place where the Holy Crown was safely secured in the fifteenth century.

now empty of their usual contents.[272] At length the queen departed from this place with her son and the crown and went to Frederick, king of the Romans and duke of Styria,[273] for he was the boy's brother. And to him she gave both her son and the crown: her son to be educated, and the crown to be kept from danger.[274]

✠ 225 (XXX): CONCERNING CERTAIN LORDS CLOSE TO THE NEW KING, AND THE COURT HELD AT BUDA FOR HIS SUPPORTERS ✠

After these arrangements, Queen Elizabeth left the king of the Romans, and with her partisans to protect her she made her way through cities and fortresses that were sympathetic towards her. She nevertheless suffered considerable persecution, not so much from the king and his foreign entourage as from the natives of her own kingdom. Many magnates were well-disposed towards King Wladislas and endeavoring to promote his interests. In this group was Simon

272. The story is truthful on the whole, but it is told here in the wrong context. It was on the day before the birth of her son Ladislas (see note 259) on the night of February 20/21 that the Queen had the crown stolen by her lady-in-waiting, Helene Kottannerin, who has left us a detailed account of the event in her memoires (see Károly Mollay, ed., *Die Denkwürdigkeiten der Helene Kottannerin* (1439-1440) [Vienna, 1971]).

273. Frederick IV (d. 1493), Habsburg Duke of Styria (from 1439), King of Germany (1440-1493), and Emperor (Frederick III, from 1452). He was a second cousin of the infant King Ladislas.

274. This treaty of great consequence, which made Frederick the guardian of the young king for the next twelve years, was signed at Wiener Neustadt in Austria on November 22, 1440. The Holy Crown was to remain in Frederick's hands until 1463.

Rozgonyi,[275] its leader and bishop of Eger, who was working together with his brothers and almost all the barons and nobles of the northern region of the kingdom of Hungary to advance the new king's party. And when the ban, Miklós Ujlaki,[276] observed that the groups of King Wladislas' partisans were increasing in size, and that the queen's party was despised, and when he determined that the infant king could then neither help nor hinder him, he defected from the queen, attached himself to the new king, and was more vigorous than anyone else on his behalf.

At that time there was in the kingdom a brave knight, János Hunyadi,[277] born in the noble and celebrated heart of the land of the transalpine people. He was a bellicose man, born to handle arms and to take charge of affairs of war, and just as water is life to fish, and roaming shady forests is life to stags, so life for him was a military expedition in time of war. The fates from on high had presumably chosen this man to be the future guardian of the realm, as his exploits demonstrate, and had brought him from foreign parts within the borders of the kingdom of Hungary. For it is said that King Sigismund, influenced by the reputation for valor of this knight's father, had brought him from the transalpine regions into his own realm, and had caused him to reside there, and that Sigismund had also granted him for his merits permanent possession of the fortification of Hunyad, where

275. Simon Rozgonyi junior (d. 1444), Bishop of Eger and Wladislas' Chancellor (see note 164).
276. See note 265.
277. Hunyad (today Hunedoara, Rumania), a village in Transylvania and the center of a royal domain, was given by King Sigismund in 1409 to a foreign-born nobleman named Woyk, who had immigrated from Wallachia and become a knight of the household. Woyk's elder son, János Hunyadi (b. c. 1407), who was soon to become the central figure of the age, began his career as a member of Sigismund's household and, notwithstanding his title from 1439 as Ban of Severin, ranked among the lesser dignitaries of the kingdom until 1441 (see Pál Engel, "János Hunyadi: The Decisive Years of his Career, 1440-1444," in *From Hunyadi to Rákóczi: War and Society in Late Medieval and Early Modern Hungary*, János M. Bak and Béla K. Király, ed. [New York, 1982], 103-123).

now a noble fortress with a delightful view has been erected.[278] And so it was that János Hunyadi was a man of not inconsiderable power in the kingdom as a supporter of King Wladislas, for by always sticking close to the side of his superior liege lord, he had already gone from strength to strength, and he had become so famous through successive promotions from the minor offices which until then had been his support that he was elevated to the rank of voivode of Transylvania.[279]

An assembly of all the leading men of the kingdom took place in support of King Wladislas' party, and the city of Buda was crowded by the arrival of many nobles. The people, too, always accustomed to rejoice in a new prince, marched with happy faces through the streets of the city. The aforementioned cardinal, the lord Dénes, and the ban, László Garai,[280] as well as a number of magnates had also come to this gathering, having been accorded the privilege of a safe-conduct. These men had been drawn there more out of love for the queen than for the new king. When they had with the other subjects entered the royal fortress, the gates that had been opened to receive them were immediately shut behind them, until such time as they promised under oath to remain loyal to the new king.[281] When this was completed, László Garai was for a while not allowed to leave,

---

278. The castle of Hunyad was erected by Hunyadi in the years between 1446 and 1452 on the remains of an old and decayed fortress of the Árpádian period.

279. Thuróczy's chronology is again confused. Hunyadi was, together with his friend Miklós Ujlaki, promoted to the Office of Voivode of Transylvania in February 1441, as a reward for their victory over the queen's followers at Bátaszék (see below, chapter 227).

280. For these persons see notes 261 and 266.

281. On June 29, 1440, the Estates of the diet at Buda vowed fealty to the future King Wladislas and declared void the coronation of the infant Ladislas. The declaration was confirmed by the sixty lords and the delegates of twenty-eight counties. The queen's partisans who had come for negotiations were also forced to subscribe to it.

until under compulsion he restored to King Wladislas the citadel of Visegrád that he held, as was mentioned earlier.

✠ 226 (XXXI): Concerning the coronation of King Wladislas and the wars that followed ✠

Now after King Wladislas took possession of the fortress of Visegrád, the repository of the holy crown was at once investigated. When the object he sought was not found inside, great confusion arose among King Wladislas' supporters: they did not want him to become king without the crown. All his people who had gathered round him, moved by goodwill towards him, were troubled, and they came together with him to Székesfehérvar,[282] where, with clerics assembled to sing aloud his praises, they crowned the king with great jubilation, using a crown once designed with remarkable craftsmanship to decorate the relics of the head of the holy King Stephen.[283]

In the meantime, all the people of Hungary were divided into two camps, and all their ties of mutual affection were undone, to everyone's detriment. And as when, long ago, Alexander the Great of Macedon had died, and his generals had torn to pieces his broad empire,[284] scorning the unity of purpose with

---

282. See notes 26 and 32.

283. St. Stephen (d. 1038), first king and founder of Christian Hungary. He was buried at Székesfehérvár in the church of St. Mary, which he had erected and where his head was venerated as a relic. The coronation of Wladislas was on July 17, 1440. Since the Holy Crown was unavailable (see notes 272 and 274), its "mystery and force" were transferred by a solemn declaration of the Estates to the substitute crown on St. Stephen's reliquary.

284. Allusion to the wars between the heirs of Alexander the Great after 323 B.C.

which, when he was alive, they had subdued, no less than with their arms, the vast earth, so the generals or lords of Pannonia[285] with dire warfare ravaged a realm that under saintly kings had been protected and had enjoyed the pleasures of peace, and had everywhere been filled with an abundance of the many products that always multiply when rivals have come to terms. Those who study and scrutinize the stars have not idly proposed that the kingdom of Hungary lay under the zodiacal sign of the Archer. For its inhabitants were always sweating under the burden of their grim arms, a preoccupation recorded in eulogies of our forefathers. And when in wars abroad they spared the blood of foreigners, they shed one another's, and raging against each other they greedily plundered the treasures amassed by their parents and by themselves. The exploits both of former generations and of our own are sufficient evidence of this, and the period of King Wladislas' reign provided convincing proof of it. For no man of spiritual or secular rank refrained from taking up arms. And every age group, quick to inflict injury, made no allowance for age, but under the leadership of discord all subjects, separated into opposing parties, kept fighting for kings with uncertain claims to the throne. Some supported King Wladislas, others endeavored to promote Queen Elizabeth and her son. And it was not sufficient for them to use a native armed force against the enemy; they employed enemies from abroad. Presently these developments kindled in the kingdom flames of extraordinary ferocity.

---

285. Pannonia, once a Roman province west of the Danube, was a favorite name for Hungary among humanist writers of the fifteenth century.

✠ 227 (XXXII): CONCERNING THE BARONS' CONFLICT
NEAR THE MONASTERY OF SZEK ✠

While all the lords and serfs disposed to be followers of the forementioned parties were by turns casting the evil eye on each other and observing one another with violent intentions, men with power in the kingdom, László Garai the ban, János Fülpös Kórógyi,[286] András Botos of Harapk, and Henrik Tamási, son of the voivode, roused to arms all their forces, intending to redress the wrongs suffered by the queen and her son, and they laid out their camp beside the monastery of Cikádor,[287] a place the common people are accustomed to call Szék. Against them with troops arrayed and banners flying came the aforementioned lord János Hunyadi, the voivode,[288] and Miklós Ujlaki, then ban of Mačva, who rushed headlong upon their camp, determined to fight bravely against them. Loud war-cries therefore resounded repeatedly on each side, and likewise drums and trumpets re-echoed from both parties. But because King Wladislas' partisans fought with greater fervor, the encampment of the other side was at once thrown into confusion, disbanded, and dispersed through unfrequented places. And once they had all lost the shelter of their camp, they ran away in scattered groups and sought refuge for themselves in hiding-places in the dense woods. The knights of the voivode and the ban pursued and slaughtered them mercilessly, as if they had come upon an enemy from overseas. It was also then that András Botos, a grim man, died a grim death, and Henrik, the son of the

---

286. Kórógy, castle in Valkó county southwest of Eszék (today Osijek, Yugoslavia), seat of the ranking noble family Kórógyi. János "Fülpös" ("son of Philip," d. 1456) Kórógyi was appointed Lord Chief Justice by Queen Elizabeth in 1440 and later became Ban of Mačva (1448-1456). For the other persons mentioned, see notes 266, 268 and 269.

287. Cikádor or Szék (today Bátaszék) on the Danube in Tolna county, a Cistercian abbey founded in the twelfth century.

288. Hunyadi became Voivode only after the battle (see note 279).

voivode, was taken prisoner. But although László Garai the ban and János Fülpös Kórógyi weighed more than the others, they nevertheless were not impeded when they conquered the enemy by resorting to flight. For having made their escape by fleeing, they never again presumed to expose themselves to their enemies in a pitched battle.[289] Lord János Hunyadi the voivode and Miklós Ujlaki the ban enriched themselves by plundering the enemy, both camp and troops, and then withdrew their army to attack the encampments at Simontornya and Siklós,[290] attempting to overpower them with a blockade. When they were unable to capture them, they departed and made their way through the kingdom, compelling each and every group of subjects to submit to the authority of King Wladislas.

✠ 228 (XXXIII): CONCERNING THE ATTACKS MADE FROM THE FORTRESS OF ESZTERGOM AND THE BLOCKADING OF THAT FORTRESS ✠

A t the same time the keeper of the fortress of Komárom[291] was Tamás Szécsi, brother of the lord Dénes, archbishop of Esztergom.[292] He was a man who in reputation, handsome appearance, and physique, deserved to be called

---

289. The battle took place during the first days of January, 1441. Though it did not prove to be decisive from a military point of view, it was of great consequence for both Ujlaki and Hunyadi, making them the heroes of Wladislas' party.

290. Simontornya Castle (see note 35) had been in the possession of the Garai family since 1427. For the castle of Siklós, see note 110.

291. Komárom (today Komárno, Slovakia), royal castle on the left side of the Danube in Komárom county. From 1439 it was under the command of Tamás Szécsi (see note 270) and his brothers on behalf of the queen.

292. Esztergom, city on the Danube northwest of Buda with a castle (still preserved in part) on the hill above it. The archbishops of Esztergom, heads of the Hungarian Church, used to reside there. In the years after 1440, the

a man, and among the other leading men of the kingdom of Hungary he did not rank last. More devoted than the others to the queen's service, he very often left the fortress of Esztergom in main force, and with fire and sword caused considerable devastation in the villages of subjects at variance with the queen and her son. And coming to the town of the hot springs (called Felhéviz in Hungarian),[293] a suburb depending on the city of Buda, he set it afire in sight of the king, reducing it to leaping flames and dark smoke. But when King Wladislas observed that his party was fighting with all its might for him, and was told that the barons of the realm who were opposed to him would be completely subdued, he collected troops of armed men and rushed forth boldly into the field. And first devoting all his efforts to capturing the fortress of Esztergom, he encircled it with a blockade. Once he had set up a defense work on St. Thomas Hill,[294] the besiegers and the besieged repeatedly attacked one another in the game of Mars, wounding each other and pouring out both their souls and their blood. When the lord archbishop Dénes saw this, he at once dissolved in sighs and tears—for he was a man innately compassionate and noble of nature, character, and life—and thought that he would be condemned by God if he did not check the progress of so great a slaughter. He therefore immediately dispatched representatives to the king, and he labored for peace and for a truce, which he also obtained. King Wladislas therefore withdrew his army, entered Zala county,[295]

Cardinal Dénes Szécsi (see note 261) held it resolutely for the queen and the infant King Ladislas.

293. Felhéviz, literally "the upper hot springs (of Buda)," a market in medieval times near the city of Buda, around the current site of Lukács Baths. Buda has been renowned for its thermal waters since Roman times. The implied "lower springs" were those at the foot of Gellért Hill.

294. St. Thomas Hill was in a suburb of medieval Esztergom called Szentamás, near Castle Hill (see note 292). King Wladislas besieged Esztergom in February 1441.

295. Zala county is in the southwest of Hungary.

and there stormed two fortifications, one called Páka[296] and the other Kigyós,[297] which were then occupied by a reckless band of Germans.[298] The king captured them and returned happily to Buda.[299]

✠ 229 (XXXIV): CONCERNING THE ACTIONS OF FOREIGN NATIONS IN THE KINGDOM ✠

After the death of King Albert, Queen Elizabeth had conferred the fortress of Zólyom[300] and other fortifications annexed to it upon a certain Jan Jiskra, called "of Brandys,"[301] a Bohemian who was expert at handling arms and greedy for plunder. And she had placed him as guardian over

---

296. Páka, in Zala county, a fortified manor-house (*castellum*) that belonged to one of the king's partisans but had been taken by the queen's party in 1440. Wladislas retook it in March 1441, along with several other castles not mentioned here.

297. Kigyós, correctly Kigyókő, a minor castle in Vas county, near the present village of Ostffyasszonyfa.

298. The Latin word *Theutunus* is used here for "German" and refers to German mercenaries who were hired by Queen Elizabeth in great numbers during the civil war.

299. About May 12, 1441. By this successful expedition the king almost broke the resistance of the opposition party in the Transdanubian region.

300. Zólyom (today Zvolen, Slovakia), royal borough with a castle. It was built by Louis I as a summer residence and was usually included, along with three other royal castles annexed to it until the mid-fifteenth century, as part of the queen's dowry. The vast forests of the region were rich in all sorts of game and were greatly valued by all Hungarian kings for hunting.

301. Jan Jiskra of Brandys (d. c. 1470), a former Hussite captain, later a mercenary leader in Sigismund's service. From 1440 on he was the chief supporter of Queen Elizabeth in North Hungary. He modestly titled himself "King Ladislas' Captain (*capitaneus*)," but in fact he governed that part of the kingdom with full authority for almost twenty more years.

all the cities in the mountains, I mean Kassa[302] and others, which were not yet disloyal to the queen and her son. When that Jan Jiskra observed that the barons were by turns offering violence to one another, he at once embarked upon a plundering expedition, invading all of the Mátyusfölde[303] and the provinces and counties in the vicinity of the city of Kassa, and almost the whole of the northern region of the kingdom of Hungary. He beat up everyone he could, and especially those whom he knew to be hostile towards the queen and her son. With hired troops from abroad, he openly travelled about in main force, roaming over the territory of Hungary, laying out a camp, and ravaging everything in his path by relentless pillaging and burning. Hence also Pongrác,[304] an inhabitant of Liptó county, and a man more savage than any foreign enemy, together with Peter Komorowsky,[305] Aksamit,[306] Talafús,[307] Rybald, Kerczky, Wryk, Zlowachko,[308]

302. Kassa (today Košice, Slovakia) was a walled royal city. It is a remarkable fact that, contrary to the great majority of the nobility, who fought for Wladislas, most of the royal cities and towns remained loyal to the queen and her young son.

303. See note 194.

304. Pongrác of Szentmiklós (today Liptovsky Mikulás, Slovakia), a Hungarian nobleman from Liptó county (d.c. 1458). Originally a captain of Queen Elizabeth, whom he betrayed, Pongrác took advantage of the troubled times and acquired great power and wealth in Northwest Hungary during the wars.

305. Peter (Piotr) Komorowsky (d. 1488), a Polish mercenary leader who succeeded in making himself lord of Likava and Árva (in Slovakia) about 1450. Later King Matthias Corvinus recognized him as *ispán* of Liptó and Árva counties.

306. Peter Aksamit (Axamit) of Kosov (d. 1458), Czech mercenary leader in the 1450s.

307. Jan Talafús of Ostrov (d. after 1462), Czech mercenary captain of Queen Elizabeth from 1440. He held for Jiskra the castle of Richnó (in Szepes county) from 1447 to 1460.

308. The last four men named here may have been commanders of minor mercenary units in the 1450s. A certain Uhrik, probably the one here called *Wryk*, is recorded as captain of the little fortress Zagyvafő in Nógrád county in 1460; the other names are not found elsewhere in the sources, although *Kerczky* may be a corrupted form of *Uderski*, who is known to have been a Polish captain

and many other Bohemians, Poles, and Slavs[309] enticed by plunder, collected some troops for protection and concentrated all
their strength on plundering the kingdom. Having established
many fortifications and wooden encampments, they terrorized
all of that part of the region in their vicinity. And so it was that a
band of foreigners with much greed plundered the possessions
that domestic wars could not exhaust. The people were being
oppressed by heavy taxes, and the repeated payment of fines
did not buy them peace. Instead, they were compelled to live
in caves in the wilderness and in other refuges in the forests, the
only places to provide them with shelter for their heads. Cities
blazed, and villages, repeatedly set alight, sent up smoke to the
sky, blackening the air in their vicinity. Throughout all of Hungary the cruel years of an evil age rolled by, and slaughter stained
with blood the barren fields of lords and serfs. How many in-
nocent people poured forth their blood or their souls? How
many were deprived of their possessions? How many women
were widowed? How many girls, blooming with virginal beauty,
were deflowered against their wills in these times, when all anyone could do in such a crisis was to save his own life, once he had
been stripped of everything he owned? Now what Count Ulrich
of Cillei, the queen's uncle,[310] did in those days to avenge her,
the old men of the kingdom of Slavonia still recall, and they relate the story to their sons, not without deep sighs. There was no
one living in a neighboring kingdom who had not shown himself to be an enemy of Hungary during her sufferings from internal wars. Such were the disturbances within the regions of the
kingdom that came and went with great storms of violence, and

---

of Jászó (Jasov, Slovakia) in the 1450s.
    309. Thuróczy uses the medieval Latin word *Sclavus* ("tót" in Hungarian)
for the Slav inhabitants of modern Slovakia.
    310. Ulrich of Cillei (see note 264) was not an uncle but a first cousin of
the queen.

that for more than twenty-eight years[311] cruelly tore Pannonia
to pieces. Many people tried frequently but without success to
check the exceedingly violent turmoil occasioned by these wars.
And had our present prince, the renowned King Matthias, about
the 1462nd year of the Lord, not forcibly compelled the end of so
much unrest, it may be said that these same disturbances would
be seething with considerable ferocity right down to this day.

✠ 230 (XXXV): CONCERNING THE SIEGE OF THE FORTRESS
OF NÁNDORFEHÉRVÁR ✠

*m*any and various events took place at one and the same
time, but they cannot be recounted together and simultaneously. For during those same years when the
late lord King Albert was dead, Murad,[312] sultan of the Turks,
subjected to his rule the whole of the kingdom of Serbia, which is
commonly called Rascia, occupying its fortresses and all its fortifications. When he heard that all the people of the kingdom of
Hungary were devouring each other in civil wars, he reckoned
that a divided people could do nothing to defend itself. He therefore decided to invade the kingdom of Hungary and to attempt
first of all to take the fortress of Nándorfehérvár[313] by siege.
Having roused to action all the military might of his domain,
and bringing with him all his engines of war, siege-machines,
and catapults, he came and attacked the aforementioned fortress
with the intention of capturing it.

311. The troubles began, as has been observed, in 1440, and came to an
end by 1462 at the latest.

312. Murad II (see note 232). He conquered Serbia from 1439 to 1441.

313. Belgrade (see note 172). The siege began in April 1440 and lasted
three months or more.

At that time the captain in this fortress was the distinguished man, János, prior of Vrana,[314] also called Jovan,[315] born of the Ragusan people, brother of Matkó, ban of the kingdoms of Dalmatia, Croatia, and all Slavonia. He was a vigorous man and fearless of character. When he saw the enemy drawing near, he went to meet him and returned to the fortress not without a fight. But since the number of enemy forces was large, he was not a match for them as far as joining battle for any lengthy encounter was concerned. He therefore went back into the fortress and duly saw to those arrangements concerned with the defense of the walls. The sultan of the Turks, on the other hand, having distributed his troops on every side and drawn up squads of soldiers to keep watch all round, kept close to the fortress with his formidable blockade. And he also set up his siege-machines and other kinds of catapults and ruinously shattered the high fortifications of the towers together with the walls, razing them down to the ground. Jovan, to be sure, and those who were with him, were by no means numbed with fear at the sight of such an enemy and by so harsh a siege. They instead swiftly performed the tasks that were their responsibility, and by working at night they repaired the walls of the fortress that had been knocked down by the sultan's daily exertions. And they very frequently burst out of the fortress like wasps and caused a great commotion amongst the enemy. When the sultan realized that Jovan's guarding the fortress was a powerful obstacle to his progress, he contrived a kind of trap in order to take it. For there is a hillock at a distance of half a Hungarian mile or less from the fortress in the direction of enemy territory, which can hide from the fortress's range of

---

314. Vrana, castle in Dalmatia near Zadar. In the fourteenth century it was the residence of the head of the Hospitallers in Hungary. He held the title of "Prior of Aurana (Vrana)" even after the castle passed to the Republic of Venice in 1409 (see note 116).

315. Jovan Tallóci (see note 168). The Tallóci brothers governed Belgrade from 1429.

view activities taking place on its far side. So in the shelter of this hillock the sultan decided to dig a long and broad subterranean tunnel penetrating right into the interior of the fortress, through which his troops could follow him in. Non-stop labor was therefore employed, and many thousands of men, digging up the earth themselves and with camels, horses, asses, and donkeys for transport, in a short time extended the channel to a point not far from the walls of the fortress itself. While this was going on, the sultan's stratagem became known to those whose chief responsibility was the safety of the fortress, either by divine command or, as certain people like to state, because an arrow, shot by some one unknown, had flown into the fortress. On this arrow a rolled-up piece of paper was found, which revealed that a channel was being dug in the spot mentioned and that it was close to the fortress. Informed as to the sultan's will in one or the other of these ways, Jovan therefore had another passage, also subterranean, speedily excavated, proceeding from the main part of the fortress in the direction of the sultan's tunnel. And he arranged for it to be set alight with saltpetre and cannon powder and other materials, and to be filled with objects capable of suddenly producing unexpected flames and thick smoke. He had the entrance leading into the tunnel skilfully and securely closed, with only a hole left open to set fire to the aforementioned materials and powders. He arranged for several guards to listen without ceasing and with exceptional attention for the enemy preparing their concealed trap. And when the enemy tunnel had reached within the walls of the fortress, up to the tunnel excavated by the fortress's inhabitants, and the noise of those digging it was heard by the guards, at once fire was brought to set alight all the explosives that had been arranged. And its fierce flames and the smoke were the cause of the sudden death of every living thing, man and beast, inside the tunnel. When the sultan himself saw that this device would not help him capture the fortress, he returned home in confusion, having lost, or so it is said, 17,000 of his people, and having devoted seven months[316] to the siege.

✠ 231 (XXXVI): CONCERNING THE WAR INITIATED BY LORD JÁNOS THE VOIVODE NEAR THE FORTRESS OF NÁNDORFEHÉRVÁR ✠

1t was after these events, but during the same period, that the lord János Hunyadi was becoming famous because of his offices as voivode of Transylvania and ban of Severin, and upon his investiture as ispán of Temes,[317] he had of necessity been made captain[318] in the aforementioned fortress of Nándorfehérvár. Then, too, the southern regions of the kingdom of Hungary as far as the Tisza river, and the whole of Slavonia[319] and all the territory situated between the rivers Sava and Drava

---

316. "Seven months" is certainly an exaggeration, as perhaps is the six-month period mentioned by other authorities (see Jovanka Kalič-Mijuskovič, *Beograd u sredimen veku [Belgrade in the Middle Ages]*. [Beograd, 1967], 110 ff.).

317. In spring 1441. An *ispán* (in Latin *comes*) was an office-holder appointed by the king or, occasionally, by a baron to govern a county (in Latin *comitatus*, in Hungarian "megye" or "vármegye"). The office of *ispán* often included command over a royal castle or castles situated in a county, and his competence was sometimes extended to more than one county. The most important *ispáns*, like that of Temes (see note 155) and of Pozsony, were considered equal to a "baron." For the banate of Severin see note 13.

318. Thuróczy here uses the Latin word *capitaneus* (in Hungarian "kapitány"), which was a general term, current since the 1390s, for all those who were entrusted with any kind of military jurisdiction, be it control of a castle, command of an army or garrison of a royal city, or the exercise of exceptional authority over a territory during wartime. For want of a better term, it is here translated as "Captain." Hunyadi became Captain of Belgrade in spring or summer 1441 jointly with Miklós Újlaki (see note 265), who shared all his dignities until 1446.

319. See note 118.

were being savagely plundered by the Turks; cities and villages and towns were being consumed by fierce fires, and possessions were being looted; people without distinction of sex and age were either being killed or led away to be sold forever into slavery; and so great was the disaster that all the inhabitants of the kingdom were overwhelmed with deep hatred, and those regions of the kingdom of which we have spoken were deserted. During all this turmoil, it was lord János the voivode who alone fiercely withstood this great persecution of the Christian religion. After many inconclusive clashes with the Turks in which he always ended up the victor, on one such occasion, when a certain commander of the Turks named Ishak,[320] who was occupying the fortress of Szendrő and other strongholds of the kingdom of Rascia, as well as all of Rascia or Serbia, given him as a gift by the Turkish sultan, had assembled a large body of his subjects and was proceeding to loot and burn out the villages lying near the castle of Nándorfehérvár and to try the courage of the new captain—then it was that lord János the voivode, aware of the enemy's plans, did not neglect to make the arrangements appropriate to dealing with so formidable a visitor. For once he had assembled an excellent garrison of armed men and had organized them in battle array, he revealed himself as an enemy to his foe in the field. An encounter between the two hostile forces took place with great violence, and when they began to fight, many were struck down from their horses. There was loud shouting as the combatants were hard pressed in the deadly battle, and countless men on both sides were killed and fell. Observing that the Hungarians were either prevailing or greatly desired to die, the Turkish commander Ishak immediately turned tail, and on his swiftly galloping horse fled as fast as he could towards the

---

320. Evrenosoglu Ishak bey, commander of Szendrő (see note 235) since 1439, former Bey of Skpoje (see Konstantin Jireček and Jovan Radonič, *Istorija Srba* [History of the Serbs], vol. I [Beograd, 1952], 363).

fortress of Szendrő, together with those of his men who had survived. Lord János the voivode and all his assembled troops pursued them at close range until they saw the walls of the fortress
of Szendrő, turning many of them into corpses. At length they
returned to the fortress of Nándorfehérvár with a victory and a
great abundance of captured loot.[321]

✠ 232 (XXXVII): CONCERNING THE WAR AND CONFLICT OF THE VOIVODE, LORD JÁNOS HUNYADI, INITIATED IN TRANSYLVANIA ✠

After this victory, which had been divinely granted to the
lord voivode, not many days passed before a second
army of the Turks crossed the Alps. Puffed up with
pride because of the glorious victories brought back previously
both from Hungary and from the kingdoms of other peoples
in their vicinity, they expected that they would perform great
deeds and that they could rely on their superior numbers and the
considerable protection afforded by their weapons. Bursting secretly through the transalpine region and rushing into the Transylvanian territories of the kingdom of Hungary,[322] they were
under the leadership of a certain voivode called Mezid bey,[323]
a severe man, and one experienced at directing military op-
érations. This cruel people, accustomed to strike without any
compassion against everything in its path, laid waste indiscriminately, using the violence of fire and sword; and age or condition

---

321. This first major victory of Hunyadi over the Turks took place near
Belgrade in the summer of 1441.

322. From Wallachia across the South Carpathians (see notes 47 and 56).

323. Mezid bey, probably Sancakbey of Kruševac in Serbia. Turk commanders were often titled "Voivode" in contemporary Hungarian, the word
(from Old Slavonic *vojevoda*, "army leader, commander") having the meaning
of "commander" in the broader sense.

did not save anyone. A few days before this murderous rush of the Turkish army, János the voivode had come into Transylvania, and having visited the city of Alba, called Gyulafehérvár[324] in the language of the people, he was carefully considering what he should do about the enemy. For because of the unexpected arrival of so numerous a foe, an opportunity to assemble troops and confront the enemy was entirely denied him. He was therefore so overwhelmed by the greatest anxiety that his features became lined and his lips were bitten from the intensity of too much brooding. Now when the Turks had already overrun many parts of Transylvania, taking away as plunder people, their goods, and their farm animals, and had come to a field near the aforementioned city of Alba so that the smoke emitted by their fires would indicate that they were not far off, lord János the voivode was strong enough to hold back others, but himself he could not; all hot for vengeance, he decided that he must confront so numerous an enemy, and with a less than adequate company of troops he rushed on to the field ready to do battle.

During those days the bishop of this city[325] was a man deserving of respect yet excessively zealous about doing things correctly. He was one of the companions of the lord voivode. When, as they proceeded, they incautiously reached the field of the village of Szentimre,[326] suddenly all the surrounding valleys discharged large throngs of the enemy who were lying concealed and waiting only for the arrival of the lord voivode. What more needs to be said? The lord voivode himself was compelled to

324. Gyulafehérvár, "the White Castle of the Gyula" (today Alba Iulia, Rumania), city on the Maros in Transylvania, see of a bishop, called "bishop of Transylvania."
325. György Lépes of Váraskeszi (1427-1442). He was notorious for bringing about the peasant revolt of 1437 by his illegal exploitation of the tithe (see note 200).
326. Szentimre (today Sîntimbru), market on the Maros near Gyulafehérvár. The battle was fought on March 18, 1442.

abandon the field and to evade an enemy for which he was not a match. All those who could, fled; but the ones who faltered in their flight were either captured or killed by the enemy. And when the bishop of Gyulafehérvár was fleeing on his swiftly galloping charger, and had fallen to the ground as the horse was leaping across a small stream, he was beheaded. This encounter encouraged the commander Mezid bey and roused him to undertake greater endeavors. He therefore proceeded fearlessly through Transylvania. He was greatly pleased about the plunder, especially that which the luck of battle had brought him, intending to hand it over untouched to his sultan, and for this there were set aside waggons with both drivers and guards.

Meanwhile, lord János the voivode very quickly gathered together every knight of those regions he could assemble in such a short period of time, and burning for revenge he at once marched out to follow the enemy. But when these developments were announced to the commander Mezid bey, he is reported to have said: "Let him come, and may he enrich us more than he has already!" At the time these words were spoken, a spy of lord János the voivode was standing in the midst of the Turks in attendance upon the commander Mezid bey, and he heard everything that was being discussed by them about fighting the war. Returning speedily therefore to lord János the voivode, he said to him privately: "You and all the devices on the arms you use to defend yourself, as well as the color of your horse, have been revealed to the commander Mezid bey; and in my presence the strongest knights, those surpassing others in arms, were chosen, and to them was entrusted the task of surrounding you as quickly as possible and of doing their utmost to hasten your death."

Lord János the voivode had amongst his other knights one named Simon, born of a family of nobles from Kamonya,[327] who

────────────

327. Kamonya, formerly a village in Zemplén county near Terebes (today Trebisov, Slovakia), then inhabited by peasant nobles (see *Introduction*). Simon

was not very dissimilar in physical appearance from himself and as strong and courageous of character as his companions. With this knight the lord voivode exchanged weapons and mount, and to protect him assigned a number of knights conspicuous for their physical strength and their desire to fight. And finally, when everything demanded by the exigencies of war had with much prudence been arranged, longing greatly to fight, he attacked an enemy who were puffed up with pride because of their previous victory, and who were drawing up their ranks in battle-formation in a certain village located in the regions mentioned above. Like what might be called a fierce whirlwind he rushed upon the enemy, actually throwing all their ranks into confusion at the first clash, and using his men's strength to divide them into various groups. Both foes proceeded over hills and through valleys, and always in this battle the sword of Hungary was raised high over the spear of the Turks.

But what help was the protective force assigned by the lord voivode to Simon Kamonyai? He was killed right at the beginning of the encounter, when the Turks loyally carried out the orders of their commander, even though many met violent deaths in the process. For he was betrayed by the emblems on the arms of his lord, whose place he had taken, and in spite of his protective escort and their trusty weapons. With this death in mind, the leaders of the armies agreed to conceal his identity from the opposite side. For it very often happens that when a leader falls, all those he led also fall.

As this most bloody battle raged on and the Turks struggled more to defend themselves than to overcome the enemy, all the prisoners that the victory had won for the Turks near the village of Szentimre were set free, and they labored with great energy

Kamonyai, obviously a retainer of Hunyadi, may have been one of them. According to Thuróczy, the victory which he won for Hunyadi by his self-sacrifice took place on March 22, 1442, only four days after the defeat near Szentimre.

to defend themselves. They savagely put their Turkish enemies to death, for they themselves were prepared to die rather than suffer the torments of captivity. When, therefore, the commander Mezid bey witnessed the very great slaughter suffered by his side, and all ranks in his army laboring to escape, he himself began also to flee, but this flight did not save him. For when he endeavored by fleeing to escape, he and his son were killed amongst others who had taken flight and whom the Hungarians pursued and put to death. He lost the booty he had taken, along with his own life and the slaughter of countless numbers of his own people.

After all the prisoners had been set free and the enemy had been plundered, lord János the voivode preyed upon the foe, whose flight saved only a small number of Turks. Successful and victorious, he pursued them all the way to the upper slopes of the Alps, and upon capturing this errant enemy, he had possession in several days of a field crowded with corpses. The fame of his great and glorious victory brought with it to the kingdom this advantage: the voivodes of Wallachia and Moldavia,[328] who in times past, when cut off from the kingdom and the kings of Hungary, had rebelled against the sacred crown and given all their military force to the sultan of the Turks, now, either won over by the military strategy of lord János the voivode or intimidated by him, reverted with their domains to their former fealty, promising under oath to furnish to King Wladislas the customary services.

---

328. The princes of Wallachia and Moldavia (see note 47).

✠ 233 (XXXVIII): WHAT FOLLOWS CONCERNS THE WAR INITIATED BY LORD JÁNOS THE VOIVODE AT A PLACE CALLED VASKAPU ✠

1 n addition to these glorious battles initiated by lord János the voivode himself, wherever any particular band of Turks rushed by any secret path to take up their usual pillaging of the kingdom, in every place they were dogged by bad luck. For they were always decisively defeated by the troops of lord János the voivode, who had been charged with the kingdom's defense. All the paths they used to invade the territory of Hungary were taken from them, and they were not permitted to flash their spears in the gleam of the sun within the borders of the kingdom. Whenever Murad,[329] the sultan of the Turks, deeply and frequently reflected upon the slaughter inflicted so often on his troops, and the great loss of life suffered by his people, and the fact that the lands of Moldavia and Wallachia, together with their masters, had withdrawn their allegiance from him, he was very much troubled and determined to exact harsh revenge against those who had offended him. He therefore assembled 80,000 of his people, chosen from those knights of his realm preeminent for their excellence as fighters, and for their leader he appointed the pasha,[330] a man second to himself in the administration of his kingdom. The sultan instructed him to invade the transalpine lands as soon as possible and to pillage them forthwith, because their voivode had defected from him. From there the pasha was finally to have his troops cross over into the Transylvanian regions of the kingdom

---

329. Murad II (see note 232).
330. Thuróczy uses the word *bassa*, a Hungarian corruption of the Ottoman Turkish word *paşa* (pasha in English), a title given to high office-holders of the Empire. The person referred to here by Thuróczy was Hadım Sehabeddin Paşa, a eunuch, and Beylerbeyi of Rumelia, i.e. the governor-general of all Ottoman provinces in Europe.

of Hungary, and there with fire and sword to exact the most severe punishments possible and to inflict the harshest retribution for the injuries caused him by lord János the voivode. This aim of the sultan not only made the peasants in those regions tremble, but even overwhelmed men of knightly rank with the most depressing speculations. Meanwhile, after an expedition by ship across the Danube near the fortress of Kisnikápoly[331] with all the people entrusted to his charge, the pasha moved freely over the whole transalpine area, which resounded with the tramping of his troops; and everyone unable to save himself by fleeing he either plundered or reduced to a corpse. Next he undertook to cross the Alps and to impose the bondage commanded him by his sultan. But lord János the voivode was ready to die rather than watch this pillaging of the people entrusted to his protection. Inspired by his previous victories, he collected together weapons and troops, ardently desiring to attack the enemy, though unequal to them in fighting power and numbers, rather than be attacked by them, and he pursued them right to the frontiers of those regions. When, however, they had reached a place called Vaskapu,[332] with a loud blast of trumpets resounding on both sides, lord János engaged the pasha in a battle that was hazardous, and decisive, and worthy of record for all ages.

From all directions the enemies charged, each side fighting vigorously. The pasha relied on the superior numbers of his people, and did not consider turning tail. Lord János the voivode wanted only to win or die, and never once considered flight. The war therefore raged on most fiercely on both sides; there was the greatest of slaughters, with many falling on the two sides, though many more of the casualties were Turks. For that reason

---

331. Kisnikápoly, Hungarian name for Little Nicopolis (see note 57).

332. Vaskapu ("Iron Gate" in Hungarian) was a common name for passes in medieval Hungary. This one lay between Transylvania and the region of Temesvár on the road between Várhely (today Sarmizegethusa) and Karánsebes (today Caranşebeş).

the pasha and the Turks were compelled to desert the field of battle and without delay to take flight, pursued by the Hungarians, who made corpses of all they could catch up with. The result was that the whole battlefield was drenched with the blood of slaughtered men and horses and crowded with numerous corpses. It gave off the stench of putrefaction when later the sun's heat grew warmer, and infected the air in the vicinity, so that no one could come near. But in routing so many thousands of the enemy and taking a great many more prisoner, and in plundering their large store of valuables and every costly piece of their army's paraphernalia, lord János should be remembered for all time as a man of conspicuous greatness, worthy of public praise. He undertook the war courageously, directed it shrewdly, fought and finished it most successfully, and brought home a remarkable victory, revealing himself as a man deserving thereafter of whole-hearted and sincere affection, not only from the people of Hungary, but also from foreign peoples.[333]

✠ 234 (XXXIX): CONCERNING THE DEATH OF QUEEN ELIZABETH ✠

𝒯hese struggles were most happily and favorably resolved within a period of two years or less during the reign of the lord King Wladislas. But all the while in the northern counties of the kingdom civil strife continued unabated, and the fact that two monarchs bore responsibility for the kingdom's defense did not please the lords of those regions as much as did the kingdom's impairment. Even the Roman curia, assailed by rumors generated by so many troubles, had as a

---

333. This notable victory took place on September 2 (or 6), 1442, by the river Ialomita in Wallachia, in a valley of the South Carpathians.

result dispatched a plenipotentiary of the supreme pontiff,[334] the venerable lord Cardinal Giuliano,[335] to calm the turmoil caused by these wars. While he was laboring to achieve peace, the queen died,[336] just when King Wladislas and Queen Elizabeth were privately very much disposed toward settling their differences, but a peace had not yet been arranged. Her death caused several of the barons who were her partisans to return to supporting King Wladislas.

✠ 235 (XL): CONCERNING THE RETRIBUTION FOR INJURIES DEMANDED OF THE TURKS BY LORD JÁNOS THE VOIVODE, AND THE SUCCESSFUL WARS WAGED BY HIM ON SIX OCCASIONS ✠

hile these events were taking place, the rule of King Wladislas was being strengthened every day and his territories were increasing. When, therefore, the king was quietly residing beneath the lofty roofs of the royal palace in the fortress of Buda, lord János the voivode roused and induced him to make war on the Turks and to repel the injuries inflicted by them on Hungary on numerous occasions. To that end King Wladislas assembled, in the third year of his reign,[337] a grand and lavishly equipped army of distinguished knights,

---

334. Giuliano Cesarini (see note 335) was appointed by Pope Eugene IV as his *legatus a latere* (or *de latere*) in Hungary, i.e. a legate sent "from his side" to represent him with full authority in the matter to be settled.

335. Cesarini (1398-1444), a cardinal since 1426 and a leading statesman of the Holy See after 1430. He came to Hungary in March, 1442, to negotiate a peace between the rival kings, Wladislas I and Ladislas V, and to organize a crusade against the Ottomans.

336. On December 17, 1442, only four days after a preliminary peace treaty had been made with Wladislas' deputies.

337. Correctly in the fourth regnal year (1443/44).

and together with lord János the voivode and several princes of the kingdom, as well as George, despot or king of the kingdom of Rascia[338] (for he had then been expelled from the government of his realm), he crossed the Danube and arrived in Rascia.[339] There it pleased King Wladislas to pitch a permanent encampment and to send the supreme captain of his army, lord János Hunyadi, to the hinterland that was subject to Turkish rule.

The king divided his entire military expedition into two parts and assigned to the lord voivode the part that excelled at bearing arms and in knightly valor. Besides this, the lord voivode was in command of several companies of his own troops whose battle-tried hands had already used their victorious weapons many times to rout the enemy. Accompanied by these men, the lord voivode passed through the kingdom of Rascia or Serbia and travelled over the whole of the kingdom of Bulgaria, which the Turks have occupied by force from early years,[340] right to the borders of Rumania.[341] And every living thing in the path of the voivode or his troops, from man to beast, was either captured or killed. Any cities, fortresses, and habitations of the Turks you care to name were captured, ruinously sacked, set ablaze, and destroyed. One of them was that city most renowned for its hot springs named Sofia,[342] filled to bursting with people and riches, which was captured and plundered,

338. George Branković (see note 170). After being expelled from Serbia in 1439, he came to live on his domains in Hungary.

339. The Hungarian army invaded Rascia (Serbia) about mid-October, 1443, and followed the ancient highway in the valley of the Morava towards Niš and Sofia. This was the beginning of the remarkable winter expedition that lasted more than three months and has been called "the Long Campaign" in recent historiography.

340. Since sometime between 1393 and 1397 (see note 81).

341. By Rumania the author did not mean present-day Rumania but the territory of the Byzantine Empire whose subjects called themselves "Rhomaioi," i.e. Romans.

342. Sofia, today capital of Bulgaria.

and reduced by fire to ashes. The conflagration of so many cities and towns gave off clouds of smoke high in the air and terrified the whole of Rumania and all the subjects in the Turkish sultan's dominions who could not put their trust in escape by sea.

Meanwhile, many thousands of the enemy, assigned to oppose him by the sultan of the Turks, kept coming up against the lord voivode. On five occasions[343] the lord voivode waged the most bloody battles with the enemy, who were always superior in number when they confronted him; and always he emerged the victor. When, on his supremely glorious and triumphant return home, he had already again reached the territory of Rascia and had measured there the ground for a camp, it was announced to him that a countless horde of Turks was hard on his heels. For, greatly enraged by so much pillaging of his realm, Sultan Murad intended to exact revenge and had to that end commanded the assembling of all the finest weaponry at his court and the entire knightly class of his realm, along with great engines of war. And the direction of this military expedition he had entrusted to his kinsman, the pasha of Anatolia,[344] who pursued lord János the voivode along the same route he had taken from the borders of Bulgaria. And when he found some Hungarians who had been wounded or were ill and had been left behind in the place where the lord voivode had pitched his camp the previous day, he ordered them brought fettered to his sultan and reproached him saying: "Let him see for himself how pitiable the people are who terrify him within his own kingdom!" To these

343. Apart from skirmishes, only three major battles are accounted for in contemporary records: on November 3, 1443, at Niš, on December 12 in the Zlatiski pass near Ihtiman, southeast of Sofia, and on January 2, 1444, on the retreat to Serbia, at the pass of Pirot near Kunovica (see Bistra Cvetkova, *Pametna bitka na narodite* [*The Memorable Battle of the Nations*] [Varna, 1979], 265 ff.). It is the last of these battles which is recounted below in some detail.

344. Thuróczy here is referring to Beylerbeyi of Anatolia, commander-in-chief of the Ottoman troops in Asia Minor (cf. note 330). According to Ottoman sources, his name was Kasïm Paşa and his office was Beylerbeyi of Rumelia.

words the sultan is alleged to have replied as follows: "It is my wish that you return home with success; when you do return, however, you alone will be the one to tell me for a fact what kind of people they are whom I am fleeing."

But when it reached the point that both enemies were resting for the night and could hear, as dawn was breaking, the sound of drums reverberating on both sides, lord János the voivode became very fearful that his enemy would evade him and rush upon the royal encampment. Preferring to have the enemy on the defensive, even though his troops were exhausted from the war's great hardships, he went unprovoked to face them. When, however, he saw that a huge horde of pagans were arrayed against him, he shook with a kind of dread, and all the troops of his army trembled greatly with fear. The lord voivode did not for that reason turn tail; instead, he displayed to the enemy the frightened ranks of his troops one after the other, and sought to rouse them by saying: "Be resolute, and let us suffer the loss of our lives before losing our usual reputation for winning! Why are you fearful of an enemy who take pride in their large numbers? Have you not already time and again put their courage to the test? And cannot one who has so often run away, now also, with God on our side, be put to flight? Never mind if death is cruel to one or another of you. For if he has eaten breakfast with me or with his comrades, he will take his supper with Christ." And when he had finished speaking, a column, greater in number than the others, which he had placed under his own leadership, began to move and rushed upon the enemy. At this sight, the other columns copied the action of their leader. A battle was joined by both sides, who craved victory, but the fighting was not on equal terms. For the pasha himself and the entire horde of Turks entrusted to his charge turned tail at the very first clash and fled precipitately.

When the Hungarians saw this they pursued them relentlessly, and what Turks there were who were not saved from in-

stant death by their horses' swift gallop died in a bloody encounter. Many thousands of pagans were killed there, for the
Hungarians had an aversion to taking them prisoner and therefore put to death all those they could catch as they fled, stabbing
them many times. This pursuit began in the evening and lasted
until the middle of the night. For the pasha himself had chosen
to begin battle at that part of the day with this object in mind: if
he were defeated in the war, at least he might be rescued from
the enemy under cover of darkness. But this plan was of absolutely no use to him. For under the light of a full moon, which
with its beams illuminated the darkness of the night, the pasha
was captured and around midnight escorted with a loud trumpet blast into the Hungarian camp, to the tent of lord János the
voivode. And thus, after successfully waging six outstanding
wars on one and the same march, the lord voivode brought back
safe and sound to the royal encampment, five months after they
had left Hungary, an army heavily laden with a very numerous
collection of men and plundered goods.[345] And as a token of
his victory he handed over to the king many military standards
or banners of the enemy. Later presented to the most glorious
Virgin Mary, patroness of the kingdom of Hungary, these were
hanging, down to our own time, in a church dedicated to her
built in the city of Buda, as a memorial and in praise of the glorious Virgin,[346] and they are proof of so many victories granted
by heaven to the lord voivode himself. They would have been
hanging there to this very day, had not dust or age destroyed
their soft fabric.

_____

345. The army arrived in Belgrade on January 25, 1444.

346. The parish church of St. Mary the Virgin at Buda, on Castle Hill (see
note 8). It is still standing in a reconstructed form.

✠ 236 (XLI): Concerning the Truces Confirmed Between King Wladislas and the Sultan of the Turks, and the Restoration of the Kingdom of Rascia ✠

Because of these many illustrious triumphs and so large a number of outstanding victories, it happened that Murad himself, sultan of the Turks, in fear and trembling sued urgently for truces, sending heralds to the king and the lord voivode. King Wladislas therefore decreed that a solemn assembly of his magnates be held in the city of Szeged.[347] Many nobles of the kingdom gathered together there from all directions; and

---

347. Szeged was an unwalled royal city at the junction of the rivers Tisza and Maros. The story of the so-called "peace of Szeged," with all the preliminaries involved, is much more complex than it was thought to be by most contemporaries, including Thuróczy, who omitted here many important facts. For a better understanding of his version, we summarize here the complete story as it has been recently reconstructed. (See Pál Engel, "A szegedi eskü és a váradi béke" ["The Oath of Szeged and the Treaty of Várad"] in Éva H. Balázs et al., ed., *Mályusz Elemér Emlékkönyv*, [Budapest, 1984], 77-96; there is a brief English version in the study cited in note 277. It should be noted that some of the main points were clarified by Halil Inalcik, "Pitanje segedinskog mira i kriza turske drzave godine 1444" [*Prilozi za orijentalnu Filologiju*, 1962-1963], 269-306). Impressed by Hunyadi's victories, the pope made preparations for a crusade as early as the spring of 1444. It was planned as a decisive blow against Ottoman power in Europe, with the main army of the Hungarians pushing forward in the Balkan peninsula towards Constantinople, and the allied fleets of Venice, Burgundy and the papacy intercepting the sultan's retreat at the Streets. Frightened by the enemy's preparations, Murad contacted his father-in-law, the Despot, George Brankovič (see note 170), who was living in Hungary and offered to return Serbia to him, provided he could prevent Hungary (and especially Hunyadi) from participating in the planned undertaking. Brankovič was not in a position to do this by himself, but he was able to bribe Hunyadi by promising him his own vast domains in Hungary if peace between Hungary and the sultan were made. Hunyadi could not prevent preparations for war in Hungary from continuing, but he induced King Wladislas to permit him to negotiate with the sultan. Then both he and Brankovič sent their plenipotentiaries to Andrianople where, on June 12, a preliminary treaty was concluded. The return of Serbia to the despot was expressly stipulated, and the other terms of the treaty were so favorable to Hungary that the sultan was reasonably certain

two leaders of the Turks came, sent by their sultan and competent to arrange the truces mentioned above. An agreement was reached for a cessation of hostilities for ten years; and the pasha of Anatolia was released by the king. The sultan of the Turks also restored to George the despot the fortress of Szendrő[348] and all the other fortifications of the kingdom of Rascia he had previously taken from him. And this armistice was confirmed by oaths, for lord János the voivode swore a binding one on behalf of the king, himself, and all the people of Hungary, and the aforementioned leaders of the Turks did so on behalf of their sultan and all the people of his realm, agreeing to observe both the ten years' truces and the other terms then promised. Would that these oaths had never been sworn! For afterwards these same

─────────

that his offer would not be refused. He confirmed it by oath and an Ottoman embassy departed immediately to have the peace ratified by their adversaries. Wladislas left Buda on July 25 and met the Ottoman ambassadors in Szeged on or about August 1. What exactly happened will probably never be known, because the negotiations were conducted behind closed doors, but the main points may be inferred from the consequences. No doubt Cardinal Cesarini, the moving spirit of the crusade and its chief proponent in Hungary, and Hunyadi played the leading roles. Hunyadi firmly intended to obtain what he had been promised and he therefore advocated acceptance of the peace offer, while Cesarini's intention to persevere with the crusade must have been no less firm. On August 4 the king took a public oath implying that any peace to be made with the Turks by himself or in his name would be automatically null. Then he moved to Várad where, on August 15, the treaty proposed by the sultan was ratified. We know only from Thuróczy that it was Hunyadi who confirmed it by his oath in the name of the king and Hungary. By the end of August Serbia together with Szendrő was in the posession of Brankovič (see next note), who handed over his domains in Hungary to Hunyadi according to their previous agreement. In the meanwhile, the peace was declared void by the cardinal and, in September, the Hungarian army crossed the Danube and invaded the sultan's territory. It was led by Hunyadi, who was persuaded to participate by the king's promise that he would receive the kingdom of Bulgaria in the event of victory.

348. Szendrő or Smederevo, (see note 235). The fortress was delivered to the Despot George by the Turks on August 22, 1444, in accordance with the terms of the negotiated peace.

truces were broken by the king and the lord voivode at the instigation of the lord Cardinal Giuliano. Just as the glory of victory
was in ancient times taken from Pompey, who had emerged as
the most victorious of all men, after he stabled his horses in the
portico of the temple of Jerusalem,[349] so, too, the initiatives in
war of King Wladislas himself and the lord voivode henceforth
turned out differently. The terms of this armistice did, however,
remain valid for the despot, for although he had been expelled
once and for all from his position of sovereignty over the kingdom of Rascia, he was restored to his previous rank as its lord
under the terms of the truces.[350]

✠ 237 (XLII): WHAT FOLLOWS CONCERNS (I) THE WAR INI-
TIATED BY THE LORD KING WLADISLAS IN PARTS OF RU-
MANIA, IN THE NEIGHBORHOOD OF THE TOWN OF VARNA
CLOSE TO THE SEASHORE, AND (II) THE KING'S UNTIMELY
DEATH ✠

When these affairs had been thus concluded, the lord
Cardinal Giuliano used all his power to insist, in the
presence of the king and the lord voivode, that they
break the armistice agreement and with their arms attack the
sultan of the Turks. For he kept saying that a promise made to
infidels should in no way have to be kept; and he said that it
was an insult to God that they were in their hearts so unappre-
ciative of that noble, God-given victory against the enemies of

---

349. However little Thuróczy may have known of ancient history, he enjoyed inserting occasional references to antiquity. Here he alludes to an early
Christian tradition that attributed Caesar's defeat of Pompey to God's anger
at Pompey's violation in 64 B.C. of the temple of Jerusalem, one of the most
sacred places of Christendom.
350. See note 348.

the Church's religion, and that they had exchanged the will of God, which should be carried out against the enemy, for the will of the enemy. With frequent persuasive arguments he pushed them to the forbidden deed; and the men whom Mars or the sword could not on so many occasions defeat, he defeated only with soft words.[351] For he promised that many Christian princes were bringing them arms, and he said that great numbers of troops were coming to them as reinforcements from Bulgaria, Albania,[352] and Thrace, and also from that most celebrated imperial city of Constantinople. The princes of these kingdoms were also promising support, and so were their peoples. At length the king and the voivode complied, won over by so confident an attitude. And as soon as many hired knights had been summoned to arms and a military encampment built, they at once sailed across the Danube near the fortress of Orsova,[353] attended by a great number of magnates of the kingdom, and rushed into enemy territory. Their camp was moved daily from place to place and every piece of enemy land they happened upon was ravaged by fire and by the plundering of moveables; some fortresses and fortifications were subjugated when their defenders capitulated; others were stormed with a powerful assault and with swords. The advance therefore seemed more and more an internal one, until they passed right through the kingdoms of Bulgaria and Rumania,[354] reached the seashore, and received the surrender of

---

351. See note 347.

352. The Albanian prince George Castriota, a firm enemy of the sultan, is known to have promised help in case of war. One cannot imagine, however, what Thuróczy meant by including Bulgaria and Thrace among the allies, as both provinces had long been under Ottoman rule.

353. Orsova (today Orşova, Rumania), a frontier castle of Hungary on the Danube. The invasion began on September 22.

354. By Rumania Thuróczy must mean some cities of the Byzantine Empire on the coast of the Black Sea, but the army did not in fact advance that far.

towns in Rumanian territory called Varna[355] and Galata,[356] which voluntarily gave themselves up, and in the vicinity of which they laid out their camp to wait for the arrival of the reinforcements promised them.

But alas! it has very often happened that when one is careless about his own army at home, he receives poor support from foreign troops when abroad. Although many spoils had, just a short time ago, been collected, and there had been many killings, as well as the burning and plundering of a large part of the kingdoms I mentioned, and the infliction of a very great number of losses, they themselves were unharmed, having been able to turn away any hostile engagement. Nevertheless, the past victories they had brought home from war with this same enemy inspired them, and for that reason they were filled with a kind of readiness to take risks, even though the promises of auxiliary troops proved false. And they also judged it to be inglorious to abandon their undertaking when they had not seen the enemy, and they therefore spent the last month of the summer and practically the entire autumn in enemy territory.

At length, on the tenth day of the month of November, which is reckoned as the vigil of the feast of blessed Martin, Murad, sultan of the Turks, came with countless ranks of armed pagans; and with his army drawn up in battle-formation he was ready to fight a pitched battle. On the other side, the king and lord János the voivode, and the other lords of Hungary who were there, had led forth from the encampment all their forces. These, with their weapons brightly shining, they divided up and arrayed in order, assigning each line a leader. They decided that their war-chariots should come behind each one of the lines at the same speed, when the time came to engage with the enemy, for the

---

355. Varna, a Bulgarian city on the coast of the Black Sea.

356. Galata, formerly a fortress in Bulgaria to the south of Varna, on the coast of the Black Sea.

Hungarians were unequal in number to the Turks and therefore afraid that the men fighting in front would be attacked by the enemy in the hindmost part of the lines.

When they had been marshalled in this formation, God from on high revealed to them in that place a sign of future disaster. For immediately after their standards or banners, flashing with gold, had been raised and unfurled by the soft gusts of winds then typical of the season, these same breezes were at once stirred up into a violent whirlwind, and as they gained in strength the banners were torn and ripped into various pieces and flew high through the air. At length, as the sound of many trumpets and drums re-echoed from both sides, and the loud battle-cries of the Turks repeatedly resounded, the two enemies joined battle. Lances were shattered on both sides, and when they broke many men were knocked from their horses. A combat of the fiercest kind raged and the greatest of slaughters ensued on both sides, though it was much greater for the Turks. For none of their lines could sustain the courageous attack of the Hungarian troops without being compelled suddenly to flee. Because, however, the Turkish lines were spread out in all directions and exceeded in number the army of the Hungarian people by more than six hundred strong, there was no use in the Hungarians pursuing their lines as they fled. For new Turkish lines would confront them on their way back from the chase, and attack them loudly in a fresh battle. Most of the day was passed in this deadly struggle, and the field on all sides was covered with many corpses, inspiring terror in both enemies. The result was that since the entire Turkish cavalry were hesitating and intent on flight, and the sultan's encampment alone was guarded by countless lines of infantry who were standing with great fear in their places, when King Wladislas saw that the enemy cavalry were retreating and that Sultan Murad and his garrison were terror-struck, he at once set in motion the column assigned to protect himself; and as the lord voivode and others pressed on with a fierce attack on another front, the king proceeded to invade the sultan's camp and to take it completely by surprise. But then, when the king came amongst the closely packed lines of infantry, he was, together with the whole of his own line, overpowered and at the same time crushed by a horde of them, and there and then killed. And to an enemy who had already been defeated and battled to a finish, and were not hoping for any victory for themselves, he provided an unexpected victory. The Hungarians therefore simultaneously abandoned the battlefield and their encampment and were made to flee, though many of those who had occupied themselves pursuing the previously routed enemy troops were unaware of the defeat of the others. They at length returned from the pursuit and in their camp abandoned themselves to sleep. But when night came, following immediately after so unhappy a day, and covered the whole world with shadows, those who, on both sides, had not yet fled their camps, kept vigils in them through the night until the dawn of the following day. They could hear, from among the corpses with which all the surrounding battlefield was littered, the cries and wailing of the countless men who had been cut down and could neither die nor live, and they themselves in their stupor scarcely hoped to see the light of day. At length, after the rosy dawn that comes between the shadows of the night and the light of day, when the very bright sun ascends above all the mountain peaks and restores the brighter day, the Turks, who were uncertain about the enemy's flight, marshalled a certain number of their lines and marched out of the sultan's camp to attack them. Advancing at a slow pace they gradually approached the Hungarian camp and carefully investigated whether it was full of troops. When they became aware of the faint murmuring of men's voices therein and observed that no one was showing signs of taking up arms or was rushing forth on to the battlefield to wage war, all the infantry of the sultan's expedition charged the camp and immediately smashed and knocked down its tents, since no one was taking any action at all to defend it. All those found alive there were either taken prisoner or put to death. There, too, in the same camp the lord Cardinal Giuliano and many other men in religious life, especially from the order of the Cseri friars,[357] are said to have died. Furthermore, the lord János, bishop of Várad, and the lord Simon, bishop of Eger,[358] as well his magnificence, István Bátori,[359] chief justice and a man conspicuous for his knightly valor, to whom also, because of his vigorous actions, the bearing of the king's banner had been entrusted at this time of terror and crisis—all these men were killed during this violent struggle.

In this way, then, the lord King Wladislas, best of kings, a man fittingly tall, dark-complexioned, with dark hair, vigorous in arms, kind to his followers, most outstanding for his honorable character, calm of mind and disposition, sadly ended both his life and his reign in his fourth year[360] as king and the 1444th year of the Lord.

357. "Cseri" (*Cheriensis* in Latin) was name used in medieval Hungary for the Friars or "Observantes," i.e. those members of the Franciscan order who observed the Rule strictly, regardless of the relaxations and changes of the previous two hundred years. The name may be derived from the place-name Cseri, a former market near Temesvár (Timişoara) where a Franciscan cloister existed in the early fifteenth century.

358. For these persons, see notes 164 and 248.

359. Bátor (today Nyirbátor), a market in Szatmár county, residence of the ranking noble family Bátori. István Bátori senior (d. 1444) had been Gentleman Carver of the King (1417-1431) and Lord Chief Justice (1435-1440).

360. An error in dating (see note 337). "Fifth year" is correct.

✠ 238 (XLIII):   Concerning the captivity of Lord
János the Voivode ✠

lthough in this disastrous war the glory of victory remained with Sultan Murad, he brought it back at the
cost of much bloodshed by his men. For his troops are
said in a trustworthy report to have received a greater number
of wounds from the Hungarians than they inflicted upon them,
and the sultan himself is reported to have received from them a
greater massacre of his people. Sufficient evidence of this is that
none of them pursued the Hungarians who later fled, for each of
the Turks had enough to do licking his own wounds.

Meanwhile, when lord János the voivode arrived in the
transalpine regions on his way back home, an enemy confronted
him at a spot where he had no cause to fear one. For Dracul,[361]
the voivode of these regions, whose escort he was hoping for,
laid violent hands upon him; and far from offering consolation to
the unhappy man, he even inflicted captivity on him. At length,
when Dracul considered that he had no reason to hold the lord
voivode prisoner, after a few days he gave him many gifts to
conciliate him, or so he hoped, and had him taken into the Transylvanian regions of the kingdom of Hungary.

✠ 239 (XLIV):   Concerning the election of Lord
János the Voivode as Governor, and the retribution exacted by him from Voivode Dracul ✠

fter this grievous war and the sad and untimely death
of King Wladislas, it was forbidden by the lord prelates
and the barons of the realm for anyone in the kingdom
to wrong another; and it was also resolved by common vote that

361. Vlad Dracul, Voivode of Wallachia (1436-1447), son of Mircea (see
note 154).

at the next feast of Pentecost there should be a general gathering of all the people of the kingdom on the Rákos Fields.[362]

The 1445th year of the Lord continued in its course and the feast of Pentecost was at hand.[363] It was a huge gathering, because of the arrival of many nobles, and it spread out on all sides over the broad expanses of the Rákos Fields. Everyone there agreed to discuss with much prudence what was in the best interests of the kingdom, and whom they could in the meanwhile elect as protector of the realm, until such time as King Ladislas, son of King Albert and a lad of five years old,[364] could develop a capacity for judgment and skill at arms.

The famous memorials of exploits achieved by lord János the voivode were hanging before the eyes of the whole community and for that reason many hoped that this high office would come to him, and it was in fact the lord voivode himself who accepted it. He was elected governor[365] of all matters touching the interests of the kingdom and the king, and because of this all the people of the kingdom of Hungary, sustained by such a protector as this, at once abandoned themselves to great exultation, loudly repeating praises to God, while the sounds of bells and trumpets rang through the air. At the conclusion of this glorious election, each of the kingdom's subjects returned joyfully to his house, while only those who believed themselves to be worthy of this

---

362. The Rákos Fields near Pest (in the neighborhood of the northeastern suburbs of modern Budapest), an open space large enough to accommodate a diet even if great numbers of nobles were to be present. Such meetings occurred on this plain so often thereafter that, by the early sixteenth century, "rákos" became a noun and a synonym for "diet." The resolution to meet there was passed at a previous diet held at Székesfehérvár in March 1446. Thuróczy is mistaken in placing the events related in this chapter in the year before, i.e. in 1445.

363. In July, 1446, Pentecost fell on June 5.

364. Ladislas was in fact then in his seventh year (see note 259).

365. On June 6, 1446. The office of Governor was newly created on this occasion. As Governor (1446-1452) Hunyadi was accorded certain royal prerogatives and in practice functioned as regent of the kingdom.

honor and had been disappointed in their hopes walked about with sad hearts, pretending to look happy.

After his election it at length pleased the lord governor to exact retribution for his confinement from Dracul, voivode of the transalpine regions, for he deeply resented the ungracious and inhospitable treatment accorded him by Dracul. Once he had mobilized a large number of armed men against him and had crossed the Alps, the governor rushed into his domain, conquered all its territory, took Dracul prisoner, and had him and his eldest son beheaded. And a certain other voivode of the same regions, the son of the late voivode Dan,[366] he had blinded. Having thus punished Voivode Dracul for his confinement, he appointed another voivode in that territory and returned to Hungary with his vow fulfilled.[367]

✠ 240 (XLV): CONCERNING THE RECLAIMING OF THE CROWN AND THE VENGEANCE EXACTED AS A RESULT ✠

During this time the lords of Hungary bore with great sadness the fact that Frederick,[368] king of the Romans, was retaining possession of the holy diadem with which the kings of Hungary are customarily crowned, and detaining the little boy-king who, by the law of nature, should have been ruling them. For they were afraid that the boy, reared in a foreign land, was becoming a different person, away from the customs

366. Dan II, former Voivode of Wallachia (1422-1431), son of Mircea (see note 154).

367. Hunyadi's Wallachian expedition took place in December, 1447, and not in the winter of 1446-1447, as was formerly believed (see Francis Pall, "De nouveau sur l'action de Iancu de Hunedoara en Valachie pendant l'année 1447," *Revue Roumaine d'Histoire* 15 [1976], 447-463). The new Voivode appointed by him was Vladislav II (1447-1456).

368. King Frederick of Germany (see notes 273 and 274).

and language of Hungarians. It was therefore agreed that the crown should be recovered or revenge sought.

And as long as the king of the Romans remained uninfluenced by the claims, he was assailed by huge losses. For in the second year[369] of his office the lord governor marshalled more troops of armed men and roamed cruelly and sternly through all the territory of Carinthia and Carniola and a large part of Styria,[370] plundering, taking men prisoner, and reducing cities, towns, and villages to blazing fires. When at length he saw that the king of the Romans was by no means moved by the pillaging of his kingdoms, he came home in triumph, loaded down with an accumulation of many moveables and prisoners.

✠ 241 (XLVI): CONCERNING THE LORD GOVERNOR'S WAR BEGUN ON THE PLAIN OF RIGÓMEZEJE ✠

hereafter the lord governor, János Hunyadi, took charge, with an excellent sense of discretion, of all the problems of the kingdom arising on every side, as a burden of responsibility imposed on his shoulders, and he protected the kingdom from enemy attack. And in these same years no opportunity presented itself to the Turks to extend their spears in an attack on Hungarian territory. At length, in his fourth year[371] of office, the lord governor, who was always taking it upon himself

---

369. Correctly in the first year (see note 370).

370. The provinces of Carinthia, Carniola, and Styria were largely in the hands of the Habsburg royal house. Thuróczy seems here to have merged two of Hunyadi's campaigns into one. He led the first in spring, 1446, before his election as Governor, against the counts of Cillei, whose lands lay scattered in the three provinces named here. In the second, in November/December, 1446, he did indeed march against King Frederick, but this time toward Austria itself, ravaging the surroundings of Vienna and Wiener Neustadt.

371. In the third year.

to attempt great endeavors by waging war, considered attacking the sultan of the Turks with a new armed expedition. He therefore assembled a large troop of knights and brought into one expedition every powerful weapon in Hungary. And when he had fortified and packed his encampment with military devices—siege-machines, harquebusses,[372] and other firearms to strike the enemy—he crossed the Danube above the fortress of Szörény[373] around the first month of autumn,[374] cruelly attacking the kingdom of Rascia on his way through, because its lord, summoned to join the expedition, had not done so.[375] He moved into enemy lands and subdued them with fire and sword, passing through not like one who intended to carry off plunder, but like one ready to occupy a kingdom.

Accompanying the lord governor were men powerful in the kingdom and outstanding because of their lineage and their ownership of lands: the lords Imre of Pelsőc, voivode of Transylvania;[376] László, his brother;[377] Imre Marcali, son of

372. It was rather late, and not before the end of Sigismund's reign, that firearms began to be appreciated in Hungary. As weapons for defending castles and city walls they appear from the 1420s only, and their use in open battles is attested in the 1440s. One of the first instances was precisely on this occasion during the campaign of 1448.

373. Szörény (today Turnu-Severin, Rumania), a Hungarian frontier castle on the Danube and residence of a Ban (see note 13). It lay on the highway to Bulgaria, and Hunyadi, on his way to Serbia, crossed the Danube well above it, at the ferry of Keve (today Kovin, Yugoslavia).

374. In mid-September 1448.

375. The Despot George was a partner of Hungary at the time of the treaty of Várad, but he had no part in the duplicity described here (see note 347). Having paid a price to recover Serbia, he continued to refrain from fighting the Turks as long as the ten year's peace lasted. Needless to say, in Hungary his behaviour was considered treacherous.

376. Pelsőc (today Plesivec, Slovakia), market in Gömör county, seat of the ranking noble family Bebek, called also Pelsőc. Imre Bebek of Pelsőc (d. 1448) was ispán of the Székelys (1438-1441) and Voivode of Transylvania (1446-1448).

377. Imre Bebek had no brother of that name. László (d. 1448) was his second cousin.

the voivode, and steward of the royal household;[378] Rajnáld Rozgonyi;[379] Tamás Szécsi;[380] Franko Tallóci,[381] ban of the kingdoms of Dalmatia and Croatia; János Székely,[382] kinsman of the lord governor; Benedek Losonci;[383] István Bánfi of Alsólendva;[384] and a great many others conspicuous for their knightly valor, audacious in war, and distinguished for their many defensive weapons. Likewise Murad, sultan of the Turks, who kept hearing that an exceedingly great hostile force was being set in movement against him, was anxious to protect himself. For he roused to action every hand in his realm that appeared able to take up arms; and he armed every knight in his nation and equipped him for war. And moving a huge army of his people, he went to oppose the approaching enemy. It was the middle of the month of October when the Hungarians' encampment was brought across the borders of the territory of Rascia and took up a position in the territories of Bulgaria subject to the sultan of the Turks. There it remained while awaiting the enemy on the plain of Merula (which in Hungarian is called Rigómezeje).[385] Finally

---

378. See note 250.

379. Rajnáld Rozgonyi (d. 1472), son of János, the Lord Chief Treasurer (see note 164)and a devoted follower of the young King Ladislas; later *ispán* of the Székelys (1449-1453) and of Temes (1457), and Lord Chief Treasurer (1470-1471).

380. See note 270.

381. See note 168.

382. János Székely of Szentgyörgy (d. 1448), a Transylvanian nobleman and brother-in-law of Hunyadi, who appointed him Ban of Slavonia (1446-1448).

383. Benedek Losonci (d. 1448), a Transylvanian magnate (see note 152).

384. Alsólendva (today Donja Lendava, Yugoslavia), castle and market in Zala county, residence of the ranking noble family Bánfi ("sons of the Ban"). István Bánfi (d. 1448) was an eminent partisan of King Wladislas I.

385. Rigómezeje, Rigómező in the modern idiom, literally "Fields of Thrushes," a Hungarian translation of Serbian, Kosovo Polje, a region in the valley of the Ibar in south Serbia (today the autonomous district Kosovo, in Yugoslavia). It is principally memorable as the scene of a decisive victory of Sultan Murad I over the allied Balkan princes in 1389.

the Thursday arrived that falls between the feasts of St. Gall the Confessor and St. Luke the Evangelist.[386] Then it was that the sultan of the Turks came and set up his lodgings not far from the encampment of the lord governor.

The light-armed troops of both sides, whom headstrong young men were leading or whose intention it was to join in close combat, were consigned to the field on either side and were split up, not without some deaths, when the two enemies charged. When, however, dawned that day, memorable for all time, of the feast of St. Luke the Evangelist, and the sun had been conveyed through the palace of the heavens and reached the noonday hours, both enemies sent forth over the surface of the plain all the power implicit in their arms and every knight in their respective expeditions. Nor was there a flute-player on either side whom, at the sight of so numerous an enemy, the fear of death had not seized in so unpredictable and critical a situation.

From all the people he was leading the lord governor organized a fighting force of thirty-eight lines, and in their midst the military standards or banners, decorated with bright gold, were carried. And every line stood protected in front by its shining arms, and their leaders, as they wheeled them round, were rousing the knights' hearts to battle with their advice and assurances.

On the other side the sultan of the Turks arranged all the troops of his army in huge lines and, when the signal to begin battle had been given, like what might be called an unbroken wall they approached at a slow pace, seizing every part of the plain situated within the Hungarians' range of vision. When it reached the distance of the flight of a single arrow, there was a sudden beating of drums on both sides, creating a terrible sound that was followed by the blare of trumpets blowing one against another. And all the battle-lines on both sides bent forward

386. October 17, 1448, the feast day of St. Gall falling on the 16th and that of St. Luke on the 18th.

their many lances, charged with all their vigor and strength, and rushed headlong into mutual slaughter as the whole plain emitted a kind of groan from so much movement. There was the loud din of lances breaking; many on both sides were precipitately knocked down from their horses, falling wounded amongst the feet of the combatants, and the whole air resounded with the terrible cries of the dying. The men on both sides were pressed together and one side did not know how to give ground to the other. Because there were so many men crowded together, one force was unable to strike at another for so long as an hour. At length the Hungarians more vigorously charged the enemy, and the Turks were scattered into a very great number of small units and driven over a long stretch of the plain by the Hungarians, who slaughtered them without ceasing. Then the Turks, aided in their turn by fresh lines of troops from the sultan's garrison, fiercely drove the Hungarians all the way back to their own camp. Meanwhile, the densest showers of arrows, fired by Turkish infantry, obscured the sun high above in the sky and cruelly struck down the Hungarians. But with 24,000 combatants or a little more, the Hungarians were too few and too oppressed to withstand an enemy swelling with more than 200,000 armed men. Yet the exceedingly large number of the enemy, the deafening clamor of their weapons, and their own innumerable wounds could not that day induce them to take flight: until the setting of the sun, with unconquered spirits, the longer their slaughter continued the less they considered surrender.

And so with great courage, but with even greater tenacity, they fought on until the darkness of the night arrived, inflicting upon the enemy a greater slaughter than they were receiving from them. The entire day was given over to the intensity of the struggle, and when countless numbers of men on both sides had been slain, and the whole battlefield was covered with fresh corpses, night came and with its shadows interrupted the armed frenzy of the two foes. But although that night the battle-lines rested a while from the labors of war, the war machines and contrivances continued the fight all night long. Immediately after the Sabbath day[387] was illumined by the rays of the rising sun, however, both enemies, inflamed with yesterday's fury, marshalled their battle-lines and rushed once again on to the plain. Battle was joined afresh, and the two sides engaged each other in this grimmest of battles, fighting with great uproar until the sixth hour of the day.[388] Meanwhile, when the sultan of the Turks saw that his lines were being thrown into disorder by the Hungarian knights, who were very few in number and exhausted, he set in motion his entire host, cavalry and infantry, and with great ferocity they rushed upon the ranks and columns of the Hungarians, and like what might be called a great deluge of water they also overwhelmed them, throwing them and their camp into disorder, and forcing men to flee who had never known anything of flight. Each and every man began to flee, and no order was maintained in the retreat. The Turks pursued them with great ferocity until the sun set. And what is more, after this there came for the Hungarians an equally cruel pursuit, because the Rascians, whom the Hungarians had offended when they first entered Rascia, confronted them when they had been fleeing for so long as a day and pitilessly despoiled, butchered, and killed them, weary from their march and stripped of all the weapons they needed to defend themselves, like sheep terrorized by wolves.

387. October 19.
388. I.e. until noon. The first hour was reckoned to be 6 a.m.

✠ 242 (XLVII): CONCERNING THE MAGNATES WHO FELL IN
THIS WAR, AND THE CAPTIVITY OF THE LORD GOVERNOR,
WHICH THE DESPOT IMPOSED, AND THE PUNISHMENTS EX-
ACTED BECAUSE OF IT ✠

*T*here fell in this war the aforementioned lords Imre of
Pelsőc; László, his brother; Imre Marcali, son of the
voivode; Tamás Szécsi; Franko the ban; János Székely;
Benedek Losonci; István Bánfi of Alsólendva;[389] and practically
the whole army of the kingdom of Hungary was wiped out.

Now when the lord governor had on his swiftly galloping
horse withdrawn far from the battlefield, away from the great
confusion of the war, and was wandering through remote areas, deserted by every knight and having laid down the arms
he needed to defend himself, he is said to have fallen into the
hands of two Turks. Moreover, since they did not at all recognize him, they hurled their spears into the ground, leaped on him
in hand-to-hand combat, and stripped him of his garments. A
golden cross was hanging from the lord governor's neck. When
one of the Turks tried to seize it, immediately a quarrel arose
between the two of them and they rushed to fight one another.
Meanwhile, the lord governor seized one of their spears during
their struggle and charged at them, so heavily striking one of
them with his powerful arm that the Turk at once crashed to the
ground dead. And when he also tried to strike the other one, he
escaped the blow by running away.

Next the lord governor proceeded further on and encoun-
tered a certain Rascian. Although the latter was roaming the
forests in search of plunder, when he noticed that a man with
a distinguished appearance and expression had come before
him, he refrained altogether from doing him an injury; perhaps, on the other hand, it was because the lord governor had

───────────────

389. For these participants in the battle see notes 376 to 384.

not yet tossed away the spear he had seized, that the Rascian by no means dared to attack him. In any case, the two men stood there wrapped in thought, when at length the lord governor asked the Rascian to guide him directly to the fortress of Nándorfehérvár,[390] promising him also appropriate payment. He at once offered to do so, but he brought the lord governor not to the place he desired, as he had promised to, but to the fortress of Szendrő.[391]

Now after it became known to George the despot that the lord governor was inside the gates of his fortress, he forgot that the courage and exploits of this man had, a few years previously, made him the new master in his kingdom at a time when he had been made to suffer defeat and exile. Enticed by the fault of ingratitude, he revealed himself to the lord governor as a thankless host.[392] For he ordered him to be detained, and did not restore him to the lords of Hungary, who were laboring anxiously for his release, until the lord governor had placed in the despot's hands his elder son, named László,[393] as a hostage for him.

Now although the lord governor was in this war attended by bad luck, all the Hungarian leaders nevertheless awaited his arrival with feelings of gratitude, because it was agreed that he had left the enemy a victory as the result of a failure of arms rather than one of courage. The proof of this is that on the lord governor's return on the feast of the Lord's birth, a great gathering

---

390. Belgrade (see note 172).

391. Szendrő or Smederevo, residence of the despot from 1444 (see notes 235 and 348).

392. No question of gratitude was involved. The despot had made a bargain with Hunyadi, and after the "Peace of Szeged" had been broken he may have thought that he had been cheated. Now he saw that his own lands were also being ravaged, and it was only logical that he should seek to obtain compensation one way or another (see notes 347 and 375).

393. László Hunyadi (d. 1457) was the elder son of the Governor. At that time he was about sixteen.

of nobles was assembled in the city of Szeged[394] to wait for him to arrive, and on his approach they met him with happy faces. Thereafter the lord governor reflected upon the ingratitude of the despot as well as the misfortune of his own captivity and, consolidating arms and troops, he proceeded to exact from the despot punishments worthy of his offense. And having marched with main force into the territory of his domain, he caused there great devastation and deprived him of all his fortresses and the domains situated around the borders of the kingdom of Hungary. And he would have destroyed more, had the despot not restored his son to him unharmed, and had the leading men of Hungary, at the request of the despot, not calmed the mind of the lord governor that was inflamed with passion for vengeance.[395]

✠ 243 (XLVIII): CONCERNING THE WARS OF THE LORD GOVERNOR WAGED WITHIN THE BORDERS OF THE KINGDOM ✠

After these many and varied events, the lord governor waged wars against Bohemians who were moving to overpower the kingdom within its borders, and he took possession of many fortifications belonging to these same Bohemians—some upon their surrender to him and others by force—which had been erected in various places to devastate

---

394. See note 347. Hunyadi arrived here about Christmas 1448, after a lapse of two months.

395. After having obtained an attainder against the despot in March, 1450, Hunyadi undertook in the spring of 1450 and the summer of 1451 to deprive him of his remaining domains. In August, 1451, however, Hunyadi accepted a treaty mediated by the Count Palatine László Garai, in which he renounced his recent occupations while retaining the lands he had obtained from the despot in 1444. He also compelled the despot to consent to a planned marriage between his younger son Matthias and Elizabeth of Cillei, who was a granddaughter of George through her mother.

Hungarian territory.[396] And he would have successfully concluded his direction of all his expeditions against these Bohemians had not leading men in Hungary attempted to betray him,
which provided the Bohemians with the help they needed. For
the more the lord governor's affairs succeeded, the more a very
great number of the lords became inflamed with secret envy of
him.

In the 1451st year of the Lord's Incarnation, the lord governor with an army comprising both many mercenaries and
troops from his own people encircled and besieged a fortification erected by the aforementioned Jan Jiskra outside the walls
of the monastery of the holy King Stephen and near the town of
Losonc.[397] When he had with his powerful assault on the place
day after day so overwhelmed its guards with thirst and fighting
that by then the governor's desire to end the siege and take the
fortification was also their hope, it at length happened that Jiskra,
who was full of pride because of support received from the royal
cities he held in the northern counties of the kingdom,[398] and

396. The Bohemians in question were mercenary troops in the service of
Queen Elizabeth and her son. They were formally under the command of Jan
Jiskra (see note 301), who succeeded in subduing a great part of modern Slovakia during the civil wars in the 1440s. As a firm supporter of the Habsburg
party he governed the lands he acquired in King Ladislas' name, and he was
reluctant to hand them over to anybody except the king, a fact that Hunyadi as
Governor of the kingdom could not help but resent. Because Jiskra continually
had difficulties paying his vice-captains, they in turn "reimbursed" themselves
at the expense of the Hungarian landowners in the surrounding counties by
plundering their lands and holding the owners captives for ransom. A vast
network of newly erected fortifications helped them to keep the region under
control. All this went on even after the peace had been formally restored in
1446, thereby exacerbating the situation. Hunyadi tried to break their power
by leading four major expeditions against Jiskra in the years 1447, 1449, 1451,
and 1452, but, he was only able to destroy a few minor fortresses.

397. Losonc (see note 152). The otherwise unknown monastery of King
St. Stephen (in Hungarian Szentkirály) was besieged by Hunyadi for a whole
month beginning on August 10, 1451.

398. Kassa and the other royal cities in the region were inclined to support

who had then been influenced by the persuasive arguments of traitors and provided with the considerable protection of his own men and of armed auxiliaries, came to bring aid to his people who had been surrounded in the aforementioned fortification. And with ranks marshalled he took up a position near the lord governor's encampment. But what wicked treachery is capable of in wartime was then revealed, when the troops of combatants had not yet been mustered and throngs of traitors had already burst out of the lord governor's camp and precipitately fled. The lord governor himself was therefore also compelled to abandon battlefield and encampment.[399] Indeed, his magnificence, István of Pelsőc,[400] fatally wounded by a random shot from a harquebus before the aforementioned fortification, with his own lips confessed this betrayal before he died. Furthermore, of the more powerful nobles of the kingdom there was killed there János Kompolti of Nána,[401] but the bishop of Eger, László Hédervári,[402] was taken prisoner, since he was lame and unable to escape.

In this way Jan Jiskra captured the battlefield and the encampment of the Hungarians along with a victory, at length attempting a heavy assault on the fortress of Gede,[403] which belonged to the sons of Loránd. But his desire was frustrated when

Jiskra and even to vote large subsidies just to protect themselves from the rule of the nobility. See note 302.

399. The battle was fought on September 7, 1451.

400. István Bebek of Pelsőc, a distant cousin of Imre Bebek (see note 376), former Ban of Macva (1447-1448).

401. Nána (today Kisnána), village and castle in Heves county, residence of the ranking noble family Kompolt or Kompolti. János Kompolti of Nána was Cupbearer to the King (1432-1438) and died as Steward of the Household (1450-1451).

402. László Hédervári (d. 1468), Abbot of Pannonhalma (1439-1447), Bishop of Eger (1447-1468), a distant cousin of the Count Palatine Lőrinc (cf. note 255).

403. The fortress of Gede near the village of the same name (today Hodejov, Slovakia) in Gömör county. Since 1439 it had been in the possession of the knightly family Lorántfi ("sons of Loránd") of Serke.

the occupants of the fortress strongly resisted, and he came before the fortress of Eger.[404] And although there the aforementioned Bishop László had wanted to hand over this fortress into the hands of Jan Jiskra to ransom himself, the captains of the fortress, since they were inhabitants of those parts, preferred the disaster that could next have followed to the distress of one man, and wanted Jan Jiskra to depart without achieving his objective.

After these events the lord governor again took up arms as well as the leadership of the peoples who were protecting the southern counties,[405] and whose knightly valor and resolute fidelity he had put to the test in previous wars. Attacking the fortifications of Jan Jiskra himself, newly erected at the monastery of Ság[406] beside the river Ipoly, and on Mt. Gácsvár,[407] and in the towns of Rozsnyó[408] and Szepsi,[409] he harried them with harsh blockades and forced them to surrender. Moreover, he besieged a fortification of Jan Jiskra that he held in Derencsény[410] and that a certain Bohemian named Valgata[411] was occupying in Jiskra's name. And since it was in a valley, a new kind of assault against it was contrived, whereby he had the valley itself below the fortification blocked with a high earthwork, reversing the course and increasing the depth of the river[412] flowing through this valley.

404. Eger, a city, castle (still partly preserved), and episcopal see in Heves county.

405. See note 10.

406. Ság or Ipolyság (today Sahy, Slovakia), market in Hont county, on the Ipoly, with a Premonstratensian monastery fortified by the Czech mercenaries.

407. Gácsvár, i.e. the castle of Gács (today Halic, Slovakia) in Nógrád county, destroyed about 1300 and rebuilt by Jiskra in the 1440s.

408. Rozsnyó (today Roznava, Slovakia), a market of the archbishopric of Esztergom in Gömör county.

409. Szepsi (today Moldava nad Bodvou, Slovakia), a market of the Rozgonyi family in Abauj county.

410. Derencsény (today Driencany, Slovakia), a village in Gömör county with a wooden fortification erected by Jiskra.

411. Martin Valgata, Czech mercenary captain in Jiskra's service.

412. Balog (today Blh) creek.

And when the flooding waters passed over the tops of the walls of the fortification, threatening all those within with death by drowning, the Bohemian occupants surrendered themselves as prisoners along with the fortification into the hands of the lord governor. Finally, he went to the city of Zólyom,[413] the nest and nurse of so much ruin, and burned it to the ground in a fierce fire. Opposite the fortress of Zólyom he had a large fortification erected and left it filled with weapons and troops, while he in the meanwhile disturbed Jan Jiskra with the din of his arms, until he forced him to seek an acceptable peace.[414]

✠ 244 (XLIX): CONCERNING THE BOHEMIANS CALLED "THE BROTHERS," WHO WERE DEVASTATING THE KINGDOM OF HUNGARY ✠

There were at that time, in addition to Jan Jiskra, many foreigners in the kingdom who had dedicated all their strength to vexing the kingdom. Peter Komorowsky[415] had subjected to his authority all of Liptó county,[416] and Pongrác,[417] a man born, as mentioned above, in Hungary, was

413. Zólyom (see note 300).
414. In the passage above Thuróczy has confused episodes from different campaigns against Jiskra. Hunyadi took Szepsi and tried to take Gács in October/November, 1449; he besieged the fortified monastery of Ipolyság in October, 1451, captured Derencsény in May, 1452, and probably destroyed Rozsnyó in July, 1452. The burning of Zólyom may also have taken place in the summer of 1452. As for the peace mentioned in the Chronicle, Hunyadi in fact entered into more than one treaty with Jiskra during these years, the last one being that of Körmöcbánya (today Kremnica, Slovakia) on August 24, 1452 (see Pál Engel, "Hunyadi János kormányzó itineráriuma [1446-1452]" ["The Itinerary of the Governor, János Hunyadi"]. Századok 118 [1984], 974-997).
415. See note 305.
416. Liptó, formerly a county in the region of modern-day Ružomberok in Middle Slovakia.
417. Pongrác of Szentmiklós (see note 304).

master of the whole of Turóc county,[418] and when usurping the fortresses of Óvár,[419] Berencs,[420] and Sztrecsén[421] he was no less savage than the others in laying waste the kingdom. These men pursued each other with mutual hatred and improved the condition of the aforementioned counties by oppressively despoiling them by turns, as well as everything in their vicinity.

There was also another class of plunderers who were ravaging the northern counties of the kingdom. These men, a kind of mob of common soldiers, prowled about with their weapons to protect them, and had acquired for themselves a very great number of dwellings, some by treachery and force of arms; some others they had modified with new construction work. With cloistered monks as their model, they also assumed for themselves a name appropriate to a brotherhood and called themselves "bratrik"[422] in their own language. Appointing captains among themselves, they kept battering all the regions of the kingdom near them with oppressive pillagings, slaughters, and conflagrations greater than any others. So great had their audacity in the kingdom grown at this point that they were openly contracting marriages, as if intending to remain in the kingdom permanently. For after the lord governor became aware that the magnates of the northern counties of the realm were setting a treacherous plot for him and that their behavior toward him reflected their envy more than a sense of moral rectitude, he was subsequently less zealous in protecting those counties.

418. Turóc, formerly a county in the region of modern-day Martin in Slovakia.

419. Óvár (Stary hrad in Slovak), castle on the Vág in Trencsén county (east of Zilina, Slovakia).

420. Berencs (Brань in Slovak), castle in Nyitra county (north of Senica, Slovakia).

421. Sztrecsén (Strečno in Slovak), castle on the Vág opposite Óvár (see note 419) in Trencsén county.

422. Hungarian plural of the Czech word bratri, "brothers;" a name of Hussite origin which Jiskra's Czech mercenaries gave to themselves.

✠ 245 (L): CONCERNING THE WAR OF THE LORD GOV-
ERNOR INITIATED IN THE LAND OF RASCIA NEXT TO THE
FORTRESS OF KRUŠEVAC[423] ✠

t the same time Murad, sultan of the Turks, was distressed that Despot George of Rascia was master of a domain so near to himself, and he had in fact formed in his
mind an intense hatred of him for setting free the lord governor.
He roused a great number of his people to take up arms, directing
them to go into parts of Rascia under the leadership of a certain
voivode of his, a man fond of war named Feriz bey.[424] And he
very strictly instructed him to repair the fortress of Kruševac located near the banks of the river Morava[425] and filled with a mass
of old debris, and from it to engage in hostilities against George
the despot. When he heard this, the despot trembled with fear,
and for a long time he was lost in thought, privately considering what he should do. For he knew that his military resources
were too small in number to be able to withstand so great a foe.
At once he regretted the wrong he had inflicted upon the lord
governor. And although he realized that in so great a crisis he
had no way to save himself except either to submit to the enemy or to get help, he did not know to whom to have recourse
for assistance. For he said to his men: "Had I not offended the
goodwill of the lord governor toward me, he would be the man
to snatch me, endangered as I am, from so many stormy troubles." When, therefore, he found no one but the lord governor
to whose protection he might entrust himself, it was more or less
with a red face that he turned to him for help. Indeed the lord
governor, who desired to wage war with the Turks more than to

---

423. The chapter is misplaced chronologically. In 1454, when the events
recounted here happened, Hunyadi was no longer Governor and Sultan Murad's son, Mehmed II (see note 439), was reigning.

424. Feriz bey, Ottoman commander. For his title as voivode, see note 323.

425. Kruševac, town and fortress on the Morava, in Serbia.

attend pleasant dances, at once ordered a very great number of the troops of his army to be called up; and with weapons ready he went himself to bring aid to the despot. The Turks also knew that the despot had obtained arms to defend himself, but they did not know that he had induced the lord governor to help him. So they waited for the enemy to arrive with their minds at ease.

Now, in order to be able to attack the enemy more quickly, the lord governor spent the whole night travelling with all his armed men and some troops of Rascians. Then both the night and the journey came to an end, and the day was near sunrise and the lord governor near the enemy. In the meantime there arose a kind of fog that prevented each of the enemies from seeing the other. When at length the fog was lifted by the rays of the rising sun, immediately the battle-lines shone brightly in their armor. When the Turkish lines saw that their enemy was near them and that the banners of the lord governor, which they had just now recognized, were being waved in the midst of the enemy lines, they turned tail and without engaging their weapons at all gave themselves impetuously to flight. All the lord governor's light-armed troops pursued them as they fled, and each one of the pursuers, who were very keen to fight, began to kill them off. So they perpetrated a very great slaughter, which lasted right until night was about to fall. And a much greater one would have followed had the shadows of the approaching night not concealed the fugitives. It was also there that the aforementioned commander Feriz bey, along with many of the more powerful men of the people entrusted to his care, were made to suffer the misfortune of captivity and were joyfully and ceremoniously exhibited to the lord governor.[426] Having obtained victory, he had

426. When the peace treaty between the despot and the sultan expired in August 1454 (see note 375), a Turkish offensive was immediatley initiated. In September, Mehmed II besieged Szendrő without success, and before his retreat he left Feriz bey behind with a large army in Serbia. Hunyadi defeated him at Kruševac on October 2, 1454.

the city of Vidin,[427] capital of all Bulgaria, destroyed by fire on his
return. Finally, after handing over all the captives to the despot,
he came successfully into Hungary with a victory procession.

✠ 246 (LI): CONCERNING THE RETURN OF KING LADISLAS
AND THE CREATION OF THE LORD GOVERNOR AS HERED-
ITARY COUNT ✠

1 n the meantime, since Frederick, king of the Romans,
was refusing to release King Ladislas to his subjects who
were peaceably seeking his return to them, at once several leading men of King Ladislas' kingdoms, as well as Ulrich,
count of Cillei,[428] assembled a large supply of threatening arms
and troops ready to inflict injuries, and with a blockade to wear
out the defenders, they completely encircled Wiener Neustadt[429]
and the king of the Romans who was inside. The result was
that the king of the Romans, who was greatly suffering at one
moment from fear and at the next from a shortage of food, was
compelled to restore King Ladislas to the leading men of his
kingdoms.[430] And so the boy prince was brought home and took
up residence in the palace of the fortress of Vienna. Many nobles
both from his own kingdoms and from foreign realms flocked
to him, for he was born of parents both outstanding and powerful, and consequently these men were exspecting him to turn
out to be a great man. It was therefore arranged that the lord

427. Vidin was capital of one of the Bulgarian principalities before the
Ottoman conquest (see note 81).
428. See note 264. As first cousin of the late Queen Elizabeth, Ulrich was
also a relative of her son, King Ladislas.
429. City in Lower Austria, in Hungarian called Ujhely or Bécsujhely, "the
new city" (near Vienna). It was Frederick's favorite residence at this time (see
notes 273 and 274).
430. On September 4, 1452.

governor, too, and all the lords and magnates of the kingdom should go there to bestow fitting honors upon the boy king and to offer their homage and fealty. The flower of the Hungarian nobility wasted no time hastening to the city of Vienna.[431] And the king's court, which was astir with activity because of the august gathering of lords, gave a place of greater eminence to these lords of Hungary amongst all the leading men of the other kingdoms of King Ladislas. And feasting his boy's eyes by looking upon them, the king himself took pleasure in the support of such great magnates. Several days were therefore taken up with the ceremonies and courtesies of life at court.

It was also then that the lord governor of his own accord put aside the burden of his office, of which he had now for eight years[432] had successful charge, and in the 1452nd year of the Lord[433] he restored to King Ladislas the kingdom of Hungary preserved by his own blood–stained efforts and those of his men, and by all possible diligence and solicitude, and the arts of war. Therefore, in a church of lofty dimensions, King Ladislas, dressed in his royal robes and sitting on the throne of his majesty, and with as many dukes, margraves, and prelates and barons of his realms as possible in attendance upon him, with great solemnity raised the lord governor to the rank of hereditary count of Beszterce,[434] for he had been brought to the favorable

431. The Hungarian lords arrived in Vienna on October 7, 1452, and were joined by Hunyadi on December 28.

432. Correctly only six and a half years.

433. Correctly the year 1453. Hunyadi must have resigned about New Year's Day, but the exact date is not known.

434. Beszterce (in German Bistritz, today Bistriţa, Rumania), a privileged Saxon town in Transylvania, was granted to Hunyadi together with its district as a "county." On February 1, 1453, he was granted the hereditary title of "Count of Beszterce," an unprecedented honor in Hungary (see note 166), intended to compensate him for the loss of his former dignity as Governor. He did, however, rule the kingdom in the absent king's name with the new title of "Captain-General of Hungary" (see note 318) maintaining control of royal

notice of the king because of the great fame of the victories he had won, which had been spread far and wide throughout the world, and because of the honor he had won by his outstanding achievements. And the king exchanged the temporary office of the governorship, which the lord governor had held until that time because of his own merits and the pressing needs of the kingdom, for a hereditary title. To the armorial emblems that the lord count had borne until that time, namely a raven holding an annulet, gold in color, which was painted on his shield, the lord king added other famous insignia, namely a red lion on the point of grasping a crown with its claws, blazoned on a white scutcheon. It was to honor his pre-eminence and rank that the king adorned the lord count of Beszterce with these insignia. At length, once all the ceremonies to confer this exalted rank had with great joy been performed, King Ladislas after a few days sent the lord count back to Hungary, honored by the royal largesse with many gifts and offerings, and accompanied by other lord prelates and barons.

✠ 247 (LII): Concerning the arrival in Hungary of Friar Giovanni da Capestrano ✠

hen the lord count of Beszterce and all the magnates of the kingdom of Hungary were happily returning to their own homes, a man of religion, friar Giovanni da Capestrano,[435] of the friars of St. Francis, dressed in the habit of his order and shining with the sanctity of his life, came with these same lords into Hungary. When the savageness of the

castles and revenues. This was a cause of growing estrangement between him and the royal court in Vienna.

435. Giovanni da Capestrano (1386-1456), a leading personality among the Observant Franciscans (see note 357), and their Vicar-General from 1449. He came to Hungary in May, 1455.

Turks was all the more fiercely being turned upon the persecution of the Christian religion, the supreme pontiff of the Roman Church, Nicholas,[436] took pains to help the Catholic people who were weathering such fearful storms and to bring together against the Turks an expedition of Christians. He had in a papal bull decreed[437] the preaching throughout all the provinces of forgiveness of sins and remission of future punishment for all those who offered to join this expedition, and, what is more, the distribution to them of a likeness of the cross, in red, against a background of white linen, which was to be placed on the left side of the chest. The lord pope had also appointed as organizer of this plan of his the aforementioned friar Giovanni da Capestrano. Since friar Giovanni was a man of great authority in matters of sacred dogma,[438] and everyone could see how his merits worked wonders for the blind, the lame, the sick, and those possessed by unclean spirits, he roused many, and especially the common people, in parts of Germany and Poland, and in Hungary, to take up arms against the aforementioned enemy.

A little before this time, upon the death of Murad, sultan of the Turks, his son Mehmed[439] had succeeded him. He was more ferocious than his father and his other predecessors in the shedding of Christian blood and in ravaging countrysides, more experienced in the discipline of affairs of war, better supplied with troops and engines of war, and more stern in his dealings with his own people. After taking control of the government of his realm, he considered as a source of reproach the city of Constantinople,

436. Pope Nicholas V (1447-1455).

437. On September 30, 1453. Thuróczy's chronology is again confused, for the papal bull was a reaction to the fall of Constantinople, recounted below in chapter 249.

438. He had been graduated from the University of Perugia in 1410, as *doctor utriusque juris*, i.e., doctor of both civil and canon law. Before joining the Order, he had intended to pursue a career as a civil servant.

439. Mehmed II, called "the Conqueror," Ottoman ruler (1451-1481), son of Murad II, whom he succeeded on February 3, 1451.

as long as it was in his vicinity and yet in foreign hands, and he always looked upon it with hostility and long gave thought to its besieging. And concealing his real purpose, with amazing and incredible speed he constructed a kind of fortification near the seashore at the mouth of the Bosphorus, not a great distance from the city.[440] This development caused great turmoil in Christendom, since the fortification appeared to promise nothing but future ruin to the city.

✠ 248 (LIII): CONCERNING THE ARRIVAL OF KING LADISLAS IN HUNGARY ✠

ext, King Ladislas, in the thirteenth year of his life, and the 1453rd of the Lord's Incarnation,[441] escorted by Count Ulrich and many other nobles of his realm, came into Hungary in that part of the year when on lords' tables meat would soon be replaced by fish.[442] Having entered the city of Buda, he was very happy to remain there.

Now during those same days the lord count of Beszterce was roaming through the southern counties of the kingdom, for he knew that a very great many lords of Hungary, and especially Count Ulrich, were not favorably disposed towards him. He was therefore fearful that they were setting a hidden trap for him with the king, into which he could easily fall were he to proceed without taking precautions. At length, at that time in

─────────────────

440. An immense fortress on the European side of the Bosporus, named Rumili Hisari ("the Castle of Rumelia") was built by Mehmed II in four and a half months, between April 15 and August 31, 1452. It was located just opposite the castle of Anadolu Hisari on the Asiatic side, and the two together were able to dominate the strait completely.

441. In fact three years later, in 1456, when the king was not thirteen but sixteen.

442. I.e. at the beginning of Lent, Ash Wednesday (February 10). From other sources we know that the king arrived in Buda on February 6, 1456.

the aforementioned year when the driver of the Titan's chariot had, during the first days of spring, left behind the home of the constellation Pisces and tied his horses to the horns of Aries, the Ram, in other words, during the holy days of Lent,[443] the lord count of Beszterce,[444] promised safe conduct, came to the king together with the barons and powerful men of the kingdom, Tamás Székely, prior of Vrana;[445] Vlad, voivode of Wallachia;[446] László Kanizsai;[447] and Sebestyén Rozgonyi;[448] and many nobles of Hungary. They surrounded themselves with their troops in shining armor and were divided into splendid companies, trusting in their strength and in the protection afforded by their arms rather than in the security provided by the aforementioned safe-conduct.[449] These magnates loved the lord count and were not afraid to place their own lives at risk to protect his. The lord count was in the king's company for several days before he finally obtained permission to withdraw and went down to Temesvár.[450]

443. I.e. about March 21, the day on which the Sun (here named "the Titan's chariot," cf. note 212) entered the sign of Aries (see note 7).

444. Hunyadi is henceforth given his new title, "Count of Beszterce" (see note 434).

445. Tamás Székely of Szentgyörgy, Prior of Vrana (1450-1467), for whose title, see note 314. He was the son of the Ban, János Székely, and so a nephew of Hunyadi (see note 382).

446. The future Voivode of Wallachia, Vlad Tepes ("the Impaler," 1456-1462), son of Vlad Dracul (see note 361).

447. László Kanizsai (d. 1477/1478), a grandson of the Steward István (see note 96), later Voivode of Transylvania (1459-1461) and Master of the Horse (1464-1467).

448. Sebestyén Rozgonyi (d. 1461), grandson of Simon Rozgonyi senior (see note 164), later Master of the Horse (1458) and Voivode of Transylvania (1458-1461).

449. They came to Buda because the king had convoked a diet for February 29, 1456. Hunyadi's relations with the court had so worsened by this time that a safe conduct from the king for himself and his followers became advisable. For the preliminaries, see note 434.

450. The castle of Temesvár (Timişoara, see note 155) was one of Hunyadi's most important strongholds in south Hungary.

✠ 249 (LIV): Concerning the assault on the City of Constantinople made by the Sultan of the Turks ✠

I n the course of the same year in which King Ladislas had come into Hungary,[451] around the first month of summer, Mehmed, sultan of the Turks, turned his arms against the Greeks and waged a formidable war against the whole of Greece, contrary to the treaties he had entered into with the emperor of the Greeks and contrary to his oath. And after collecting countless troops from every source and setting in motion all the instruments of war in his kingdom, with a blockade by land and sea he violently and arrogantly attacked that most celebrated city of Constantinople, formerly called Byzantium, child of the ancient emperors and mistress of the world. And with the unremitting attacks of his arms he so devastated the sad city, which was begging for reinforcements from Christian kings and yet was abandoned by everyone to disaster and destruction, that even women were compelled to come to its defense. But what good was it for the Greeks to raise a mismatched hand against so many countless foes? Devising a new kind of assault, the sultan had subterranean tunnels and trenches excavated, which he used for an ambuscade; and when the sea had been spanned both with chains and by a bridge, and wooden towers had been erected to such a height that they were taller than the walls of the city, which were exceedingly tall, and from their tops the Turks were with thick showers of arrows striking everything that was being mobilized in the city, he caused, with the additional use of an assemblage of siege-engines and ballistas of many kinds and of unforeseen size, the city's walls to be reduced to debris. At length, with the walls for the most part in ruins on the ground, the sultan, to the exceedingly loud noise of drums and trumpets,

---

451. Correctly three years before, in 1453.

set in motion all the main strength of his expedition to invade the interior of the city, and after the 4th day of the siege he took the city with the use of the utmost force and in one final struggle.[452] And once its emperor had, when the enemy entered the city, been many times wounded and slain,[453] everything of beauty the sultan of the Turks found in the city, both of God and of men, he handed over to be pillaged by the unclean hands of the Turks. The city's leading citizens were taken prisoner and brought to him, and the cruel prince had them most miserably strangled; the tombs of saints he had overturned and their relics sunk in the sea. Who can put into adequate words, who can mourn, who can describe the fall of so great a city, the disaster, so very much to be lamented, suffered by the Christian religion, and the countless and enormous crimes indiscriminately perpetrated with brutality and wickedness by a rabid enemy against the sacred and profane, and against men and women alike?

✠ 250 (LV): CONCERNING THE SIEGE OF THE FORTRESS OF NÁNDORFEHÉRVÁR BY THE SULTAN OF THE TURKS ✠

King Ladislas was staying in the fortress of Buda and the 1455th year of the Lord was passing,[454] when it was heard that Mehmed, sultan of the Turks, was threatening to invade the kingdom of Hungary and intended to storm the fortress of Nándorfehérvár[455] as soon as possible. This news caused not only the common people of Hungary but also all the neighboring regions and practically the whole of Christendom to

---

452. On May 29, 1453. In fact, the siege began on April 2 and lasted fifty-eight days.

453. The last Byzantine Emperor, Constantine XI. He fell on the last day of the siege.

454. It was in fact the same year as above on chapter 248, i.e. 1456.

455. Belgrade (see note 172).

become very anxious and apprehensive. For the ferocious blockade of the city of Constantinople was vividly imagined by all
Catholic people and seized everyone with great terror. Indeed,
once the sultan of the Turks had obtained his victory over the
Greeks, it was as if he had become some other man, and swelling
with ambition and a very haughty pride, he thought that the triumphant times of the late Alexander the Great of the Macedo-
nians had come back for him.[456] For he is supposed to have said:
"One God rules in the heavens; it is appropriate that only one
prince rule the earth."

When these rumors were reported to King Ladislas, at once
the young prince became profoundly frightened, and Count
Ulrich, whose actions reflected the German spirit of warlike
courage and whose advice guided the king, was no less disturbed. They did not therefore discuss the protection of the kingdom nor did they ready their arms to withstand the enemy, but,
as if unaware of the rumors, they withdrew one dark night from
the fortress of Buda and proceeded to the city of Vienna by an
indirect route.[457] And the fortress of Buda remained closed and
without appropriate defense beyond mid-month, and although
the fearful rumor of the arrival of so large an enemy force daily
became more widespread, no one was moved to take up arms
against it.

At length, upon the arrival of that part of the next summer
when the ears of corn in the fields, brought forth from the living soil, were already turning yellow, and Phoebus was causing his chariot to be drawn through the field of the constellation
Gemini, the Twins,[458] the aforementioned sultan of the Turks,

---

456. Mehmed II was known to be an admirer of the ancient Macedonian
King, Alexander the Great (d. 323 B.C.).

457. The king and the Count of Cillei left Buda in early June, 1456.

458. I.e., during the zodiacal period (see note 7), between May 21 and June
22. The date is wrong, however, as the Ottoman army arrived before Belgrade
in the first days of July and began the siege on July 4.

along with his terrible and multifarious engines of war and more than 400,000 Turks,[459] attacked the aforementioned fortress of Nándorfehérvár by encircling it with a terrifying blockade. The tops of their innumerable tents, spread out over the level ground of the plain far and wide on all sides, could be seen from the lofty walls of the fortress. Indeed, no one could with his eyes take in the masses of the enemy. What is more, the sultan had brought many ships constructed after the pattern of sea-going vessels, and with these he had so fortified the Danube and Sava rivers flowing alongside the fortress that no one could use a boat to bring aid to it. With the greatest labors he had brought devices and siege-machines and ballistas, so many in number, so great in size, and of a kind and magnitude that no one could ever believe they had been transported for the destruction of a fortress. These were with astonishing quickness assembled near the fortress of Kruševac,[460] for because of their size they could not have been conveyed from distant parts. At length these machines were placed opposite that part of the fortress facing the plain. Some of them repeatedly struck the solid walls of the castle; others kept shooting stones the size of a bushel high into the air, which fell down with formidable impact within the walls of the fortress, instantly killing, like a thunderbolt, every living thing they hit.

And so day and night the siege-machines discharged violently and repeatedly, resounding with a thunderous noise, and their terrifying din could be heard as far away as the city of Szeged and in other cities far and wide, distant more than twenty-four Hungarian miles.[461] And the uninterrupted firing

---

459. An exaggeration, not unusual in medieval chronicles. The actual size of the Turkish army may have been around 80,000, still a sizeable force at that time.

460. See note 425.

461. One Hungarian mile is equivalent to about 8.5 kilometers, and the twenty-four miles given by the chronicler is therefore 204 kilometers or 127

of the siege-machines gave off incessant smoke, and the thick murkiness of its clouds darkened the air once splendidly clear from the golden radiance of the sun. The swift breezes were tainted with the sulphurous stench, and neither the intensely hot summer's day nor the darkness of night brought any rest to the besiegers and the besieged, for the whole time was spent in deadly struggle.

The tops of the noble towers were collapsing under the massive impact, the walls were being shattered, and the lofty defensive walls protecting the fortress and its inhabitants were being razed to the ground. What more can be said, except that the besieged, utterly dazed by a profound fear of death, were waiting only for their last day?

Rumor of this most bitter and powerful siege spread through all the counties of the kingdom, but the Hungarian lords had fallen prey to a kind of torpor, as if in a deep sleep, and were not bringing any armed assistance to the city that was about to be lost. At last a man of innate courage and military expertise, the aforementioned lord count of Beszterce, went to oppose this awe-inspiring method of laying siege, escorted by a modest number of troops and intending to fight to the finish with an exceedingly numerous foe. A very great number of Hungarians assembled, people who were marked with the sign of the cross by the aforementioned friar Giovanni da Capestrano[462] and were

---

statute miles. In fact, the distance by air in kilometers between Belgrade and Szeged is somewhat less, about 170 kilometers.

462. In September, 1455, Pope Calixtus III (1455-1458) had sent his legate, Cardinal Carvajal, to Hungary and Poland to preach a crusade against the Ottomans. Papal sponsorship was proclaimed at Buda on February 15, 1456, and the recruiting of crusaders in Hungary was entrusted by the legate to Capestrano (see note 435), famous for his talents as a preacher of hypnotic power. During the following months he gathered together an army consisting mainly of peasants and artisans from the southern counties who were full of enthusiasm but unskilled in fighting. They wore, like former crusaders, a large cross sewn on their garments.

ready to fight for the name of Christ, and from Polish regions there came some three hundred crusaders. Although the lord count, as was mentioned above, had been relieved of the responsibilities of government, he was nevertheless unable to endure not attacking the enemy, impelled as he was by his usual restless energy. He therefore searched for a way by which he could remove the enemy's ships from the aforementioned rivers and bring armed assistance to those laboring under the blockade.

Eventually, after hunting down some ships, he loaded them with armed troops and crusaders and at length dispatched them along the river Danube against the enemy vessels. The result of this manoeuvre was that both enemies were brought together in a naval battle. Amongst the Turks their loud battle-cry abounded, and the Hungarians, too, with loud voices called upon the lord Jesus for assistance. Since both enemies had been deprived of escape routes, there commenced some very fierce fighting. The ships of both sides were conveyed here and there over the deep waters of the Danube, and many men, mortally wounded, were falling from them into the river. The clear water of the Danube turned blood-red from the immense slaughter, the result of the shedding of so much blood, and meals for the voracious fish were made of combatants on both sides.

At length, after the drawn-out struggle of the fight, the Hungarians were victorious; and charging very fiercely against the Turks, they cut apart their ships, which had been fastened together with iron chains, and set them alight.[463] After this became known to the sultan of the Turks, he is supposed to have said: "Now it will be more difficult for us to have our way."

Having achieved a glorious victory in the naval engagement, the lord count at once approached the fortress and brought solace to its captains, who were by now in a state of shock and confusion and awaiting no other fate but death. "Why," he said,

---

463. On July 14, the eleventh day of the siege.

"are you terrified? Is it just the Turks you now see? They are the very ones we have very often routed; and we have ourselves sometimes fled before them. Why does the sight of them, whom you have many times seen, upset you? Have you not personally experienced their arms and their fighting power? Let us then put our trust, my dear sons, in Christ, for whose name we have very frequently shed our blood, and let us fight all the more courageously with his enemy and ours! Did not Christ die for us? Let us then also die for him. Be therefore resolute and courageous in war. The enemy, as we know, is afraid. And if God is with us, this enemy can easily be crushed. For he is in the habit of turning tail, and is not ashamed to give way, take flight, and return home a fugitive. What further need is there of discussion, seeing that you, too, have found out these things by trial while enduring, under my leadership, the long weariness of war?" And so, with these and a great many more words, and by his very presence, the lord count restored them to a state of no little aggressiveness. In addition, he strengthened the fortress with fresh troops and also brought into it a very large number of crusaders. And although they were of common birth and ignorant of the use of arms, the lord count trained them for war as best he could.

Before this, the sultan of the Turks had heard that his father Murad, while alive, had devoted seven months to a siege at the base of the fortress of Nándorfehérvár and had not at all been able to take it, and he had withdrawn from it without a victory and with disgrace.[464] Consequently, with the leaders of his army in attendance upon him, the sultan of the Turks immoderately criticized his father and said that he could capture this same fortress in fifteen days. When the voivode of Anatolia,[465] the most exalted of the sultan's commanders, heard him boasting in this way, he obtained permission to speak first and replied

---

464. In 1440 (see note 313).

465. The Beylerbeyi of Anatolia (cf. note 344, and for the title "Voivode," note 323). Ottoman sources mention only the death of the other Beylerbeyi, Dayï Karaca Paşa of Rumelia.

to the sultan's remarks as follows: "Mightiest Sultan, it would be in my best interests to say something agreeable in the presence of your dignity, but I am afraid that the future outcome of this undertaking may convict me of telling your clemency a lie. Yet we should know that the Hungarians surrender their fortresses with greater reluctance than the Greeks."

The tops of the noble towers had by now been knocked down and the defensive walls were largely reduced to rubble on the ground, and the moats and embankments of the fortress were filled up and the ground made level, so that there was no barrier at all to stop the enemy's incursion. When the fifteenth day of the siege, which I mentioned above, had begun to dawn, immediately the sultan, while the sunrise was still glowing brightly, mobilized all his hordes of people with the sounds of beating drums and blaring trumpets all round. And with a frenzied charge, he attacked the fortress, penetrating into its midst with a bloody slaughter. Now although the Hungarians were too few to join battle with so numerous an enemy, they nevertheless defended themselves with all their strength. And very often proclaiming the help of the lord Jesus, they keenly concentrated their efforts on the enemy's destruction. So the lethal war was renewed, with fighting in the streets of the fortress. The bodies of many men who had been killed fell on both sides, and the loud, confused sound of much shouting and of the clanging of countless swords re-echoed in the air. Frequently were both enemies, one after the other, compelled to retreat.

Friar Giovanni da Capestrano was also there. As if in a trance, he and other friars, who with him had prostrated themselves on the ground, were with groans offering prayers, their thoughts and hands raised up for help from on high and their eyes fixed on heaven. Indeed, with the prophet they might have said: "I have lifted my eyes unto the mountains, whence help shall come to me."[466] The lord count of Beszterce was, with

466. A quotation from the Vulgate, Ps. 120 (121):1.

threats in one place and warnings in another, urgently pressing his men to fight. Likewise Mihály Szilágyi,[467] the captain, and László Kanizsai,[468] two young men of surpassing knightly courage, as well as the armed troops that the lord count had brought along with them, and also the companies of crusaders, all took up a position on the ruined walls of the fortress and were fighting with great ferocity.

First the Turks, who had very often been driven out of the fortress and had re-entered it as the result of a dreadful struggle, were stronger than the Hungarians. Now a very great number of houses in the fortress were set alight and were spouting fierce flames. Then a great many of the sultan's standards were held aloft on the walls of the fortress as a sign of victory; and then the Hungarians, deprived of all hope of offering resistance, were forced to withdraw, if there was any place for them to retreat to, for the vision of imminent death was for each of them fast becoming a grim reality. Finally, when they saw that flight could not save them but that death alone would be their solution of so great a crisis, they once again loudly invoked the name of the lord Jesus, readied their arms and joined their shields, and rushed against the enemy with as powerful an assault as possible.

The deadly struggle was therefore resumed, with many on both sides pouring forth their blood and their souls. And the help of God was not wanting. For in a short time all the Turkish ranks were thrown into disarray by so strong and vigorous an assault by the Hungarians, and were forced to turn and flee.[469] The

---

467. Mihály Szilágyi (d. 1461) of Horogszeg (a village in Temes county, northeast of modern-day Kikinda, Yugoslavia), the husband of Hunyadi's sister, Erzsébet Szilágyi, at this time Captain of Belgrade, later Ban of Mačva (1457-1458), Governor of Hungary (1458), and Count of Beszterce.

468. See note 447.

469. Thus far the final assault on the fortress on July 21 has been described. What follows refers to events of the next day (see note 470).

Hungarians for that reason regained their fierceness, and as if aided from heaven with fresh fighting spirit, they pursued them at sword point for a very long time, until all the siege-engines and the other catapults that the Turks had employed to destroy the fortress were deprived of the soldiers manning them. The Hungarians therefore set alight all the defense works the Turks had erected, and with iron nails firmly closed the siege-engines' apertures that were designed to discharge fire.

There was no pause in the fighting as long as daylight lasted, but the struggle that had previously taken place in the narrow streets of the fortress was thereafter continued for a time with much severity on the broad plain, until night arrived and with its darkness separated the two foes. But how the sultan, under cover of that night's thick shadows, slipped away by flight below the fortress, no one is in a position to state for certain. Nevertheless, to God's glory and the consternation of the sultan, suffice it to say that, deprived of all his war engines, and having abandoned all his siege-machines and the other kinds of catapults he had brought there, he returned to his own land after a huge slaughter of his own people.[470] And what is more, thereafter any mention of this fortress, made by anyone in his presence, was to him never welcome.

In spite of what has been written here, certain people have said this about the sultan's flight: that he had been wounded in the chest by an arrow during the fierce heat of battle when he was mustering his troops for the fight, and had then fallen to the ground more dead than alive. And his men had picked

---

470. On July 22, some units of Capestrano's irregular army ventured an attack on the Ottoman army, worn out by the long and unsuccessful siege but still far superior in number. Soon the Turks were ready to launch a counteroffensive, and Hunyadi had to intervene to prevent a catastrophe. Against his better judgment he ordered a full assault that, curiously enough, led to a remarkable victory in the end. The following night the sultan struck camp and vanished. These details are related in the chronicle too briefly and rather inaccurately.

him up and carried him to their tents. But when it had reached nightfall, the Turks had seen that both the commander of Anatolia and indeed all their nobles had been killed in the war, that they themselves had suffered the greatest of slaughters, and that the sultan himself had hardly any pulse, as if he were half-dead. And terrified they would be attacked by the Hungarians come morning, they had begun to flee. Carrying the sultan with them so that he would not be made more ill by the labors of the journey, they had encamped beyond their fortress called Zrnov.[471] And when the sultan had there recovered consciousness and had asked where he now was, and they had pointed out the place to him, he had said: "And why or how did we come to this place?" "We were decisively defeated," they said, "by the Hungarians, and the commander of Anatolia and practically all the leaders of your army have been killed. We also suffered a great slaughter; and, what is more, we imagined that your serene highness was dead instead of alive. And so we fled until we reached this place." The sultan had in his turn also inquired if the siege-engines and the other devices had also been abandoned there; and when they had replied that indeed everything had been left there, the sultan at once had said, afflicted with profound bitterness of heart: "Bring me poison that I may drink it and die rather than return to my kingdom in disgrace!"

In this way, then, did the sultan of the Turks end his fight with the Hungarians below the fortress of Nándorfehérvár. And he, who with arrogant attitude and proud gaze wished alone to rule the whole world, was decisively defeated by divine judgment at the hands of a rustic band that were better with hoes than weapons. And he who had very joyfully arrived to the sound of many trumpets and many drums, fled shamefully in the silence of the gloomy night.

---

471. The fortress of Zrnov, south of Belgrade, was built by the Turks in the 1440s.

✠ 251 (LVI): Concerning the death of Lord János Hunyadi, Count of Beszterce ✠

After this victory the lord count of Beszterce fell ill. From the early days of his youth he had completed so many important tasks in wartime, but he had not yet succumbed to old age.[472] He was, however, weary from the uninterrupted burden of bearing arms and the fulfillment of his responsibilities, and he was drained of strength. He fell ill there, and after suffering from the illness[473] for a few days, he was at length taken to the town of Zemplén,[474] and with the commendation of that man of God, the aforementioned friar Giovanni da Capestrano, he gave his spirit back to his Savior. There arose a loud lamentation throughout the whole of Hungary, and the land was distressed, as was the rest of Christendom, and grieved exceedingly when it heard that its champion had died. Moreover, even the stars fixed high in the heavens announced his death in advance, for a remarkable star with a tail had appeared in the heavens prior to his passing.[475] Even Sultan Mehmed mourned, though put to flight by this lord count below the aforementioned fortress of Nándorfehérvár just before his death. When the death of the lord count was announced by Despot George of Rascia to the sultan as if to console him, it is reported that the sultan remained silent, with his head motionless, for a full hour, and that he, although the count's enemy, suffered greatly at his passing and said to the messenger that from the beginning of time there never had been such a man in the service of a prince. That man

472. Hunyadi's exact age is not known, but he must have been about fifty at this time.
473. A plague had broken out in Hunyadi's camp soon after the battle. He fell ill on August 5.
474. Zemplén or Zimony, today Zemun, opposite Belgrade (see note 172), a market in Szerém county. Hunyadi died there on August 11, 1456.
475. An allusion to Halley's comet, which returns every seventy-five years. Its perigee was May 27, 1456.

alone, amongst all the mortals of our generation, demonstrated how correct Solon was in ancient times when he denied supreme happiness to Croesus, king of the Lydians and the richest of all kings, who was questioning him about this. Is it not the case, for instance, that Tellus, the most outstanding of all the Athenians, whom Solon placed above Croesus in happiness after he had seen the latter's treasure-chambers, was provided for by the supreme creator of the world with children, for whom everyone had the highest hopes? Is it not also the case that the count lived a life redolent in all respects of much glory and fame, and that a most illustrious death came to him as his lot just as it came to Tellus, when it brought to a close his life following the conquest and rout of so great a sultan, with the greatest of praise for the victory he was always striving for, when he could still taste the sweetness of his triumph, and with his good name intact?[476]

At length his body, while his family and followers shed many tears, was carried to Gyulafehérvár[477] and honorably buried. Now the lord count died in the 1456th year of the Lord's Incarnation, when Virgo had the sun as a guest in her heavenly bed. When the aforementioned friar Giovanni da Capestrano observed him laboring to breathe his last, he is reported, after commending him to God, to have repeated this sorrowful epitaph: "Hail, heavenly circle of light; you have fallen, corona of the kingdom! You have been extinguished, lamp of the world! Alas! the mirror into which we were hoping to look has been shattered. Now that your enemy has been decisively defeated,

---

476. In a confused way Thuróczy is here referring to a story he found in a Latin translation of the Greek historian Herodotus (c. 484–c. 420 B.C.). According to Herodotus, the Athenian Solon was asked once by King Croesus of Lydia whom he considered to be the happiest man in the world. It must have been the Athenian named Tellus, Solon answered, whose city was prosperous, who had fine sons and grandchildren, and who died gloriously in a battle in which the enemies of Athens were routed.

477. Gyulafehérvár (Alba Iulia) in Transylvania (see note 324), in whose cathedral Hunyadi's tomb is still to be seen.

you reign with God and celebrate your triumph with the angels, O good János!"

The lord count was a man of moderate height, with a large neck, curly chestnut-colored hair, large eyes, a look of calm assurance, a ruddy complexion, and so appositely and elegantly proportioned in the other parts of his body that he was recognized as a man of the first rank and importance in the midst of large numbers of people. He had two sons, to whom all of Hungary was looking with unrestrained longing. For the merits of their father compelled everyone to love them, and people observed that they had also inherited the courage and character of their father. The elder of these was called László,[478] who was the same height as his father and a most outstanding young man amongst all his contemporaries for his courage as a knight, the integrity of his character, and his kindness and generosity. The younger son, Matthias,[479] was still a boy when his father passed away. While alive his father was profoundly fond of this boy and his youthful agility commended him in the eyes of everyone. All who looked at him foresaw that he would be a great man.

478. László Hunyadi (see note 393).

479. Matthias I, later surnamed Corvinus, the future King of Hungary (1458-1490). He was born on February 23, 1443, and was ten or eleven years younger than his brother László.

✠ 252 (LVII): CONCERNING THE DEATH OF FRIAR GIO-
VANNI DA CAPESTRANO ✠

Now those who during life have together fostered a mutual love in Christ are not parted from each other at
the time of cruel death's dire examination. For friar
Giovanni da Capestrano, the man previously mentioned, whose
name deserves to be written in the catalog of saints,[480] and who
had been attached to the aforementioned lord count of Beszterce
in sincere affection and love, did not live for many days after
the passing of the lord count. Greatly desiring to live in a starry
dwelling more than in an earthly one, he restored his poor body,
now separated from his soul, to the earth of which it had been
made, as his spirit flew up to heaven.[481] Buried in the convent of
the Observant Friars Minor established in the town of Ujlak,[482]
in whose habit he imitated the life of his holy father Francis, his
body was renowned because of countless miracles, and its fame
has not ceased right to the present day.

✠ 253 (LVIII): CONCERNING THE RETURN OF KING LADIS-
LAS TO HUNGARY AND THE BEHEADING OF THE COUNT
OF CILLEI IN THE FORTRESS OF NÁNDORFEHÉRVÁR ✠

The next thing to happen was that, when news of this
great victory had been spread extensively throughout
the world, to the joy of all adherents of the Christian
religion, King Ladislas, upon hearing that the sultan had been
put to flight and that the lord count had indeed died, decided to

---

480. Capestrano was not canonized until 1724, but cf. note 482 below.

481. He died on October 23, 1456, ten weeks after Hunyadi.

482. Ujlak, today Ilok, (see note 265); for the Observants, see note 357. The
miracles at his sepulchre were registered between 1458 and 1461 with a view
to initiating his canonization.

return at once to Hungary.[483] In the meantime, Count Ulrich of Cillei was with much agitation reflecting upon the feelings of resentment that had for a long time been conceived against the late lord Count János, and upon the means by which he might generate these same feelings against the count's sons, now that their father was dead. For he was of the opinion that they were being led by youthful passions, and for that reason he thought he could the more quickly employ some treacherous plot to ruin them. Since he was the most ambitious of men and puffed up with pride more than any other man, Count Ulrich had previously taken it ill that the lord Count János was governor of the kingdom of Hungary. Indeed his judgment was that this distinction belonged to him more than to anyone, by right of consanguinity.[484]

Then another cause of envy had arisen: at the time when the late lord Count János was still discharging the office of governor, he had, while exacting penalties from the king of the Romans for not restoring the crown and the king's son, incurred Count Ulrich's animosity, as a partisan of the king of the Romans. A third cause for rancor between Count Ulrich and the sons of the late lord Count János was the allegation that Count Ulrich, as a man filled with ambition and of haughty heart, was laboring to bring back under his own power both the supporters of the crown and everything that was rich, beautiful, and agreeable in Hungary—those very things under the direction of the young counts' faction. These grudges in no small way kept gnawing away inwardly at count Ulrich's mind, and he much wanted to

---

483. King Ladislas arrived in Pozsony by August 30 and in Buda on September 15, 1456. He appointed Count Ulrich of Cillei Hunyadi's successor as Captain-General (see note 434) and he reclaimed from his son, László Hunyadi, the royal castles held by his father in his capacity as Captain-General. This was the cause of the dissension between them, and by omitting this from his list of causes in this chapter, Thuróczy is revealing his own bias in favor of the Hunyadian dynasty.

484. For his relationship to the king, see note 428.

make an end of things. For it is reported that he had said: "I am the man who will banish from the land this language that only dogs should talk." Count Ulrich's venemous manoeuvres did not escape the notice of the young counts. They were therefore made to think bitter thoughts of him, and all the common people of Hungary looked upon him with contempt.

At length the year of the lord Count János's death passed,[485] and it was the time when summer, with autumn approaching, was hastening to its last days. Then it was that King Ladislas and Count Ulrich of Cillei, closely surrounded by a very large number of German crusaders,[486] took ship across the depths of the Danube and came into Hungary with a great clamor. And having first occupied for some days the palace in the fortress of Buda, they at length moved down to a town called Futak.[487] Now this unwalled town[488] was situated alongside the aforementioned river in Bács[489] county, on fertile soil, with streets in all directions. After they reached this town, there was celebrated there by royal edict a solemn gathering of the nobles of the entire kingdom. And as the gathering daily increased in size because of

485. Thuróczy obviously thinks that the events recounted below took place one year later, but see note 486.

486. The crusaders in question were recruited abroad in the spring and summer of 1456, but they did not arrive in Hungary until autumn, amidst rumors that their delay was intentional (cf. note 462).

487. Futak (today Futog, Yugoslavia), a market on the Danube in Bács county. From October 13 to November 8, 1456, the king stayed in Futak, where he held a diet.

488. Thuróczy here uses the Latin expression *Oppidum campestrale* (translated as "unwalled town") which is a literal translation of the Hungarian word *mezőváros* and seems to be his own invention. Its equivalent in other Latin texts is always simply *oppidum*. The Hungarian term is derived from the words *mező* ("field, an open place") and *város* ("a city"; originally "a place fortified with a *vár*, i.e. with a castle"), and described any city, town, borough or market that was unwalled, in contrast with a *civitas murata* (a walled city, in ancient Hungarian *kulcsos város*, "a city which has a key").

489. Bács, formerly a county in south Hungary (today part of Yugoslavia) between the Danube and the Tisza.

the arrival of many leading men, Count László, who feared the fickle disposition of King Ladislas and a trap by Count Ulrich, surrounded himself like his father with a numerous armed guard before approaching the king. Afterwards it pleased King Ladislas to view in the fortress of Nándorfehérvár what was left of the power of the Turkish sultan. And so the king and Counts Ulrich and László proceeded there together, and all the crusaders who had come from Germany followed them by ship. In the meantime, those to whom the king's intention was evident kept saying to Count László: "You are in serious trouble, for Count Ulrich has corrupted the king's mind against you and has persuaded him that you and all the other Hungarians should be deprived of the official posts you have held till now, and that these same dignities should be assigned to Germans who are more acceptable to the royal will than are Hungarians, and that you should be expelled from this fortress as soon as possible. Sufficient evidence of this is the fact that these German crusaders have been brought hither exclusively for this purpose." When he heard these remarks, the young man was very much troubled and wrapped in thought wherever he went. And his supporters tried to persuade him that Count Ulrich should be killed as soon as time and place afforded an opportunity. This question went on being discussed in secret, with many of the leading men of the kingdom who shared the same anxiety praising murder as an appropriate course of action. So, with very frequent and persuasive arguments they impelled the young man, who was hot-tempered and much given to rash behavior, and who could scarcely control the unruly impulses of his own youthfulness, to commit a crime of very serious consequences.

The days of the year had now arrived when the renowned bishop Martin, long since raised up from his humble earthly dwelling and conveyed to the lofty mansions of heaven, used to turn the sweet-flowing must into good-tasting wine; and it was the Monday following his feast.[490] That day, very early in the morning, after the dawn had been dispersed by the rays of the sun, Count László proceeded to the residence in the fortress assigned to accommodate Count Ulrich and approached the count to have a private talk with him, or so it is said. But oh, the hostile succession of fate's decrees! Oh, most accursed envy, fuelled deep in the breast over long periods of time by hidden nourishment! Oh, envy, you who immediately turned our old enemy into a serpent and thereby caused the fall of our first parents from the delights of their abodes and the lofty summit of goodness, and who had flooded the hearts of both counts with so much rancor, that each one, though he concealed his desires, deeply craved the murder of the other! What was going on, deep inside you, while the two counts, Ulrich and László, conversed, under one roof and behind closed doors, became clear as they vented their anger upon each other. Contending first with threatening words and in the end with shining weapons, each one wet his sword in the blood of the other. Now when noise of the struggle within reached the ears of those faithful to Count László who were standing before the entrance, they were quick to break down the door of the dwelling and search out the cause of the unexplained clamor. When they saw the two counts sweating from their encounter, they at once drew their swords, rushed upon Count Ulrich, who was defending himself with all his strength, and struck him down after he had been wounded severely in the foot by the blow from a spear. Next, they there and then beheaded him as he lay prostrate on the ground. They

---

490. In 1456, the Monday after St. Martin's Day (November 11) was November 15. But Cillei, whose murder is recounted next, was in fact killed on November 9, 1456, the Tuesday before Martin's Day. He and the king had entered Belgrade the day before, but Thuróczy passes over the fact that their army remained outside the walls and that their followers were immediately disarmed. Thuróczy tries hard to diminish the responsibility of the young Hunyadi for the death of Ulrich of Cillei, but all the facts clearly point to a premeditated murder on his part.

sensed how great the fear was which at that very moment shook the king, the barons of the kingdom, and the Germans attached to the king, and with how much terror their every inward organ quaked, when they saw unsheathed swords, stained with human blood, gleaming throughout the streets of the fortress, for they all were thinking that they would drink from the same cup from which Count Ulrich drank.

Now Count Ulrich was a man of becoming tallness, of appropriate proportions in countenance and body, thin of face, fifty years of age or less, congenial, and very amorous. He used to adorn his hair and have his beard plucked out by the roots so that his lovers would not think him older than he was.[491]

✠ 254 (LIX): CONCERNING THE PARDON GRANTED BY KING LADISLAS TO COUNT LÁSZLÓ FOR THE DEATH OF COUNT ULRICH ✠

A t length, after a delay of this kind in the fortress of Nándorfehérvár, the king and Count László headed off in the direction of the fortress of Temesvár, together with the other barons, that is, the count palatine, whose name was László Garai;[492] Mihály Ország of Gut[493] and Pál Bánfi of Alsólendva,[494] stewards of the royal household; the knightly

---

491. This remark reveals Thuróczy's bias against the count, who obviously had a clean-shaven face like other Europeans of his class, in contrast with the Hungarian fashion of wearing a beard (see note 216).

492. See note 266.

493. See note 165.

494. Pál Bánfi of Alsólendva (d. 1471-1477) was a younger brother of István Bánfi (see note 384). From 1437 he frequently held high offices in the royal household, ultimately serving as Steward (1455-1458) together with Mihály Ország.

members[495] of the king's court; and very many leading men of the kingdom, who were in attendance at the royal court. For this fortress, which surpasses all others in Hungarian territory, was constructed with a famous defense work in the southern counties of the kingdom, near the bank of the river Temes,[496] in a quite charming spot. When they had drawn near this fortress, Count Matthias and the lady Erzsébet[497] his wife came to meet the king dressed in black garments as an expression of grief for the passing of the late lord Count János. When the king had been ushered into the lofty palace of the fortress, they received him with extraordinary hospitality, as befitted his royal rank. And there, with the barons of his realm standing on either side, King Ladislas pardoned Count László, who prostrated himself asking for forgiveness, and showed him clemency for the rash deed he had committed in killing Count Ulrich, the kinsman, as was said, of the king. And in order that the king himself would not at any time be regarded with mistrust by Count László, should the count's brother die and László exact vengeance, the king adopted both counts, László and Matthias, as his brothers, with an oath of loyalty sworn upon the most holy body of Christ. And by the same oath he gave his word[498] that never in the future would he, as long as he had his wits to guide him, wish to exact any compensation in kind from these same counts. And as a sign of his most illustrious adoption of them as brothers, he ordered the two counts to be stripped of the mourning garments they were wearing in memory of their father's death, and he had them, instead of himself, dress in clothing overlaid with reddish

---

495. See note 9.
496. See notes 155 and 450.
497. Erzsébet Szilágyi of Horogszeg (d. 1483), widow of János Hunyadi and a sister of Mihály Szilágyi (see note 467). Both her sons inherited the title of Count of Beszterce (see note 434) from their father.
498. In December, 1456. One must not forget that, after Cillei's murder, the king had fallen into the hands of László Hunyadi, remaining virtually his captive until he took the oath referred to here.

purple. But oh, hateful garment, glowing on the surface with a rosy redness, while beneath the surface the marten-pelts from which you had been cut were afterwards transformed into fox skins! Oh, cunning fraternal agreement, to be rejected by every good man! And alas for the oath, which you need not have taken and which will be remembered with shame, sworn by you, king, upon such dear, such pre-eminent, such exceedingly holy, and such dread relics! Alas, unspeakable crime! since long ago a simply worded promise made by the divine kings of Hungary was kept more steadfastly than you have kept your oath! Can it really be that the oath you broke did not cause the loss of your life, when the last day of the first year of the oath you swore did not pass without your simultaneously departing, by divine retribution, from your realms and your life?[499]

✠ 255 (LX): Concerning the vengeance exacted by King Ladislas from Counts László and Matthias ✠

When these arrangements between the king and the counts had been completed in the order described, the king and Count László came to Buda and were happy to remain there. Trusting in the royal oath, Count László was favorably disposed toward the king. Had the king formed any fierce resentment whatsoever against him because of the death of Count Ulrich, László thought it would be ended. Besides, he had placed no small hope in this matter in the count palatine, László Garai, mentioned above, whose daughter he had arranged to take as his consort[500] while her father was still alive.

---

499. An allusion to the king's early death; see chapter 257 below.

500. Apart from Thuróczy's remark, nothing is known about this marriage, not even the name of the bride (cf. note 506).

For he thought that if the king were roused to anger against him, the palatine, who guided the king, would restrain him and come to the count's assistance. Deceived by this hope, Count László therefore suspected no malice at all on the king's part when he saw that the king was being influenced to treat him with continued good will. But what profit was it to him to place his trust in the count palatine, when for the murder of Count Ulrich, who was his uncle,[501] the count palatine was endeavoring more than King Ladislas to exact a cruel vengeance? The count palatine, and Pál Bánfi,[502] and many more who in the use of their weapons were the servants of flattery rather than the king, and all those who had been unable when he was alive to give vent to the rancor they had conceived against Count László's father, with frequent words of persuasion assailed the king to exact from Count László punishments for his crime. For they kept saying: "You are the king, and all Hungary follows him. Arrogant because of the support of leading men and the common people, he has in return committed these outrages at your side on your kinsman,[503] Count Ulrich. You should be afraid that this presumptuous man may do the same thing to you. You are king, but you will never rule in the kingdom of Hungary so long as he remains alive." The young mind of King Ladislas was influenced by frequent words of persuasion, and a small spark, which had, as it were, been buried in oblivion in the king's breast and was growing, began to blaze up under the frequent blasts of persuasion. Once they discovered that the king's mind had been influenced by their entreaties, they kept seeking an opportunity whereby they might the more quickly be able to obtain what they desired, for they were afraid that the plot they had secretly concocted would be uncovered.

---

501. Thuróczy is in error. Garai and Cillei were first cousins, Garai's father having married Anna of Cillei, an aunt of Ulrich (see note 219).

502. Pál Bánfi of Alsólendva (see note 494).

503. For this relationship, see note 428.

In the meantime it was announced that the Turks were threatening to burst across the borders of the kingdom. Wishing to imitate the character of his father, Count László arranged to hire a very great number of mercenaries from the northern counties of the kingdom as far as the city of Pest,[504] and prepared to meet the Turks, having obtained from the king permission to withdraw.

But the ones who took pleasure in the adversities of Count László kept counselling the king not to allow him to depart before he had arranged for Count Matthias to come to the royal court in his brother's place. And to Count László, on the other side, they kept making suggestions, saying: "If you intend to leave the king, bid your brother come to him before you have said your farewell. For it is permitted that one of you always be at his side. Once you have organized the affairs of your brother at the royal court, you will be able to depart; and if in your absence anything contrary to your interests is ever raised with the king, your brother, and we with him, shall smooth away any difficulties." And by this cunning the plotters were hoping that they could at a more favorable moment trick the two counts, and their expectation did not prove vain. For immediately after the king's will in these matters was declared to Count László, he, unaware of the plot and forgetting what his father had said to him —that he take precautions never to be confined within the precincts of the royal palace at the same time as his brother—wanted Count Matthias to come there before he departed. After this became known to the lady Erzsébet, mother of the counts, she at once began to fear and, as if foreseeing future events, she was insistent that Count Matthias not hasten there for the time being, as long as his brother was residing in the court. But because the

---

504. Pest (today the "Inner City" [Belváros] of Budapest on the left side of the Danube) was virtually a royal borough until the times of Matthias Corvinus, who surrounded it with walls and equal in rank with the city of Buda. For the expression "northern counties," see note 10.

fates bring their work to its conclusion, whether that be good or bad, Count Matthias complied with the orders of his brother rather than the prohibitions of his mother, and was sent away by her with tears before coming to the king.

When the two brothers were within the confines of the royal court, it was the time when the Lenten fast had brought those observing it near its mid-point, and the Monday immediately following the third Sunday in Lent,[505] illuminated by the brilliant rays of the sun, had reached midday. Then it was that Count László, summoned to a meeting with the king, was taken prisoner there and then in the royal residence, while László Garai, the palatine and his father-in-law,[506] and one, as has been said, whom he intimately trusted, made known the reason for his misfortune, and in the presence of Pál Bánfi, Jan Jiskra,[507] Benedek Turóci,[508] and a German named Lamberger.[509] Count Matthias on the other hand, who was unaware of what was being done to his brother, and whose child-like innocence was no help to

---

505. March 21, 1457, the Monday after the third Sunday in lent, is here called *Oculi mei* Sunday, from the first word(s) of the psalm verse with which the Mass for that day began. March 21 was indeed the date of the royal charter, used by Thuróczy as a source, which contained the story of László Hunyadi's felony and his execution, but the event recorded here took place a week earlier on March 14.

506. The fact that Thuróczy here calls Garai the father-in-law of László Hunyadi seems to indicate that the planned marriage mentioned earlier (see note 500) had in fact taken place.

507. For Pál Bánfi and Jan Jiskra, see notes 494 and 301.

508. Benedek Turóci (d. 1465), a former retainer of Cillei and *ispán* of Varasd on his behalf. In 1456 he entered royal service and later became Steward of the Household (1462-1465). His ancestors were members of a minor noble family in Turóc county (see note 418), but he was not a kinsman of the chronicler, whose name likewise indicates that his forbears had been landowners in the same county (see Introduction).

509. Friedrich Lamberger (d. 1471), a German kinght from Carniola and a retainer and counsellor of Ulrich of Cillei, was in royal service from 1456. He became lord of Csáktornya (today Čakovec in Yugoslavia) and Steward of the Household (1466-1468).

him, was shut up in a house assigned to accommodate him in the fortress of Buda. In the end both were separately compelled to endure continuous confinement.

When night came and changed the light of day into shadows, Miklós Ujlaki,[510] voivode of Transylvania, put on his cuirass and came there with an escort of his followers, eager to see the outcome of an event of such importance. He was at once admitted to the fortress of Buda, for that Miklós, the voivode, was no less eager for the fall of Count László, and he participated in the plan concocted to murder him. For since he was a man greedy for esteem and burning with no ordinary ambition, and born of the exalted blood of his parents, he took it ill that the late lord Count János and his sons enjoyed a name and title of greater eminence in the kingdom and in the eyes of the king.[511] And thereafter he was made to feel for them no ordinary envy.

Soon after the next day had dawned, the following had the misfortune of imprisonment inflicted upon them: the lord János, bishop of Várad;[512] Sebestyén Rozgonyi; and László Kanizsai[513] —men distinguished in the kingdom both for their blood and for the estates they possessed, and excelling in knightly prowess— and also Gáspár Bodó of Györgyi,[514] a man not least esteemed by the council; György Modrar,[515] possessed of great wealth;

---

510. See note 265.

511. This is not quite true. Though Ujlaki was a high-born and amibitious magnate with count palatines among his ancestors, he did not hesitate to co-operate closely and even in a friendly way, over a long period of time, with János Hunyadi, who was of a more humble origin but no less ambitious. Their estrangement began only after 1453, when Hunyadi, ever determined to maintain his power, started alienating even his former friends and allies.

512. János Vitéz of Szredna (d. 1472), Bishop of Várad (1445-1465) and Keeper of the Privy Seal (1453-1472). He was known as a man of learning and as a patron of humanist scholarship and art. Born to a family of minor gentry in Slavonia, he owed his career to his friend, Hunyadi, who chose him as a tutor for the young Matthias Corvinus.

513. For Sebestyén Rozgonyi and László Kanizsai, see notes 448 and 447.

514. Györgyi, formerly a village near Mágocs in Tolna county (today in Baranya county) and seat of the knightly family Bodó. Gáspár Bodó of Györgyi

the two Páls, surnamed Horvát;[516] and a certain German named Frodnohar[517] —all knights outstanding for their skill at arms—in addition to certain other men who had been either advanced or reared from infancy by the late lord Count János, and influenced to feel a personal loyalty to and friendship for Counts László and Matthias. When at length the third day[518] of the detention of the counts had passed the hour of vespers, and the chariot of the sun had come close to the evening hours, Count László was handed over to the mayor and aldermen of the city of Buda to be punished with death.[519] And under the custody of many armed guards he was brought before the fortress of Buda, opposite the

---

(d. after 1492) was at this time a young retainer of the Hunyadi house. He later became Gentleman Carver of the King (1459-1461), Master of the Horse (1461-1463), and Steward of the Queen.

515. Pál Modrar, by mistake given here the Christian name György (d. c. 1459), originally a wealthy citizen of Kassa and a partisan of Jiskra, who helped him to acquire the lordship of Nagyida (today Vel'ká Ida, Slovakia). After 1450 he joined Hunyadi's party.

516. "Horvát" is the Hungarian name for the Croats. In the medieval period it was a common surname for anyone who came from Croatia or had anything to do with it. Of the two Pál Horváts mentioned here by Thuróczy, only one can be identified with certainty. This was Pál or Pavao Spirancic (d. 1463), called also Pál Horvát in official records. Probably a retainer of the Hunyadi house, he was made Captain of Damásd (1458) and of Diósgyőr (1458-1459), Ban of Croatia and Dalmatia (1459-1463), and even Count of Cetina and Klis in Croatia. The other Pál Horvát may have been Count Paul IV of Corbavia, a Croatian magnate, but there is no known evidence to connect him with the Hunyadis.

517. Wolfgang Frodnohar (d. after 1465), probably a knight of German origin, who may also have been a retainer of the Hunyadis. He received as a royal grant, perhaps from King Matthias Corvinus, the lordship of Bednja in Slavonia.

518. March 16, 1457.

519. By a special privilege granted by King Ladislas V, the city of Buda, represented here as it usually was by its mayor and twelve aldermen (see note 228), was authorized to carry out any kind of capital sentence on a criminal arrested within its boundaries. It was because of this privilege that László Hunyadi was placed in the hands of the city authorities.

building named the Frisspalota,[520] and there and then beheaded.

Now at the time of his beheading something occurred that must be related as a miracle of no small significance. For when Count László was beheaded and was already prostrate on the ground, with his hands tied behind his back, following the triple wound of the beheading that had been inflicted upon him, at once he rose and stood erect under his own strength, and he said in a quite intelligible voice that he was not legally bound to give any further satisfaction beyond the three prescribed wounds required at his beheading. At length, with all the bystanders aghast at this strange occurrence, he fell on his face when suddenly he had moved forward and after several steps had trampled upon the garment in which he had been dressed. And at the command of certain bystanders who took pleasure in what had happened, the remains of his beheading were destroyed.

But alas! the grief! alas! the sorrow! And alas! how much distress did this count's death cause for those who loved him! In fact, you could have seen practically every Hungarian, noble and peasant alike, walking about with head bowed, hands joined, and wrapped in thought as if in the grip of a deep sleep. And you could have seen fresh floods of tears running down the faces of many. For it may be said that if the agitation of the people of Hungary had not been calmed by frequent public proclamations and by terrible, intimidating threats, and if Count László himself had not been brought for his execution at a suitable hour of the day to St. George's Square, where once the thirty-two knights were beheaded,[521] all the peasants themselves would have snatched him and thereby prevented his losing his life. For at that time many had come together into the city for the tillage of the vineyards,[522] and they felt so much affection for him, that

520. The Frisspalota ("new palace") was a magnificent building constructed in 1420 by King Sigismund. It was destroyed during the siege of 1686.

521. In 1388 (see note 67).

522. In the Middle Ages an extended viticulture flourished on the slopes of the hills around Buda, an area that is today primarily residential.

it would have been no additional burden for them to shed their blood and die of a thousand wounds to avenge him. And this was the reason why Count László was beheaded not in the otherwise usual spot and about the last hour of the day.

Now after he was beheaded, he was immediately wrapped in a black covering, placed on a bier, and brought to the church of St. Mary Magdalene.[523] And throughout the entire night guards kept watch. Finally, just as the first light of dawn was breaking forth, he was unceremoniously interred in the church of the most holy body of Christ,[524] where lay buried the aforementioned thirty-two knights, whom the late King Sigismund, in a fit of anger, had beheaded.

Count László was, as has been said, not unlike his father in height, with a round and swarthy face, long hair like chestnuts in color, kindly of gaze, broad of shoulder, vigorous in bearing arms, quite daring, and as kind to his own people as to foreigners.

✠ 256 (LXI): CONCERNING THE VENGEANCE AND THE WARS WHICH FOLLOWED IN THE KINGDOM UPON THE DEATH OF COUNT LÁSZLÓ ✠

n ow what did the inducement to so great a crime profit those who with their words of advice perverted the youthful mind of King Ladislas to violate his oath? Had

---

523. The church of St. Mary Magdalene, of which nothing except its tower has been preserved, was the parish church of the Hungarian citizenry of Buda in the northern quarter of the city. The other parish on Castle Hill, that of the Germans, was the Church of the Holy Virgin (see note 346).

524. The Blessed Sacrament Chapel (see note 69).

it pleased God's judgment, it would have seemed more in accord with man's way of thinking that they, and not King Ladislas, would have suffered retribution for the aforesaid perjury. But one may think that the fates by this course were setting the stage for future developments. And yet the ones who had been responsible for this crime won for themselves disgrace and hatred among the people; and many others, even those who had no share in these affairs, endured because of them loss of life and possessions alike, as those loyal to Count László exacted revenge in continued warfare for the murder of their lord. Indeed, there immediately arose in the kingdom a bitter outbreak of violence, and indiscriminately harsh punishment was exacted for the counts' sufferings. And in fact Mihály Szilágyi of Horogszeg,[525] the uncle of the counts, brought together troops comprised of warlike men from both native and foreign peoples, and attacked the Transylvanian regions of the kingdom. And in a few days he subjected to his rule all the cities and towns of that land, and he converted for his own use and that of his supporters all the royal proceeds generated by that part of the kingdom and belonging to the king's treasury. But should it please anyone to record for future memory what others did with fire and sword and by general plundering, who were distressed by the counts' misfortune and held in their control strong fortifications throughout the regions of the kingdom, he would tell his descendants a story that ends in many sighs of grief.

---

525. Mihály Szilágyi of Horogszeg (see note 467) took over the leadership of the Hunyadi party after László's execution.

✠ 257 (LXII): CONCERNING THE LOT OF THE OTHER PRIS-
ONERS AND THE DEATH OF KING LADISLAS ✠

At length, when a few days had passed following the death of Count László, the lord bishop of Várad, as required by his honorable rank, was assigned to the lord Dénes, archbishop of Esztergom,[526] to be held in captivity at the king's pleasure. Count Matthias, too, was kept under watch night and day, in a small house constructed beside the Istvánvár[527] and looking out towards the lower hot springs.[528] The other captives were also confined apart from Count Matthias and held in accordance with the king's wishes.

Day followed day, and it was the 1458th year of the Lord.[529] The spring of that year, clothed in its lovely dress of flowers, had already passed beyond its later stages and had made way for the fruitful summer. When the sun had passed beneath the horizon, and the night that followed immediately upon the feast of the most holy body of Christ[530] had fallen with dense darkness, and a moderate cloud-burst was striking the fortress of Buda, all the prisoners who had been housed within the high walls of the fortress, with the exception only of Count Matthias and Pál Modrar, who remained the king's prisoners, escaped to Alhéviz, the lower hot springs, letting themselves down the overhanging walls of the fortress by using two linen sheets, or some such thing. Now when the escape of his prisoners became known to

526. See note 261.
527. The Istvánvár, or more commonly Istvántorony ("Stephen's Castle/Tower"), was a part of Buda Castle that is no longer extant. It was a kind of keep, built at the south end of the castle in the mid-fourteenth century, and named for Duke István of Slavonia (d. 1354), brother of King Louis I.
528. "The lower hot springs" of Buda, in Hungarian Alhéviz (cf. note 293), around the modern-day "Rácfürdő" baths.
529. The events related here occurred in the same year, i.e. 1457.
530. June 17, 1457, the day after the feast of Corpus Christi.

King Ladislas, he took it very ill, as did those who had been responsible for their imprisonment, and he was very much afraid.
For the aforementioned Sebestyén Rozgonyi and László Kanizsai were powerful in arms and they were fortunate in having
many kinsmen in the kingdom. The king and the barons associated with him were therefore fearful that these men would
the more quickly rise up to avenge themselves. Because of this
the king quickly armed all his partisans and without any delay crossed over to the city of Vienna,[531] bringing with him in
the same carriage Count Matthias unbound and Pál Modrar in
many iron shackles, for the latter was well supplied with gold
and the king hoped he could extort huge sums from him. At
length, after staying for a short period in Vienna, he proceeded
into Bohemia, leaving Count Matthias under a strong guard in
the fortress of Vienna. But while he was maintaining royal state
in the city of Prague, the king was afflicted with a sudden and
grim disease, and as he breathed his last, that was the end of his
life and his perjury.[532] Now whether, as is held by some, he died
from a deadly poison administered by George of Poděbrad,[533]
previously governor of this kingdom, or because God had called
him, I cannot myself say for a fact.[534] For often many tell different
stories, but who is able to trust them all?

King Ladislas' body had grown to a suitable height; his hair
was bluish-grey and curly, his face was white and tinged with
red, and his nose, which was straight and perfectly centered,

531. Thuróczy is in error. The king had left Buda as early as May 27, arriving in Vienna in the first days of June.

532. Ladislas was crowned King of Bohemia on October 28, 1453, and
spent more than a year there. In autumn 1457, he returned to Prague, where he
died a few weeks later on November 23, 1457, not (as Thuróczy writes at the
end of this chapter) 1458.

533. George (Jiří in Czech) of Poděbrad (d. 1471), a Czech magnate, regent
of Bohemia from 1444 to 1458, and then king (1458-1471).

534. Though his illness had the symptoms of plague, there were rumors
that he had been poisoned.

bulged out slightly at its midpoint. Compared with other young men of his age, he was no less attractive for his moral integrity and his sagacity.

King Ladislas died in the 1458th year of the Lord, the eighteenth of his life and of his rule over his kingdoms, when the autumn of that year had filled in the sphere of its last moon, on the same day on which he had, the previous year, taken the aforementioned oath, as has already been stated, to counts László and Matthias.[535] He was interred in Prague, in a parish church, to await there the final resurrection.

✠ 258 (LXIII): CONCERNING THE ELECTION OF THE LORD COUNT MATTHIAS AS KING ✠

N ow when from foreign reports news of the death of King Ladislas reached the kingdom of Hungary, it saddened many, but especially those who had successfully urged the murder of Count László, since they could see that the avengers of the blood shed by this count desired more eagerly still to break out with even greater force and achieve the vengeance they longed for. And this would have happened, had the general congregation, which had been proclaimed throughout the whole kingdom of Hungary for all the nobles to settle the affairs of the kingdom and elect a king, not restrained the minds of the avengers that were burning for revenge. At length, when this general congregation was with a very turbulent crowd of nobles thronging all the streets of the city of Pest on the appointed days—at a time when the swift and clever pens of the notaries

---

535. As to the date, otherwise unknown, of the king's ominous oath, Thuróczy provides useful information, if only one could be certain of its accuracy.

had recently begun to inscribe the 1458th year of the Lord—the aforementioned Mihály Szilágyi, uncle of Count Matthias, as has been said, who with the count's mother had been born of one and the same womb, came to this concourse of nobles, bringing with him a large force of men and arms.[536] And accompanying this Mihály Szilágyi were men powerful in the kingdom, in whose hearts were enduring memories of the meritorious kindnesses of the late lord Count János - these were the lords Tamás Székely, prior of Vrana; Sebestyén Rozgonyi; László Kanizsai; and Pongrác of Szentmiklós;[537] as well as a whole company of nobles from Transylvania and the southern counties of the kingdom. When on their arrival in the city of Pest they had chosen suitable accommodation for themselves, and the night coming first after their retirement had revealed the stars of the heavens that had been hidden from human sight during the brightness of the day, the Almighty from on high covered the deep River Danube in the depths of that night with such firm and solid ice, that when the next day dawned, everyone wishing to cross the Danube, now that every ship had been moved away, proceeded on foot on the surface of the ice, as if over an unploughed field, for the water was no obstacle to them. Moroever, the lords László Garai, palatine; and Miklós Ujlaki, voivode; Pál Bánfi of Alsólendva, who was steward of the royal household,[538] as has been said; and certain other men of no great importance, who

536. The diet was held at Pest in early January, 1458. Szilágyi arrived there on January 20.

537. For Tamás Székely, Sebestyén Rozgonyi, László Kanizsai, and Pongrác of Szentmiklós, see notes 445, 448, 447, and 304.

538. Bánfi's office in the Household was that of *magister ianitorum regalium*, "head of the royal janitors," which has been translated here as Steward of the Royal Household. Like other office-holders of the Household, the steward was a regular member of the royal council. Note that for English translations of Hungarian offices, suggestions proposed by Erik Fügedi (*A 15. századi magyar arisztokrácia mobilitása* [Social Mobility in the Hungarian Aristocracy of the Fifteenth Century] (Budapest, 1970) have usually been adopted.

had been responsible for the misfortune of counts László and Matthias, were in the fortress of Buda, and they were filled with fear at the actions of Count Matthias's uncle. Now who would have thought that they were shaken by a little fear and anxiety, when they saw that those who would exact retribution for the crime they had committed were flourishing, with considerable strength in arms and with the largest possible troop of men eager to fight, and that they were indeed close at hand? And had they hoped that there might be some protection for them on the Danube river, their hopes were frustrated when they saw that the river was covered with closely packed lumps of ice. And had they not been encouraged by the prerogative accorded by the general congregation, and the promise given them by Mihály Szilágyi himself, it may be said that they would have placed no trust at all in the strength of the high walls of the fortress of Buda and would perhaps have scattered during the darkness provided by the first night, to search out places safer for themselves. At length, reassured as to their security, they went down to the city of Pest, and in company with those who were there, they attended to the election of a king, expending more days in uninterrupted discussion.

Mihály Szilágyi and all the people united with him, as well as practically the whole assembly of the nobles of Hungary, kept urging that Count Matthias be elected king. But as long as László Garai, palatine, Miklós Ujlaki, voivode, Pál Bánfi of Alsólendva, and all their company thought they could afterwards receive a heavier punishment for the crime they had committed, they did not willingly give their assent to the proposition that Count Matthias should have the royal dignity; nor did they by choice absolutely refute it, as long as they, with bands of partisans all around them demanding vengeance for Count László's death, were being jostled along in the midst of this uproar. At length they relied on more sensible advice, taking their chance whether they would lose their lives and their possessions. Having first received a loyal oath from Mihály Szilágyi that never thereafter would this crime be laid to their charge, and that never would any punishment by way of retribution for the murder of Count László be exacted from them and their heirs, they, too, agreed that Count Matthias should be elevated to the royal throne. And what were they to do, except agree, when the entire Hungarian people walking through the broad streets of the city, as well as a crowd of children running about here and there, kept saying and loudly shouting: "We want Matthias to be king; God has chosen him for our protection; and he indeed is the one we also choose." For all the people participating in this congregation, except for those who were anxious and fearful because of the crime committed against him, were moved by love to want him, so that they wished for his elevation to the royal state more than all delights. Therefore a noble council of lords who were prelates, barons, and leading men of the kingdom was brought together, and it pleased all the Hungarian people that Count Matthias be adorned with the royal dignity and rule the kingdom of Hungary; and they also took an oath of loyalty, promising alike to revere and fear the king's sceptre. And because they considered Count Matthias in his boyhood unable to sustain the weight of the troubles of so vast a kingdom, so great were the problems confronting him, they placed his uncle in charge as governor of the kingdom and of the elected king, until the chariot of the sun had completed five annual journeys.[539]

But, remarkably, this most solemn election was up to that time conducted in an inner chamber and a report of it had not yet reached the people. And now the church of Pest[540] burst forth into solemn song, chanting praises to God for so desirable

539. Both the election of the king and that of the new governor took place on January 24, 1458. The governorship was the office created for Hunyadi in 1446 (see note 365).

540. Probably the parish church of Pest, which still survives in its medieval form next to the Erzsébet Bridge.

an election. When news of it did come to the notice of the commons, the whole Hungarian people rejoiced greatly; and the air around reverberated with the sound of church bells ringing everywhere, the very loud blast of trumpets, and the music of many pipes, and also the loud sound of voices breaking out into song and publicly singing in praise of God. Messengers ran about everywhere, bringing the joyful news of the election to those who were absent and returning laden with many gifts. After the twilight of the approaching night arrived, the night itself was passed festively with the kindling of many fires, and was transformed, so to speak, into a counterfeit day as many a pile of firewood blazed. Indeed, one may presume to say that from the beginnings of Hungarian history never was an election of any king celebrated with so much rejoicing and so much splendor.

✠ 259 (LXIV): How the Lord King Matthias was released from captivity and brought back into Hungary ✠

Now after so auspicious an election achieved the result which had been hoped for, Mihály Szilágyi, who was haughty because of the support of the common people, and unwilling to stay away from the royal palace he had occupied in Buda, was pleased to enter the counties of many lords of Hungary and take possession of them for the new prince. László Garai,[541] the palatine, who by ancient custom of the realm exercised superintendence over them, nevertheless surrendered them to him with feelings of dejection, while ostensibly doing so on his own initiative, and secretly departed from that place to a region which for him was more secure. When this was

541. See note 13.

done, Mihály Szilágyi went to the grave of Count László, and
having the corpse exhumed, he mourned together with all those
who were gathering round. And at length he had it conveyed
to Gyulafehérvár[542] in Transylvania, and arranged to inter it
with many funeral rites next to his father's tomb. At the same
time he tried to keep the elected king away from the influence of
George of Poděbrad. For, because of his control of many cities
and his many blood-relationships in the kingdom of Bohemia,
that George of Poděbrad was richer than all the nobles of that
land. And when the late king Ladislas was seized during infancy, George held the office of governor of the kingdom of Bohemia. After the king's death, however, omnipotent Fortune did
not prohibit his sitting upon the royal throne in the kingdom.[543]
  Certain people say that it was under these circumstances that
the elected king had come into the hands of this George: while
Matthias still had the title of count, King Ladislas had given orders, near the end of the closing days of a royal festivity of his,
to bring the count from the citadel at Vienna before him in the
city of Prague. And on the day when King Ladislas had died,
Matthias had been brought within the walls of the city of Prague.
And upon the death of King Ladislas, he, along with the rest of
the affairs of Bohemia, had come under the control of George of
Poděbrad. Now others have tried to persuade me that the release
of the new king occurred in the following way: immediately after King Ladislas had breathed his last, George of Poděbrad had
carefully kept secret the news of his death, had slipped the dead
king's signet-ring from his fingers, and had had a letter written,
to which he at length had caused the seal to be affixed, and which
he had entrusted, under the counterfeit name of King Ladislas
himself, to the ones who had been given responsibility for the

542. Gyulafehérvár (Alba Iulia), was the burial place of the Hunyadi family (see note 477).
543. George of Poděbrad was elected king only after Matthias' release on
March 2, 1458.

custody of Count Matthias. This he had done so that, as soon as they had seen the letter, they would hand Count Matthias over to the bearers of the letter, who would come with him right to the city of Prague. For when King Ladislas left the fortress at Vienna, he is said to have left this seal behind, as an indisputable sign for the guardians concerning the affairs of Count Matthias. The guardians had therefore accepted as true the false commands in the letter and had shown themselves prompt in carrying them out. Count Matthias, however, under the direction of the messengers, had not yet reached the borders of the kingdom of Bohemia when they had been confronted by a very large number of armed Bohemians sent by George of Poděbrad, in whose midst Count Matthias had safely ridden right to Prague. Indeed, when George of Poděbrad saw him, he was exceedingly pleased, for he was thinking he could receive a lot of gold for his ransom. But after he heard that Count Matthias had been elected king of Hungary, he often arrogantly lectured the new Hungarian king and persuaded him to make a marriage with his daughter, having won him over in many a conversation; nor thereafter, when Matthias was returning home, did George permit him to depart without paying a very large amount of gold.[544]

At length, in the first year of the elected king, when the freezing cold weather of winter, dispersed by a warm west wind, had flowed as a stream into the deep valleys from the lofty mountain peaks, after the chilly snows had melted, and when the eagerly awaited mildness of spring was loosening the beaks of small birds to sing their charming songs, the new king, with an armed escort of Bohemians, was brought with great joy to a town called Strážnice in Moravia, located next to the Morva river.[545] There a concourse of his nobles, filled with boundless delight, at once

---

544. Poděbrad in fact compelled the betrothal of his daughter Catherine to King Matthias; and he kept for himself the high ransom obtained for the king.

545. On February 9, 1458.

surrounded him, and finally in their joyful company he rode happily to the fatherland he longed for. Now when he reached the fortress of Buda,[546] immediately a gathering of many nobles awaiting the arrival of the king they desired was adorned with great splendor as the court of this king.

✠ 260 (LXV): WHAT MIGHT BE CALLED A BRIEF SUMMARY OF CERTAIN CAMPAIGNS OF THE LORD KING MATTHIAS ✠

his man was naturally disposed to be a king in every way, for amongst all the Christian princes of his age, he alone is the one whose career as king is marked by exalted and glorious deeds. Is it not the case that Mehmed, sultan of the Turks, who lived in this age of ours and had caused the whole world to tremble violently from terror of him, and who because of the greatness of his deeds deserved to be called Mehmed the Great, is reported to have said about this king: "I and he, of all the princes of the world, are the ones who deserve to be called princes." Is it not also the case that it is proper for a prince to behave appropriately in councils of state, to be lenient and most merciful toward wrongdoers, resourceful and provident when administering the affairs of his kingdom, vigorous of mind, bold at undertaking great and difficult matters, tireless in enduring labors, clearheaded in anticipating and forestalling events, prudent in avoiding dangers, perceptive in uncovering and overturning the plots and plans of the enemy, wonderfully skilled in

546. On February 14 the king was solemnly enthroned in the Church of St. Mary in Buda. He was not crowned, however, because the Holy Crown of Hungary was in Emperor Frederick's hands (see note 274).

every military matter and in all the operations under his direction, a master of dissimulation, eager for boundless glory, and—shall I say?—born to rule?

This king had the beginnings of his reign disrupted by his subjects; but after he grew in strength and discretion, as if emerging from some terrible flood, he smoothed out all his difficulties with an excellent sense of moderation. During the first years of his reign, in a mighty war he routed a large army of Turks,[547] which had rushed to pillage Szerém county[548] and had by force taken the fortresses of Kölpény[549] and Zentdemeter[550] beside the bank of the river Sava. During these same years he also, sometimes with force, at other times with guile, restrained and put an end to the ambitious greed of Frederick, emperor of the Romans, who was burning for the sceptre of the kingdom of Hungary and wishing to rob the king himself of his royal eminence, having been afforded an opportunity to do so by certain barons.[551] At length, having turned his sword against the Bohemians and Poles who with the greatest depradations and conflagrations, as was mentioned above, were harassing the kingdom, with admirable swiftness he restrained them after much slaughter; and with the support of a very small number of knights he sacked their strong dwellings and fortifications, and he compelled those who survived the slaughter to wander through the wilderness and the depths of the forests and to flee the kingdom.[552] Furthermore, with what one might call a fine sense of discretion

547. In October, 1458.
548. See note 123.
549. See note 176.
550. Szentdemeter or Szávaszentdemeter (today Mitrovica, Yugoslavia), a city with a castle on the Sava and the site of ancient Sirmium.
551. Emperor Frederick III was elected King of Hungary on February 17, 1459, by a group of rebellious magnates led by the deposed Count Palatine, László Garai. The revolt was crushed in two months.
552. Matthias' wars against Jiskra and the Czech mercenaries in North Hungary (see note 396) lasted from 1458 to 1462.

he also restrained and allayed the storms of wars, which from the times of the late King Wladislas had occurred sporadically and turbulently in the kingdom; and he established an excellent peace, desired for so many years, throughout all the territories of his realm. Next, after assembling a powerful expeditionary force, he ranged over a very large part of Serbia, and returned home victorious, having subjected the land there to great devastation by fire and sword.[553] Only after this expedition, when the sweat on his horses had not yet dried, did he attack the kingdom of Bosnia, which we also call "Rama",[554] and which was then subject to the dominion of the Turks. And by force he obtained the surrender of the fortress of Jajca,[555] which had very strong natural defenses and the protection of high walls, as well as the surrender of other fortresses in this land. And admitting to his grace and authority all the troops of the sultan of the Turks who were assigned from his court to the custody of these fortresses, and whom the Hungarians had not put to the sword, he brought them with him resplendent in purple garments, and reported a most commendable and a new kind of victory.

---

553. Serbia was entirely under Ottoman domination after the fall of its capital, Smederevo, in 1459. Matthias led an expedition to north Serbia in August, 1463.

554. "Rama" ceased being a current political or even geographical term long before Thuróczy's time. It had been the Hungarian name for Bosnia in the twelfth century, and it was preserved only because the kings of Hungary continued to use the title, among others, of "King of Rama" (*Rex Ramae*) until as late as 1918.

555. Jajca (Jajce in Serbian), a town and castle on the Vrbas in Bosnia. Matthias took it on December 25, 1463, after a siege of two months. His campaign was a reaction to the conquest of the kingdom of Bosnia by the Ottomans in the spring of that year.

✠ 261 (LXVI): CONCERNING THE AUSPICIOUS CORONATION OF THE LORD KING MATTHIAS AND CERTAIN OF HIS EXPEDITIONS ✠

*m*eanwhile, after the holy diadem of the kingdom of Hungary had with great difficulty been recovered from the hands of Frederick, king of the Romans,[556] King Matthias, in the sixth year of his reign[557] and the 1464th year of the Lord's Incarnation, on the day of the Lord's supper,[558] was with great solemnity auspiciously crowned according to the customs observed on other such occasions, in the presence of the lords spiritual and temporal of all his realm, and of the leading men of his kingdom, who rejoiced at his coronation.

After this, with the clamor alone from one of his expeditionary forces he struck terror into Mehmed, the aforementioned sultan of the Turks, who at the assault on the fortress of Jajca was pressing hard with formidable engines of war; and he compelled him to abandon in that place all the different kinds of siege-machines and catapults Mehmed had brought there, and the sultan himself to retreat from below the fortress without a victory.[559] Eventually, with great glory for his deeds then following, he surrounded with main force a certain Bohemian called Svehla,[560] an outstanding general and powerful because of the many troops he had assembled, who was seditiously striving to plunder the kingdom of Hungary in the town of Kosztolány or Szentvid,[561]

---

556. By the treaty of Wiener Neustadt, ratified on July 19, 1463, Matthias had to pay 80,000 gulden for the Holy Crown and for the city of Sopron, pledged to Frederick in 1441. He also had to consent to Frederick's continued use of the title of King of Hungary (see note 551).

557. The seventh regnal year, in fact.

558. On March 29, 1464, at Székesfehérvár.

559. At the news of Matthias's advance, the Sultan retreated from Jajce on August 23, 1464 after a ten-week siege.

560. Jan Svehla (d. 1467), a Czech mercenary captain.

where defensive works had been prepared for him. The king overcame his resistance and, having captured and hanged him and a great many of his accomplices on a forked frame, he exposed them to the blowing of the winds.[562] He also caused the suffocation, from the poisonous stench of his prisons, of a very large number of Svehla's other associates who had been captured. At length, under the influence of some derangement of the mind, an insurrection against his royal eminence was set in motion by all the nobles from the Transylvanian regions of the kingdom, and by the entire populace, when they had elected a new prince for themselves and, having been formed into many companies, were with ranks in battle-formation striving to prevent His Majesty from entering. At once the lord king, like some kind of violent whirlwind, rushed towards them with his own armored ranks, even though he was outnumbered. Without joining battle at all, they were in fact struck with extreme fear and fled like wild animals at the sight of a lion.[563] At length, the lord king subdued them just as he pleased. Because of this a number of them lament down to this day the villeinage they thereby endured.

But without his troops having been refreshed at all by any respite, he turned the reins of his horses towards Moldavia,[564] namely the region subject to the sacred crown of the kingdom of Hungary, which was then in revolt. When he had crossed the Alps[565] and had with main force traversed a large part of this

561. Kosztolány or Szentvid (today Vel'ké Kostol'any, Slovakia) a market on the Vág in Nyitra county, where a band of Czech mercenaries constructed a fortress in the 1460s.

562. Kosztolány was taken on January 29, 1467.

563. The revolt in Transylvania was suppressed in September, 1467.

564. On the prince of Moldavia and his alleged status as a vassal of Hungary, see note 47.

565. The East Carpathians (see note 51).

land, and in a certain town of the region, called Banya,[566] had received hospitality with all his men, Voivode István,[567] lord of these territories, united a large number of his people and in the quiet of the night rushed upon the royal army. He set the town on fire and roused to arms the Hungarians who were distracted by both sleep and wine. Voivode István had chosen to attack the royal army under cover of night, so that if he should fail in battle, at least the darkness would assist him. Nevertheless, he was mistaken in this. For suddenly the king with the sound of drums and trumpets mustered his whole army and with a furious charge rushed upon the enemy lines in the light provided by both the moon and the fires in the town. And after there had been much fighting on both sides, and the greatest of slaughters had been inflicted on the Walachians, Voivode István was compelled to flee, and the king thereby won an outstanding and memorable triumph.[568] From that place he also brought back to Buda a great many military standards as a sign of his famous victory, which were placed with great solemnity in the parish church of the most glorious Virgin Mary[569] and are on display even today.

At length, following his glorious victory, the lord king, at the urging of holy mother Church and in response to the entreaties of Frederick, emperor of the Romans, continued his war of seven years against the heretic Hussites in Moravia and Bohemia;[570]

---

566. Bánya or Moldvabánya in Hungarian (Baia in Rumanian), a town on the Moldova in Moldavia (today in Rumania).

567. The Voivode István III of Moldavia, called "the Great" (cel Mare) (1457-1504), then a Polish vassal.

568. On December 15, 1467. Contrary to the official view of the Hungarian court, it was more a defeat than a victory, and the voivode did not accept Hungarian suzerainty until 1475.

569. See note 346.

570. Matthias launched an offensive against Bohemia in the spring of 1468. Fighting lasted for almost seven years, until the end of 1474. He had been encouraged to go to war by Emperor Frederick as well as by Pope Paul II (1464-1471), who had accused King George of heresy and proclaimed a crusade

and always ending up the victor, he brought under his rule the whole margraviate of Moravia, all of Silesia, and Lusatia, too, and deserved to be elected king of Bohemia and to enjoy dominion and supremacy over those lands. Because of this, to adorn and dignify his most celebrated election, in the city of Olomouc[571] the hymn inscribed below was sung in a new version:

On the seventh of May,[572] with the greatest devotion, we have been delighted to observe a feast that anyone should revere, a feast unexpectedly worthy of the victorious and blessed cross.

The people who call Bohemia their homeland, bishops of the true faith, barons, and mighty companies from Christian cities were at liberty to meet.

The church of Olomouc, constructed high on a hill and piously filled with laymen and clerics, resounds with prayers to the Lord.

The Holy Spirit, invoked continually, is believed to have granted so many righteous souls the

---

against him. The king's real aim was, however, the acquisition of the Bohemian crown. Indeed, in May, 1469, he was accepted by the Catholics as King of Bohemia.

571. Olomouc (Olmütz in German), a city in Moravia where a final peace was ratified on July 21, 1479, between Matthias and George's successor, King Wladislas of Bohemia (1471-1516), a son of King Kazimierz IV of Poland. According to the treaty, both kings were to continue to style themselves King of Bohemia. The lands of the Crown of Bohemia were divided between them, the Margraviates of Moravia and Lusatia and the Duchy of Silesia being ceded to Matthias, and Bohemia proper to Wladislas.

572. Thuróczy is in error. This panegyric describes the festivities in Olomouc, celebrating Matthias's election as King of Bohemia on May 3, 1469, and his coronation there on May 13.

power openly to proclaim: Behold, it is resolved that Matthias be chosen.

The chosen one quickly takes up these clear expressions of their wishes. Shaken in his mind by commands from heaven and prayers on earth, he bows down before you, Christ the merciful, and obeys.

Worthy of praises, the mighty Matthias generously agrees to add to the kingdom of the Pannonians the crown and title of the Bohemian kingdom.

Let us all give glory to Jesus for his gifts, and let singing and a blast of trumpets resound, so that there may come to us a just man, inspiring terror in our enemies.

May this king lift up our faithful spirits when afflicted; and may he restrain and destroy, as vigorously as possible, hostile heresies and their sects.

Sooner will Xanthus relinquish its moist water, and Arcturus throw away his wagon, than the prince would, on your account, forsake God's cause and his peoples.

✠ 262 (LXVII): CONCERNING THE TREASON COMMITTED BY CERTAIN LORDS OF HUNGARY AGAINST THE LORD KING MATTHIAS, AND CERTAIN OF THE SAME KING'S VICTORIES ✠

At the time when the lord king was with successful outcome directing his affairs with respect to the kingdom of Bohemia, certain of the lords of Hungary, but especially those whom the king's benevolence had raised up to exalted rank—and most of all János, lord archbishop of Esztergom,[573] and János, lord bishop of Pécs,[574] both of whom had been born in Slavonia of the lesser nobility and called to mind the king's kindnesses without any sense of gratitude—had not only disrupted the king's affairs in Bohemia, but had tried to rob the king himself of his sceptre and his rule in Hungary. To disgrace the king they brought into the kingdom through the land of Szepes[575] the illustrious Kazimierz,[576] a son of King Kazimierz of Poland, who was full of pride because of his Polish followers and arms, and they placed in his hands the fortress of Nyitra.[577] There the lord King Matthias blockaded him, relying on the troops of a knight he mistrusted, and when Kazimierz was under siege, the king so harassed him with fighting and lack of food, after annihilating an exceedingly large number of Poles, that both he and his men despaired of their safety and were forced to fear the loss of their lives more than that of their possessions. And the lord

573. János Vitéz (see note 512).

574. János Csezmicei (1434-1472), Bishop of Pécs (1459-1472), a nephew of Archbishop János Vitéz, better known under his humanist name, Janus Pannonius, as a Latin poet of the first rank.

575. Szepes or Szepesség (Zips in German) formerly a county in north Hungary on the Polish frontier (today in Slovakia).

576. Prince Kazimierz, a younger son of King Kazimierz IV of Poland and a nephew of the former King, Wladislas I of Hungary (see note 246). He came to Hungary in October, 1471.

577. Nyitra (today Nitra, Slovakia), an episcopal see with a castle on the Nitra.

king would have harassed him more had he not been uncertain about his troops, and had the darkness of night not rescued Kazimierz from the midst of the king's blockade. It was because of such a fate that Kazimierz, fighting with his men in Hungary, not only failed to capture the sceptre of Hungary, but on his return scarcely brought home to his father news of his own survival.[578]

At length, after so awe-inspiring a victory, the lord king rushed upon the fortifications of the Poles in Zemplén and Sáros[579] counties, which they had erected to harass those regions, storming and razing them to the ground.[580] And subjecting the Poles who were guarding them to the harsh bondage of defeat, he sent them right to Buda to announce his glorious triumph. He next with a great clamor of arms directed a numerous army of his people into Poland to exact retribution for his injuries; and in that kingdom he caused, with firebrands and much depredation, the exaction of unspeakable punishments for the opprobrium he had suffered.

At length he heard that King Kazimierz of Poland was engineering a revolution in Silesia. Having therefore assembled from both his own courtiers and from hired troops an army not at all like the one the king of Poland was leading against him, he advanced and entered Silesia, pitching a permanent encampment near the walls of the city of Breslau.[581] On the other side came the king of Poland, bringing together in one expedition all the powerfully armed troops of his domain, namely Poles, and Ruthenians, Lithuanians, and Tartars, and he stationed all the forces of his camp a mile or less from the Hungarian encampment. And

---

578. In December, 1471.

579. Zemplén and Sáros, former counties in northeast Hungary on the Polish border (today in Slovakia).

580. In November/December, 1473.

581. Breslau, in Hungarian Boroszló (today Wroclaw, Poland), an important German city in Silesia.

although so large a number of people inspired terror in the lord King Matthias and his people, he did not therefore take to flight, but thoughtfully considered what the enemy would do first.

And so a certain number of days passed, and as they sped by, neither the king of Poland nor his troops ventured to attack or set eyes on the Hungarian camp. But the lord king did not play the same role in his expedition as did Kazimierz, for immediately after he saw that the king of Poland was the victim of idleness with respect to his weapons, he gave his attention to the battlefield and began to disturb the enemy camp. In fact his troops, who came out of the camp as if they were so many wasps, were killing and capturing Poles concerned with the quest for food; and they drove them in a mass towards the king's camp in such large numbers that when captured they were repugnant to their captors. The lord king therefore decided that they were not to be taken prisoner, except for those he judged worthy of captivity because of their pre-eminent rank. But any other captives who might appear had only to be cut on some part of their face and at length sent away, so that when they returned home their scars would be their evidence that they saw the Hungarians. Furthermore, the lord king simultaneously overwhelmed and scattered the pair of camps of the king of Poland that were supplying him with victuals. And having in the meanwhile dispatched his magnificence, István Zápolyai,[582] hereditary count[583] of Szepes and supreme captain of his expedition, together with a certain part of his army, to Poland, which was then deprived of the pro-

---

582. István Zápolyai (d. 1499), a gentleman of humble origin from Pozsega county and a favorite of Matthias, who elevated him to the rank of Count of Szepes in 1465 (see note 583). He later became Count Palatine (1492-1499) and the greatest landowner in Hungary.

583. *Comes perpetuus* was the Latin title for hereditary counts (see notes 166 and 434), as opposed to the simple *comes*, which only signified an office (see note 317). Szepes county (see note 575) was given by Matthias to the Zápolyai brothers as a hereditary lordship.

tection of its troops, he carried out there the greatest devastations with fire and sword. With such violent onslaughts as these the lord King Matthias harassed the king of Poland and so exhausted him that the latter was strongly moved by the distressing hunger suffered by people and horses and sought peace instead of war. Afterwards, when both kings with an equal number of troops convened on the battlefield under the shade of the tents set up just for this meeting, that excellent peace, which could not be achieved through arms, was achieved through the personal participation of the kings.[584] And there the lord King Matthias brought the king of Poland into his tent and treated him with elegant hospitality, as all the counts of the king of Poland, Poles and also Ruthenians, Lithuanians, and Tartars, expressed wonder and astonishment at both the dignified generosity of the lord King Matthias and his self-control.

Next, returning from this place, he besieged and captured, in the harsh winter cold, a fortress of the Turks called Sabač,[585] near the banks of the River Sava, constructed by them very carefully and strongly of wood and earth, and fortified with towers and embankments and valleys, and also with troops.

After this he assembled a superb expedition of choice and outstanding troops, and for reasonable cause attacked with main force the domains of Frederick, emperor of the Romans. Although there was in this struggle often a fight to the finish, the lord king nevertheless always won a glorious triumph, taking by force almost all the cities of the duchy of Austria, and many also in Styria and in Carinthia, which were richly supplied with guards and arms for defense, and impressively and strongly constructed with encircling walls and closely spaced towers;

---

584. On December 8, 1474. The events recounted above took place during the previous four months.

585. Sabač, located west of Belgrade, was besieged from the end of December, 1475, and captured on February 15, 1476.

fortresses that were very well fortified he stormed, and he subjected to his own absolute authority the land and water of those
regions. Included among the cities he took by force were those
most celebrated and famous ones, Vienna and Wiener Neustadt,
which were superior to the others in the size and height of their
defensive walls, outstanding for the rank and intelligence of their
citizens, abundantly rich in possessions, noteworthy for the at-
tractiveness of their locations and their pleasures both in town
and in the environs, and captured during no period of human
history by any king or emperor. He advanced to attack these
cities with the splendid siege-engines of his troops, and after
their capture he spared, because of his natural disposition to
clemency and goodness, the possessions and lives of the citizens
who were struggling against him. And so it was that in the city
of Vienna, after its capture, this poem was published in praise of
the lord King Matthias:

> Learn, mortals, not to put too much trust in
> walls; captured Vienna teaches what walls can
> do. Of what vigorous courage and the king's
> right hand can do, famous Vienna is its own
> example. O wonderful clemency of a king too
> much disposed to kindness! Accustomed to
> conquer all, he knows not how to harm.

The splendid news concerning this king flew through the
world, and his sword inspired neighboring regions with terror. Nor did Mehmed the Great, whose spear spared no one,
ever dare to try this king's fighting power in a pitched battle.
And when from below the fortress of Jajca, mentioned before,
and from Moldavia, he energetically took to his heels before the
king's sword,[586] returning to his own land without fulfilling his

---

586. An allusion to the Moldavian expedition of a Hungarian army led by

desire, the fates made this king a victor. Hence it was that to
glorify his deeds these verses were composed: By some strange
fate there has recurred the most celebrated victory of the Huns,
which once took place in King Attila's time.[587]

The royal treasury[588] and table of this king are resplendent
with so many decorations and jewels, with so much paraphernalia, and so many gold and silver vessels and cups, that none
of the kings of Hungary is believed to have possessed objects reflecting such great splendor. Evidence of this is that noble diet
celebrated by the king and the illustrious Wladislas, son of the
king of Poland, in the city of Olomouc.[589] There in the palaces
and streets the lord king displayed for men to look upon so many
novelties, in gems and precious stones, and in gold and silver, I
mean vessels and cups and other ornaments of the royal tables
and residences, in an astonishing and hitherto unseen multitude,
that Xerxes,[590] former king of the Persians and of Babylon, is
scarcely believed to have displayed so many splendid possessions at that memorable banquet of his for the princes of his

the Lord Chief Justice, István Bátori junior, in August, 1476. Sultan Mehmed II,
who had gone personally to conquer that country, retreated before the arrival
of Bátori.

587. The reference to Attila was the greatest possible praise Thuróczy
could imagine, Attila being the founder of the empire of the Huns in the fifth
century and considered an ancestor of the kings of Hungary (see *Introduction*).

588. In the early times of the Árpádian dynasty, *Tárnok* (*tárnokok* in the
plural, in Latin *tavernici*) was the name of a special group of royal serfs charged
with guarding the kings' storehouses and with transporting the goods kept in
them. After the thirteenth century their name was preserved in only two in-
stitutions. One was the baronial office of Lord Chief Treasurer, formerly their
head under the Hungarian title, *tárnokmester* ("Master of the Tárnoks," *magister
tavernicorum regalium* in Latin), and the other one was the Royal Treasury, called
tárknokház ("the House of the Tárnoks," *domus tavernicalis* in Latin); spelled
thauernicalis in the text of Thuróczy's Chronicle translated here. The Royal Treasury was in Buda Castle, the kings' residence, and contained many valuables,
including the royal charters and rolls.

589. In 1479 (see note 571).

590. The Persian King Xerxes, called Asuerus in Thuróczy's text and Ahasuerus in the Bible (see note 92).

realm. Who, moreover, is able to describe fully the countless multitude of devices, cannons, siege-machines, and other catapults that the lord king is accustomed to bring on his expedition to destroy enemy fortifications and fortresses, for no one saw all of them together in one and the same place? It may be said, however, that in these things, too, he surpasses all the kings of Christendom.

Many and various things should be related concerning this king, which in view of their magnitude and their novelty are worthy of his zest for life, but since the glory of his great deeds demands a unique style and narrative, as well as a greater herald than I am, accounts that will be recorded about the king in greater detail I leave to my authorities, begging pardon for the temerity that compelled me to pen the aforementioned comments. They will go on to describe all the same deeds one by one in a loftier and worthier style, as they came to pass, while also in greater detail recounting the hostilities which roused the king against the emperor of the Romans.

THANKS BE TO GOD!

www.ingramcontent.com/pod-product-compliance
Lightning Source LLC
Chambersburg PA
CBHW020402100426
42812CB00001B/160